LIBERATORS

LIBERATORS

FIGHTING ON TWO FRONTS IN WORLD WAR II

Lou Potter
WITH William Miles
and Nina Rosenblum

HARCOURT BRACE JOVANOVICH, PUBLISHERS
NEW YORK   SAN DIEGO   LONDON

Copyright © 1992 by Lou Potter, William Miles, and
Nina Rosenblum

Library of Congress Cataloging-in-Publication Data
Potter, Lou.
    Liberators/fighting on two fronts in World War II/by Lou
  Potter, William Miles, and Nina Rosenblum.—1st ed.
      p.   cm.
    Includes index.
    ISBN 0-15-151283-3
      1. United States. Army. Tank Battalion, 761st—History.
  2. World War, 1939–1945—Regimental histories—United
States.   3. United States. Army—Afro-American troops—
History—20th century.   4. World War, 1939–1945—
Participation, Afro-American.
    I. Miles, William, 1942–   . II. Rosenblum, Nina. III. Title.
  D769.306 761st.P68   1992
  940.54′1273—dc20   92-18791

Designed by Lydia D'moch

Printed in the United States of America

First edition
A B C D E

PREFACE

The genesis of this book can be found in the work of documentary filmmakers William Miles and Nina Rosenblum. Their film *Liberators: Fighting on Two Fronts*, broadcast as a special presentation of the Public Broadcasting System's *American Experience* series on Veterans Day, 1992, recounts the World War II saga of all-black army units, in particular the 761st Tank Battalion, whose emblem was the black panther and whose motto was "Come Out Fighting." The 761st distinguished themselves as "spearheaders" for General George S. Patton's renowned Third Army. This volume was written by Lou Potter; interviews and additional research was conducted by Miles and Rosenblum.

The exploits of the men of the 761st—the first African-Americans to be trained to fight in armor—caught the attention of filmmaker/historian Miles in 1976, during the development of his four-part public television series *A Different Drummer*, a comprehensive survey of black Americans' service in the armed forces of the United States. He was particularly intrigued by the veterans' recollections of the liberation of the Dachau death camp and their connection with Patton. The former aspect of the Black Panthers' story was of special interest in that few of the millions of words written about the Holocaust refer to the involvement of African-American GI's in freeing survivors of the atrocities of the "Final Solution." The battalion's connection to World War II's most celebrated field commander was of more than passing interest in light of the Academy Award–winning film *Patton*, in which the 761st's considerable contributions to the general's success were totally ignored. Miles concluded that though the Dachau story was included in *A Different Drummer*, the men of the 761st richly deserved a film of their own, which would detail the battalion's quite remarkable history.

The reasons for finding these tankers worthy of such a project are indeed compelling. They survived nearly three years of training in the racist backwaters of Texas and Louisiana with their dignity as individuals and their esprit de corps intact. Nor did they allow the inherent—and constantly manifested—institutionalized bigotry of the United States Army to deter them from the pursuit of excellence. When, in 1944, the Panthers were sent—at Patton's request—into the European Theater of Operations, they carried out their duties in a manner that far exceeded all expectations but their own. They fought through six nations in the course of an unparalleled 183 consecutive days on the front lines in near continuous combat. During these six grueling months, the 761st cracked open the Germans' vaunted defenses on the Maginot and Siegfried lines, played a heroic role during the Battle of the Bulge, and fought farther east—within sight of Czechoslovakia—than any other American outfit on the western front. In the spring of 1945, they led the way for U.S. forces in the liberation of two of the Nazis' most notorious concentration camps, Buchenwald and Dachau.

Bill Miles shot the first footage for the film during the summer of 1982, when a group of battalion veterans returned to Europe to revisit some of the sites in France, Belgium, Luxembourg, and the Netherlands where they had battled the Wehrmacht four decades earlier. In Paris, they laid a wreath at the Arc de Triomphe and were cited by the French government for their gallant actions in freedom's cause. As they traveled through towns and villages where they had fought—and some of their comrades had fallen—there were impromptu reunions with local citizens who witnessed the combat in 1944–45 and well remembered these African-American warriors. One encounter—in Tillet, France—was particularly heartwarming. During January 1945, tanker Horace Jones had been billeted for a week in the home of the Nelissen-Radelet family. A special and enduring relationship was established between the black GI and his Belgian hosts. For nearly forty years, Jones and his friends maintained a correspondence. Their tearful reunion was a moment of rare and real emotion.

While Miles went on to produce and/or direct such acclaimed films as *Paul Robeson: Man of Conscience, Black Champions, Black Stars in Orbit*, and *James Baldwin: The Price of the Ticket*, his determination to enter the Panthers' saga in its rightful place in the historical record never wavered. His dedication to this project did, in fact, redouble after he contacted and became friendly with a Buchenwald survivor, Ben Bender. Bender, in a published letter to the editor of the *New York Times*, had refuted the legend that he and his fellow inmates were freed by the Red Army and had vividly recalled their liberation by the black tankers of the 761st. Liberators and liberated would come to share Bill Miles and Nina Rosenblum's dream. The film thus reflects a special camaraderie between the documentarians and their subjects.

Rosenblum had been asked by Miles to codirect *Liberators* because of his high regard for her socially conscious productions such as *America and Lewis Hine*—a portrait of the pioneering realistic photographer—and the award-winning *Through the Wire*. The fact that this team—a black man and a Jewish woman—worked in tandem to tell a story of great significance to both ethnic groups resonates on both an artistically and a politically symbolic level. Aspects of the story were not new to Rosenblum. Her father, Walter Rosenblum, was the most highly decorated World War II cameraman and one of the nation's foremost still photographers; while working as a combat photographer for the War Department, he had documented the capture of Dachau by American forces.

In 1985, Miles and Rosenblum began the always difficult and problematical task of raising full production funding for the project. Ironically, this quintessentially American story came to the screen as a result, in large part, of the early financial support of broadcast organizations in Germany, France, the United Kingdom, and Australia. Later, the Corporation for Public Broadcasting and New York's public station WNET/13 came aboard.

At this time, Lou Potter, a twenty-five-year veteran screenwriter/producer whose films and series have won a score of American and international awards, was working in an office adjoining that of Miles and Rosenblum. After the completion of *The Exiles*, an Emmy Award–winning documentary on the impact of refugees from Hitler's Europe on American life and culture, written and coproduced with Richard Kaplan, Potter joined the *Liberators* project as a screenwriter.

In autumn 1991, Jewish survivors of Dachau and Buchenwald were reunited, under the auspices of the production team, with members of the 761st. The dramatic and poignant event received widespread media coverage, which led to Harcourt Brace Jovanovich's decision to employ the publishing medium in making this exciting and previously untold story available to the widest possible audience in this country and abroad.

This book will recount the concentration camp experiences of Ben Bender and other survivors, such as Abe Chapnick—also liberated from Buchenwald—and Samuel Pisar, freed from Dachau. It also focuses on the yeoman service-in-arms of such Panther veterans as Staff Sergeants E. G. McConnell, Johnnie Stevens, Leonard "Smitty" Smith, and Walter Lewis, and the battalion's white commanding officer, Lieutenant Colonel Paul Bates.

This is their story.

ACKNOWLEDGMENTS

I would like to acknowledge the invaluable contributions of my editor, Claire Wachtel, assistant editor Ruth Greenstein, and my agent, Edythea Ginis Selman, in shepherding this volume from idea to reality.

Lou Potter

. . . .

I would like to thank liberators E. G. McConnell and Leonard "Smitty" Smith and survivor Ben Bender for the inspiration to create *Liberators*. I also thank all the veterans of the 761st Tank Battalion who helped make the film and the book possible, with special thanks to my loving family, Gloria, Brenda, Debra, Ben, Chris, and Akira. I thank my literary agent, Edy Selman; Harriet Obus, for excellent research; and Charles E. Inniss, who understood what it meant to be fighting on two fronts.

William Miles

. . . .

I wish to express my gratitude to William Miles, who asked me to join him in creating *Liberators* for television. I thank the liberators and survivors who revisited Buchenwald for the film—Ben Bender, Leonard Smith, and E. G. McConnell—and all the liberators and survivors who gave so generously of their time, for believing in the production.

I am indebted to Claire Wachtel, our wonderful editor, assistant editor, Ruth Greenstein, the very talented book designer Lydia D'moch, and the HBJ family, as well as our literary agent, Edy Selman, for making this book possible. I also thank Denzel Washington, Suzanne DePasse, Suzanne Coston and DePasse Entertainment; Kareem Abdul-Jabbar, Richard Rubenstein and Laurel Entertainment; Judy Crichton, executive producer of *The American Experience*, and Bill

Baker, president; George Miles, chief operating officer; Mel Ming, director of technical and corporate support; Jon Olken, director of marketing; Harry Chancey and Fred Noriega, executives in charge at Thirteen/WNET; and Nicolas Pavicevic, director of operations, for their commitment to the project.

Our creative team, including John Crowley, Daniel V. Allentuck, Lou Potter, Steven Olswang, Arthur Schlenger, Margaret Crimmins, Kevin Keating, Nancy Schreiber, Richard Adams, Larry Banks, Rosa Howell Thurston, Craig Russell, Eva Fogelman, George Tooks, Robin Stouber, Vivian Wan, Karen Williams, Rosa McKenzie, librarian Harriet Obus, music service director John Adams, and composer Harold Wheeler, must also be recognized for their superb work.

We thank our international coproducers—Channel Four, U.K.; WDR, Germany; LA SEPT, France; SBS, Australia; the Corporation for Public Broadcasting, Thirteen/WNET, and *The American Experience*—along with our funders, including Jackie Donnet of The Donnet Fund and Charles Inniss of Brooklyn Union Gas, for their support for the project.

We are grateful for the aid of the U.S. Holocaust Memorial Council, Neil Goldstein, Sybil Milton, and Genya Markon. I also must thank Ira Schreck, Esq., Howard Rappaport, Esq., and Andrew Lund, Esq.; Michael Shepley, Terry Williams, and the Public Relations Department of Thirteen/WNET; Magdeleno Rose Avila of Amnesty International; Joe Hicks, director of the SCLC; Danny Goldberg, director of the ACLU Foundation of Southern California; Colonel Jesse J. Johnson and Dr. Leroy Ramsey, military historians; and Debbie Gruber of William Morris Agency, for all they have done on our behalf.

And most of all, I thank my family—my parents, Walter and Naomi Rosenblum, my sister, Lisa Rosenblum, Esq., and my husband, Daniel V. Allentuck—for their constant support and guidance.

Nina Rosenblum

INTRODUCTION

We live, Americans in all our millions, in an oddly amnesiac nation. Those who neither recall nor understand their collective past are condemned, so the philosopher Santayana implied, to endure repetitive tragedy in an eternal present. The Third Reich had its Jews, Slavs, homosexuals, and Gypsies. Now, as another wave of racism threatens to deluge the Western world, more than a few citizens of the "New Germany" revile the Turks, Poles, Vietnamese, and Africans living within its borders. In France, strident voices of reaction rail against Algerians and other "outsiders." Racial incidents occur with distressing frequency in such traditional bastions of tolerance as Sweden and the Netherlands.

In America, where the open expression of bigotry seems again to be edging toward respectability, a majority of Louisiana's white voters cast their ballots for a candidate whose résumé highlights his leadership in the neo-Nazi movement and the Ku Klux Klan. A huge turnout of African-American electors contributed to David Duke's failure to claim the statehouse. From Brooklyn's Bensonhurst and Crown Heights to such seemingly unlikely venues as Portland, Oregon; Dubuque, Iowa; and Las Vegas, Nevada, racial tensions grow and flare, not infrequently into deadly violence. In May 1992, impoverished South-Central Los Angeles erupted in flames and semiautomatic-weapon fire as long-festering discontents and animosities exploded in a rash of extreme violence. This fury, a result in no small measure of years of government-ordained policies calling for not so benign neglect of the needs and legitimate aspirations of America's poor and nonwhite masses, was ostensibly triggered by a series of events—beginning on a freeway and culminating in a suburban courtroom—that seemed to make a mockery of Constitutional provisions mandating color-blind justice and equal protection under the law for each and every citizen. It should be noted that while blacks, perhaps, made up the majority of those participating in the disturbances, many Hispanics and whites took part as well.

The 761st Tank Battalion, Camp Hood, Texas, 1943.

The United States, freedom's land, has always housed a large contingent of decidedly unequal persons, a continuing reality proving that the "melting pot" exists only in metaphor and that a blood-and-tear-stitched quilt—its patches tinted in black, brown, yellow, and red—remains a more accurate representation of the national experience.

As this is written, our citizenry still revels in a splendid victory over Iraq, another in a string of third world enemies—Panama, Grenada, Nicaragua, El Salvador, Mozambique—subdued under U.S. sponsorship. We dance to the tunes of glory, though our foe's ascendance to a threatening position of power was, arguably, the result of our own leaders' geopolitical opportunism and naïveté. The triumph in the steaming sands—though honest folk may differ on its roots, morality, and ultimate consequences—resulted, to an appreciable degree, from the dedicated efforts of African-American GI's, male and female, bivouacked for months in a most inhospitable Arabian desert, and from the leadership of a clearly capable African-American chairman of the Joint Chiefs of Staff, General Colin Powell.

The foreparents of contemporary white Americans would have consigned the idea of such a circumstance to the realm of traitorous fantasy. The foreparents of contemporary black Americans would have found such a state of affairs incomprehensible.

The nation's seemingly ungrudging recognition of the role of African-American enlisted personnel and officers in the Persian Gulf reflects a historical irony of some significance, namely that the objectives of the nonviolent civil rights movement for racial integration should come closest to realization not in the groves of academe, on the factory floor, in the corporate boardroom, or in the union hall, but on the field of battle.

These pages will travel part of the long and tortuous highway that begins on Bunker Hill and, for the moment, ends near Baghdad. The epic of the 761st Tank Battalion includes, as perhaps its proudest moment, the coming—in the eleventh hour—of one despised and rejected people to the rescue of another, who have been maligned and murdered throughout all the history that we know.

In *Mein Kampf*, Adolf Hitler set forth the equation that has linked racism with its anti-Semitic variant for centuries:

> It was and it is Jews who bring Negroes into the Rhineland, always with the same secret thought and clear aim of ruining the hated white race by the necessarily resulting bastardization, throwing it down from its cultural and political heights and himself rising to be its master. . . . It is positively a sin against all reason; a criminal lunacy to keep on drilling a half-born ape until people think they have made a lawyer out of him. . . . It is against the will of the Eternal Creator if his most gifted human beings by the hundreds of hundreds of thousands are allowed to degenerate into the morass of proletarianism while the Hottentots and Kaffirs are trained for intellectual professions . . . training exactly like that of the poodle.

In our rather tragic present, when black and Jewish Americans indulge in conflict that, in the final analysis, gives joy and comfort only to those racists and anti-Semites who are their common enemies, there is reason to remember a period in the not too terribly distant past. A time when those of both groups who were progressively inclined attempted with some success to collectively comprehend their horrific historical experiences. A time when there was an effort as well to honestly consider their differences and points of antagonism in a spirit of conciliation and rectification rather than usually unproductive confrontation. Just as many black Americans in the late forties and early fifties were strong advocates of the establishment of a Jewish homeland, likewise during the fifties and sixties Jews were in the forefront of those whites who locked arms with African-Americans in their courageous struggle against bigotry and segregation. Two young Jewish men from New York City, Michael Schwerner and Andrew Goodman, along with their black comrade James Cheney, would lose their lives during the Freedom Summer of 1964 in the battle to secure for Mississippi's African-Americans that most elemental of democratic freedoms, the right to register and vote.

The pages of this book will speak also of the failure, for three decades, of this nation's military and political leadership to recognize officially the significant role played in the Allied victory over fascism by the Black Panther battalion, liberators of Buchenwald and Dachau. This refusal, apparently rooted in racism, to acknowledge a major African-American chapter in a proud historical record is, though regrettable, hardly rare. It merely reflects the malignancy that has prevented this nation from becoming a true, not an imaginary, exemplar of freedom to all the world.

Above all, however, we sing in this volume of arms, and of the Black Panthers of the 761st Tank Battalion, who bore them so bravely in what many consider to be the last "good war" we won.

LIBERATORS

CHAPTER 1

Name in a footnote. Faceless name.

Moot hero shrouded in Betsy Ross

and Garvey flags—propped up

by bayonets, forever falling.

Robert Hayden,
"Crispus Attucks"

WPA painting of Crispus Attucks,
the runaway slave who was first to die
in the American Revolution, 1770.

The saga of the 761st Tank Battalion can best be viewed as a way station along a historical continuum that begins on the fifth day of March, 1770. Workers in Boston, Massachusetts, had for years fiercely resented a British government policy that permitted soldiers to take jobs with private employers during their off-duty hours. Clashes between civilian workmen and redcoat "scabs" were frequent and often bloody. On Monday, March 5—following a weekend of sporadic fistfights—a detachment of soldiers converged with a crowd of unarmed workers led by Crispus Attucks, a runaway slave. Harsh words and threats were exchanged. Several of the soldiers panicked and fired their muskets into the group of civilians. Attucks fell dead, followed by James Caldwell and Samuel Gray. Two other men later perished from their wounds. John Adams would write of the incident: "On that night, the foundation of American independence was laid."[1]

Though the name Crispus Attucks, first that day to fall in the Boston Massacre, has long occupied a place in the popular pantheon of Revolutionary War heroes, he need not stand alone as an African-American token in those ranks.

On June 17, 1775, the Battle of Bunker Hill placed regular troops of the British army against ragtag elements of the Massachusetts militia. Sensing victory, the British commander, Major John Pitcairn, leapt atop a wall, shouting, "The day is ours!" A black freedman, Peter Salem, raised his rifle to his shoulder and fired a single shot, mortally wounding the major and decisively turning the tide of battle. Also that day, another freedman, Salem Poor, received a special commendation for leadership and courage.

The story of African-American participation in the War for Independence is complex, marked by twists and turns in policy on the part of the Continental Congress, the several states, and General George Washington, the army's commander in chief.

In the summer of 1775 South Carolina's Senator Edward Rutledge proposed to the Second Continental Congress that all blacks, slave or free, currently serving in the army be summarily dismissed.

Less than a month after Salem and Poor were honored at Bunker Hill, Washington's headquarters issued an order forbidding recruiting officers from accepting any "stroller, Negro or vagabond" into the ranks of the Continental Army.

Rutledge's bill reflected the apprehension of most white Southerners—and many in the North as well—that placing weapons at the disposal of blacks, slaves particularly, was an open invitation to insurrection. So deep-seated was this fear that in 1778, the government of South Carolina threatened to defect from the revolutionary cause and cast its lot with the redcoats if its slaves were armed. Colonel John Laurens, on duty in South Carolina, wrote to General Washington that "reason had been drowned by the howlings of a triple-headed monster in which prejudice, avarice and pusillanimity are united."[2]

Though Congress would vote down Rutledge's proposal, Washington unilaterally terminated all black enlistments. On October 13, 1775, his decision was ratified by the legislators over the protest of some generals, such as John Thomas, who asserted—as recorded in Morris MacGregor and Bernard C. Nalty's invaluable *Blacks in the United States Armed Forces*[3]—that Negroes made just as good soldiers as whites and had "already proven themselves brave." Three months later, responding to protests from African-American servicemen, Washington reversed his decision and issued orders authorizing black recruitment.

By 1777, soldiers of color were much in evidence on the battlefields. A Hessian officer fighting with the British recorded in his diary: "The Negro can take the field instead of his master, and therefore there is no regiment to be seen in which there are not Negroes in abundance and among them are able-bodied and strong fellows."[4] As this statement indicates, many slaves entered the army as substitutes for their masters; often they received their freedom in return for placing their heads on a potentially deadly block. Virginia would, in fact, mandate that freedom be accorded to all slaves enrolled in the service by those who held them as property. Free blacks either volunteered or were conscripted. Only Maryland, in 1780, gave slaves the right to enlist of their own volition.

The British, recognizing the slave system as a potential weakness in the rebels' armor, attempted to exploit it. Their commander in chief, Sir Henry Clinton, declared in June 1779 that any blacks serving in the Continental Army who were captured would be sold as slaves, but "any who desert the rebel standard will have their freedom secured." Though this offer, combining the carrot of freedom with the stick of slavery, did not result in widespread defections from the ranks, it remained a matter deserving serious consideration by Washington and his staff.

In May of 1780, South Carolina's shortsighted policy of adamantly refusing to arm its blacks proved disastrous. After a month-long siege, made possible by the Britons' extensive use of freed slaves as support troops, Charleston, the state's premier city, fell to the enemy. Rubbing salt into the wounds of the vanquished, the redcoats dispatched squads of African-American soldiers to confiscate the city's cannons. Hundreds of their fellows seized the opportunity to escape their masters and join the British forces. The Battle of Charleston was, however, a unique event. Overwhelmingly, slaves showed little inclination to rally behind the Union Jack.

Within the rebels' ranks, meanwhile, not all the officers in the Continental Army were pleased to have African-Americans under their command. Referring to reinforcements of Massachusetts militiamen sent to Fort Ticonderoga in August 1777, Brigadier General William Heath wrote to Samuel Adams: "I saw a number of Negroes . . . generally able-bodied, but for my own part, I am never pleased to see them mixing with white men."[5] General Philip Schuyler, that same month, complained that the high number of African-American reinforcements was "a disgrace to American arms." One wonders if Schuyler moderated this judgment when, the following October, these same black troops played a major role in the crucial victory over General Burgoyne at Saratoga.[6] Also that autumn, African-American forces fought valorously in the battles of Brandywine and Fort Mercer. During the excruciating winter of 1778, nearly four hundred black soldiers endured the privations of Valley Forge with George Washington. Their desertion rate was reported to be considerably lower than that of their white comrades.

As the war progressed, major black participation was noted in the June 1778 Battle of Monmouth Courthouse, where seven hundred African-Americans fought under Washington's command. That August, in the Battle of Rhode Island, a unit of 125 newly recruited black infantrymen held off, for four hours, a combined force of experienced British and Hessian soldiers, making possible the escape of a major component of the Continental Army from a well-laid enemy trap. In November 1780, the Army of Louisiana, made up in the main of African-Americans, captured Mobile and Pensacola. Six of its black officers were decorated for bravery.

The final battle in the War for Independence was fought at Yorktown on September 19, 1781. A slave, James Robinson, was awarded a gold medal for conspicuous bravery under fire.

Though at least five thousand African-Americans bore arms during the Revolutionary War and participated in some fifty engagements with the enemy, their nation—as it would time and again—quickly forgot the contributions of its countrymen of color and deemed them unfit for future military service.

The Militia Act of 1792 restricted membership to "each and every white male citizen of the respective states . . . of the age of eighteen and under the age of forty-five." Secretary of War Henry Knox declared in 1798 that "no Negro, Mulatto or Indian shall be enlisted in the corps of Marines." This proscription stood until 1942. Also in 1798, Secretary of the Navy Benjamin Stoddard barred Negroes and mulattos from service in that military branch. This edict, though, was interpreted somewhat loosely, and African-American sailors were allowed to serve on a few vessels throughout the nineteenth century.

The army's all-white policy would be breached only in Louisiana (and to a lesser extent in Georgia and North Carolina), where in 1804 some fifty-five free nonwhite males, all with previous military experience, petitioned Governor William C. C. Claiborne to be permitted to offer their services as a unit of volunteers. Subsequently, a "Mulatto Corps" of militiamen was organized in New Orleans.

So matters stood until the nation was threatened by its former colonial master. The climactic battle of the War of 1812 was fought at New Orleans, and the difference between American victory and defeat may well be attributed to the courageous efforts of the relatively large number of black Louisianans who fought in that engagement.[7] General Andrew Jackson, early on in the war, had warned Governor Claiborne of the pivotal role the area's black population might play. "They are either for us or against us," Jackson wrote. "Distrust them and you make them your enemies: place confidence in them and you engage them by every dear and honorable tie to interests of the country who extends to them equal rights and privileges with white men."[8] When on January 8, 1815—two weeks after the signing of an Anglo-American peace treaty in Ghent, Belgium— Jackson, unaware the war was over, faced the invaders outside the Crescent City, two battalions of African-American troops were at his side. One of these was commanded by a black man, Major Joseph Savory. Jackson was not sparing in his praise for their accomplishments:

> **To the Men of Color:** Soldiers! I collected you to arms. I invited you to share in the perils and to divide the glory with your fellow countrymen. I knew that you loved the land of your nativity and that like ourselves you had to defend all that is most dear to you. But you surpass my hopes. I have found in you, united in these qualities, the noble enthusiasm which impels men to great deeds.[9]

Five years after the war to sustain this nation's liberation was successfully concluded, the American military's racial pendulum took another characteristic swing:

7

No negro or mulatto shall be received as a recruit in the Army of the United States of America.[10]

Adjutant General's Office of the U.S. Army,
February 18, 1820

In 1828, Andrew Jackson was elected President. Despite his earlier paean to African-American troops, the policy of exclusion remained in force throughout Old Hickory's eight years in the White House. Whatever Jackson's personal racial feelings may have been, his first allegiance—as with most elected officials, before or since—was to the political realities of the moment. America was a society looking, in the main, toward economic prosperity, powered, in large part, by the locomotive of uncompensated human labor. Significantly, Jackson's vice-president during his first term was John C. Calhoun, the powerful South Carolina senator and architect of the South's philosophical, judicial, and legislative defenses of slavery.

Though some establishment voices—like Old Hickory's White House predecessor, John Quincy Adams, along with such conscientious abolitionists as William Lloyd Garrison and the former slave Sojourner Truth—were articulating a strong and well-reasoned antislavery position, the power brokers of the 1820s and 1830s, and most of their white constituents, were quite comfortable with the "peculiar institution."

Black laborers at the docks, circa 1864.

• • • • • • • •

Action! Action! . . . is the plain duty of the hour. There is no time to delay. Liberty won by white men would lose half its luster. . . . Who would free themselves must strike the blow. Better even to die free than to live slaves. The Counsel I give comes of close observance of the great struggle now in progress and it is your hour and mine. I now . . . feel at liberty to call and counsel you to arms. . . . I urge you to fly to arms and smite with death the power that would bury the government and your liberty in the same hopeless grave. The chance is now given you to end in a day the bondage of centuries, and to rise in one bound from social degradation to the plane of common equality with the other varieties of men.[11]

*Frederick Douglass,
March 1863*

Frederick Douglass, a self-taught slave from the eastern shore of Maryland, had escaped to the North in 1838. He rose quickly to national prominence as an abolitionist firebrand and an uncompromising advocate for the rights of African-Americans, slave and free. A charismatic personality, Douglass, with his intellect, eloquence, dignity, and personal courage, inspired throughout much of the nineteenth century both black Americans and those whites who had come to realize that freedom is a concept blind to color, gender, or religious persuasion.

Well over a century after the fact, this nation's panoply of entertainment and information media has begun to pay serious attention to the part played by African-Americans in winning and securing their own freedom from involuntary servitude. Within the past half decade, mass audiences have enjoyed and been educated by the acclaimed feature film *Glory* and the Public Broadcasting System's highly successful documentary series *The Civil War*. The saga of the 54th Massachusetts Regiment is now part of the patriotic public domain. The men of this regiment, recruited by the indefatigable Douglass, particularly distinguished themselves in July 1863, during the important Battle of Fort Wagner, outside Charleston, South Carolina. Under the leadership of Colonel Robert Gould Shaw, the 54th drove the Confederates from their stronghold; in the process, half of the regiment's men were killed, wounded, or captured. Colonel Shaw was among those slain. Sergeant William H. Carney received the Congressional Medal of Honor for his courage under fire.

The First South Carolina Volunteers—composed of newly freed slaves—fought gallantly in major battles and raids in the South. In one of their most daring exploits, the regiment made a lightning strike into Florida, capturing and holding the city of Jacksonville until ordered, for logistical reasons, to withdraw. Their commander, the Boston abolitionist Colonel Thomas Wentworth Higginson, has told their tale with respect and dignity in his classic work *Army Life in a Black Regiment.*[12]

It is necessary to examine the circumstances that led to the enrollment, during a fraternal struggle of horrific proportions, of 186,000 African-American combat troops, 200,000 black civilians in support and service units, and 29,000 black seamen aboard the vessels of the United States Navy.

Frederick Douglass had long viewed the prospect of war, and later its reality, as a blessed event that must inevitably result in his people's freedom. He unceasingly agitated for blacks to be enlisted in the Grand Army of the Republic, meeting with Abraham Lincoln in the White House in an unsuccessful attempt to convince the President to cease his opposition to both immediate emancipation and the recruitment of African-American troops. Lincoln's preoccupation, in the early phase of the war, with keeping the border slave states in the Union precluded his assenting to the black leader's petition. It must be noted that Lincoln, though he abhorred slavery, was not an integrationist like Douglass. The President believed that a "colonization" program—the voluntary repatriation of blacks to Africa—offered the best possible solution to the nation's racial dilemma. However, abolitionists, black and white, adopted and ardently seconded Douglass's call to arms. His own community reacted enthusiastically to its acknowledged spokesman's militant stand.

Recruiting offices in Northern cities were besieged by black would-be enlistees. According to Douglass scholar Philip Foner, "Philadelphia Negroes offered to go South to organize slave revolts."[13]

Only with the Emancipation Proclamation of January 1, 1863—twenty-one months into the war—did the Lincoln administration revise its policies. Congress soon after resolved that "the President of the United States is authorized to employ as many persons of African descent as he may deem necessary for the suppression of this rebellion."

Some in the army's high command welcomed the new forces, though the opinions of many liberals were not without a measure of condescension. An aide to Major General David P. Hunter of the Department of the South wrote:

Aftermath of a Union Army assault on a South Carolina town, 1864.

Suddenly released from the cruel restraints of chattel slavery and still pursued into freedom by the curse of that ignorance which slavery fostered as its surest weapon and effective shield, the Major General believes that the disciplines of military life will be the very safest and quickest school in which these enfranchised bondsmen can be elevated to the level of our higher intelligence and cultivation.[14]

Charles G. Halpine,
Assistant Adjutant General

As large numbers of black recruits arrived on military installations in Union territory, they faced, as they would again in future times, the enmity of white civilians and police. A white contemporary observer described the situation as the result of "an intolerant prejudice against the colored race which deny them the honorable position to which every soldier is entitled, even though he gained that position at the risk of his head in the cause of the nation. A large class [exists] that believes that the Negro race does not possess the necessary qualifications to make efficient soldiers and that consequently the experiment would end in disaster."[15]

11

Union soldiers at Camp William Penn,
Philadelphia, Pennsylvania.

The performance of African-American fighting men would prove the nay-sayers wrong. In May 1863, six hundred black soldiers lost their lives in the battle for Port Hudson, Louisiana. Their units—the 1st and 2nd Louisiana Colored Regiments—comported themselves in a manner that typified the devotion of black troops to the Union cause. They were saluted by General Nathaniel Banks: "The highest commendation is bestowed upon them by all officers in command. The history of this day proves conclusively that the government will find this class of troops effective supporters and defenders."

Harriet Tubman, chief conductor of the Underground Railroad and a towering figure in the struggle against slavery, made notable contributions to the Union cause. Throughout the war she served, without pay, as a spy and scout. Tubman also organized recently freed slaves into an intelligence service that provided the Union forces with valuable information from behind Confederate lines. In June 1863, she personally led a contingent of troops in a raid up the Combahee River in South Carolina, which destroyed millions of dollars' worth of Confederate property and resulted in the escape of over seven hundred slaves. At war's end, "General" Tubman, as she was now known, began a futile thirty-seven-year struggle to be compensated by the government for her efforts. Eventually she received a small monthly pension, based on her deceased husband's service in the Union Army, not on her own manifold contributions to the cause.

African-American troops participated in over three hundred battles with Johnny Reb. Sixteen black soldiers and four black sailors were awarded the Congressional Medal of Honor for their conspicuous bravery above and beyond the call of duty.

In the immediate post-Appomattox period, the presence of black outfits in the Union force occupying the old Confederacy infuriated an unrepentant white population, now demoralized in defeat. These units were removed from Southern and border states as soon as it was militarily feasible.

The Reorganization Act of 1866 established four black contingents in the regular army—the 24th and 25th Infantry Regiments and the 9th and 10th Cavalries.

●　　●　　●　　●　　●　　●　　●　　●

> Just a Buffalo Soldier
> in the heart of America,
> stolen from Africa,
> brought to America.
> Said he was
> "Fighting on arrival.
> Fighting for survival."
> Said he was
> "a Buffalo Soldier
> in the war for America."
>
> *Noel George Williams and Bob Marley,*
> *"Buffalo Soldier"*

It is not difficult, with the benefit of more than a hundred years of hindsight, to condemn the record of the Buffalo Soldiers from atop a politically correct pedestal. Inarguably, there is something beyond tragedy in the sight of one oppressed people killing another in the name of their mutual oppressor. Their actions must be viewed, however, within the context of their times.

During the years these men rode and marched the plains, mountains, and deserts of the Southwest and the West, freedmen in the South were enduring the cruelly thwarted promise of Reconstruction. They returned to virtual peonage in the subsequent, often bloodily accomplished, so-called Redemption of the Confederacy's values, power structure, and prejudices. In the North, the postwar era's continuing economic instability would, to a great extent, decimate an embryonic entrepreneurial black middle class fighting to sink its roots into most unreceptive soil. The continuing arrival of destitute European immigrants brought new competition and new hardships for the African-American working class. Given the plight of his civilian brothers and sisters, it would not be surprising if the black professional soldier viewed his lot as being relatively secure, privileged, and honorable.

The relationship between black and Native American populations had always been rather problematic. There were tribes like the Cherokees, Chickasaw, and Choctaw, who held relatively large numbers of slaves—though, in the main, they treated their bondsmen with greater respect and gave more privileges than did most white slavemasters. Other tribes, like the Seminoles and Creeks, had admirable records for taking runaway blacks into their midst, and intermarriage was far from uncommon. Nonetheless an equation of shared oppression would not have leapt immediately to the minds of the Buffalo Soldiers, whose nickname was bestowed by their Native American adversaries. Stationed on remote and dangerous outposts in the West and Southwest, they wore the colors of an army that had won black people's freedom. The enemy of that army was, therefore, their enemy as well. The Buffalo Soldiers' Native American foes regarded them, not without reason, as "black white men."

These highly professional outfits battled the Cheyenne, the Mescalero Apache, the Arapaho, and the Sioux. They fought Geronimo, Sitting Bull, Black Kettle, and a host of other war chiefs. Between 1870 and 1890, thirteen Buffalo Soldiers received the Congressional Medal of Honor. Colonel Benjamin Grierson, the organizer and longtime commander of the 10th Cavalry, was

> gratified to be able to refer to its splendid record of twenty-two years service to the government . . . rendered at the most isolated posts on the frontier with the most warlike and savage Indians of the plains. . . . The men have cheerfully endured many hardships and

Sergeant John Denny,
Congressional Medal of Honor
winner, 1894.

Buffalo soldiers, 1870.

Black soldiers at evening mess in Camp Alger, Virginia, 1898.

privations, and in the midst of great danger steadfastly maintained a
most gallant and zealous devotion to duty and they may well be proud
of the record made and rest assured that the hard work undergone in
the accomplishments of such important and valuable service to their
country is well understood and appreciated and that it cannot fail—
sooner or later—to meet with due recognition and reward.[16]

The phrase "sooner or later" in relation to this nation's appreciation of the
sacrifices made by its servicemen of color has, far more often than not, meant
later—very much later.

The United States Military Academy at West Point, New York, was established in 1802. By 1941, only five African-Americans—Henry O. Flipper, John
H. Alexander, James D. Fowler, Benjamin O. Davis, Jr., and Charles D. Young—
had graduated and received commissions. All were ostracized by their white
fellow-cadets during their time at the academy. Young, a member of the class

16

of 1889, rose to the rank of lieutenant colonel. He fought guerrilla insurgents in the Philippines with the Buffalo Soldiers and later served as military attaché in the United States embassies in Haiti and Liberia. In 1917, with the country entering World War I, Young expected to be offered a post commensurate with his record and proven abilities. Instead the army abruptly retired him, stating that he was physically unfit for duty. In protest, the colonel rode his horse five hundred miles—from Wilberforce, Ohio, to Washington, D.C.,—to show that his health was not impaired. The black press and leadership raised their voices in his support. The army reinstated Colonel Young, and he was assigned to Fort Grant, Illinois, where he trained African-American troops for the duration of the war.

As the nineteenth century neared its end, the United States, urged on by jingoistic and bellicose politicians and press, provoked a war with Spain. The Buffalo Soldiers, if viewed through present-day lenses, again occupied a rather unenviable political position. They fought for the liberation of Spanish colonials who, at war's end, would find, instead of freedom, further subjugation within America's own newly constituted empire: Cuba, Puerto Rico, Guam, and the Philippines.

The sixteen volunteer African-American regiments raised during the Spanish-American War lived in a completely segregated world, with little or no off-the-battlefield fraternization with their white comrades. Their performance, along with that of the regular army's black units, was repeatedly commended.

Summarizing the 24th Infantry's conduct during the decisive July 1, 1898, Battle of Santiago in Cuba, Captain Benjamin Leavell stated: "It would be hard to particularize in reporting upon the men of this company. All . . . showed a desire to do their duty, yea more than their duty. . . . Too much cannot be said for their courage, willingness and endurance."[17]

In the public memory, the centerpiece of the Spanish-American War is the almost mythologized charge of Teddy Roosevelt and his Rough Riders up the strategically crucial San Juan Hill, near Santiago. Contrary to popular perception, the future President and his men were hardly fighting alone. With Roosevelt's 1st Volunteer Cavalry were four other units, including the 10th Cavalry of Buffalo Soldiers. Major General Joseph Wheeler would say to them:

> You forded the San Juan River and gallantly swept over San Juan Hill, driving the army from its crest. Without a moment's halt, you bravely charged and carried the formidable entrenchments of Fort San Juan.

The 24th Infantry in Cuba, 1898.

. . . You, in the darkness of night, strongly entrenched the position your valor had won, you continued the combat until the Spanish Army of Santiago succumbed to the superb prowess and strength of American arms. Peace promptly followed and you return to receive the plaudits of seventy millions of people.[18]

One person whose plaudits the men of the 10th Cavalry did not receive was Colonel Theodore Roosevelt. Never one to share a spotlight willingly, Roosevelt claimed that some of the African-American troops were "laggards," who remained at the rear during the clash. This version of events was thoroughly discredited by many officers on the scene, who stated that the blacks at the rear were ammunition carriers, not fighters, and were positioned precisely where they were supposed to be. Five 10th Cavalry "laggards" would be recipients of the Congressional Medal of Honor. In the aftermath of the war, the 24th and 25th Infantry Regiments would serve in the Philippines, battling guerrilla resistance to the world's newest colonial power.

On July 28, 1906, Companies B, C, and D of the 24th Infantry arrived at Fort Brown, in Brownsville, Texas. They had hardly settled in their new quarters, when civilian harassment and attacks began. A contemporary report states: "Incidents of friction were numerous and notorious enough to be the cause of much discussion in the barracks room."

During the afternoon of August 13, a rumor swept through town that a black soldier had grabbed a white woman by the hair and dragged her down a street. The community was outraged, and the men of the 24th feared violent reprisal for a deed that had never been committed.

Shortly past midnight, a group of men—witnesses varied on their number, some recalling as few as nine, others as many as twenty—began firing in a white neighborhood adjacent to the camp. One white civilian was killed, two were injured. Suspicion immediately fell on Companies B, C, and D, none of whose members, then or ever, admitted to participating in the attack.

Despite the absence of either corroborative or noncircumstantial evidence, the army—through administrative procedures rather than public and legally exacting courts-martial—dishonorably discharged the three companies' entire component of 167 enlisted men. This extremely harsh collective punishment was meted out after a Cameron County civilian grand jury—which could hardly have been expected to be sympathetic to the accused—thought the army's case so flimsy that they refused to return any indictments.

African-American reaction to the railroading of these troops was swift, angry, and loud. The nation's most prominent black spokesman, Booker T. Washington, who rarely took militant stands, was moved to write Secretary of War William Howard Taft: "I hope some plan will have been thought out by which to do something that may change the feeling the colored people now as a whole have regarding the dismissal of the three companies. I have never in all my experience with the race experienced a time when the entire people have the feeling they now have regarding the administration."[19]

Persistent pleas for justice from Washington, his fellow black leaders, and the African-American press struck no responsive chords in the War Department or in Theodore Roosevelt's White House.

Following two extremely suspect investigations, Roosevelt reported to the Senate on January 14, 1907, that the punishment was indeed justified. Two weeks later, a majority of the Senate Military Affairs Committee sustained the official position. Four less gullible senators, including Joseph Foraker of Ohio and Morgan Bulkeley of Connecticut, called, in a minority report, for the reinstatement of the soldiers and the restoration of all their civil rights. The dissenting committee members found that testimony failed to identify the individuals who participated in the shooting or to show that any of the discharged soldiers engaged in a "conspiracy of silence" to protect the perpetrators. The testimony, the senators continued, "is contradictory and much of it unbelievable so as not to be sufficient to sustain the charges." The controversy, however, soon died out.

On April 28, 1972, Secretary of the Army Robert Froehle, at the urging of the Congressional Black Caucus, admitted the service's egregious errors in the case of the Brownsville Raid and issued honorable discharges to the 167 members of Companies B, C, and D. Only one veteran, eighty-six-year-old Dorsey Willis, was still alive to savor his long-belated vindication.

. . . .

The south does not want colored men to get any kind of military training; nothing frightens it worse than the thought of millions of colored men with discipline, organizing power and a dangerous effectiveness. This is why Senator Vardaman [of Mississippi] is so bitterly opposed to Universal Military Training.[20]

Dr. J. E. Spingarn,
Chairman, NAACP, 1917

During the first months of 1917, as America moved toward entering the Great War in Europe, the question of how to utilize its black male citizens in the coming struggle was a matter of great debate. Among the issues considered were: Should they be drafted and, if so, where, given regional prejudices, should they train, and for what roles should they be readied—combat, support, or both? Congress, in the end, enacted a military draft law that made no mention of race.

On August 23, 1917, a bloody episode in Texas focused the nation's attention on black servicemen and appeared to justify Southerners' fears. One month earlier, the 24th Infantry's 3rd Battalion—645 men strong—arrived at Fort Sam Houston from Camp Narriboda in Minnesota. They were proud men, members of a unit that had fought and died for its country with honor and distinction, at home and abroad, for half a century. They perceived themselves to be first-class citizens and were not prepared to accept the Jim Crowism rampant in their new

Houston riots court martial at Fort Sam Houston,
November 1, 1917.

environment. This attitude, predictably, clashed with that of their Texas hosts;
trouble came immediately. There were brawls over the troops' refusal to abide
by laws mandating segregated seating on Houston's streetcars. Fights broke out
when they refused to drink from "colored" water fountains. So tense was the
situation that the fort's commanders—fearing that the 3rd Battalion would re-
taliate against civilians over their mistreatment—confiscated the infantrymen's
weapons.

During the afternoon of August 23, a black soldier intervened in the arrest
and beating of a black woman by a Houston policeman. The officer struck the
soldier and, when he fled, fired several shots in his direction, all of which missed
their target. Rumor carried a different story back to Fort Sam Houston: a member of the 3rd Battalion had been murdered in cold blood by a cop. That night
an estimated one to two hundred African-American troops decided to take their
revenge.

The men raided the fort's armory, stole guns and ammunition, and made
their way into town. The result was the largest and most violent clash between
black troops and white civilians in United States military history. The soldiers
marauded through the streets, firing into houses and bars, taking aim at

21

pedestrians. When the battle subsided, fifteen white civilians—including four policemen—lay dead. Twenty-one whites were wounded. Four of the men of the 3rd Battalion lost their lives during that terrible night.

Following an investigation, fifty-four soldiers were convicted by a court-martial of mutiny and murder. Forty-one were sentenced to life imprisonment at hard labor. Thirteen were condemned to die on the gallows. On December 22, 1917, a hangman carried out the death warrants. Two more courts-martial resulted in sixteen additional death sentences. In September 1918, six of these men were hanged; the punishment of the others was reduced to life in prison.

Writing of the incident in *Strength for the Fight*, Bernard C. Nalty observes: "The mutiny sent the same kind of shock waves through the military that Nat Turner's rebellion had inflicted on pre–Civil War Southern society. The War Department had to overhaul its plans and avoid large concentrations of black combat troops. [After the hangings] military leaders also became concerned about the loyalty of black Americans."[21]

Conscription of African-Americans, however, was already in force, and they continued to be drafted. Three hundred eighty thousand enlisted men and twelve hundred officers—a minuscule percentage of the black population—would serve their country in the "War to End All Wars." All would be placed in rigidly segregated units. According to MacGregor and Nalty in *Blacks in the United States Armed Forces*, only one in nine African-Americans served in combat out-fits; the rest were "uniformed laborers."[22] None of the black units in the regular army were sent abroad, a result, in all probability, of high command mistrust generated by the Houston riot.

Prior to the United States' joining in the Allied cause, the NAACP's chairman, Dr. J. E. Spingarn, had forcefully pressed the army to establish a base where black officers could be trained. In 1917, such a facility—the Colored Training Camp—went into operation near Des Moines, Iowa, over the objections of local whites. Its first class included four recent Harvard graduates and two Harvard Law School students, along with a host of graduates of the nation's black colleges and universities. The *New York Tribune* reported: "No drill is held, no outdoor exercise is taken, without an admiring audience of the colored folk of Des Moines watching their dusky brethren in Khaki. No member of camp can walk through the town without a dozen small darkies trailing wistfully at his heels."[23] After a year, the Colored Training Camp was incorporated into a centralized officer candidate school, where the African-Americans were instructed separately from their white counterparts.

Colonel Charles Young, 1917.

Despite the high caliber of the majority of black officers-in-training, Colonel P. D. Lochridge, acting chief of the War College Division, would write in October 1917: "Colored officers should be limited to the grades of first and second lieutenants, as it is not believed that a sufficient number of colored men can be obtained [who are] capable of commanding companies. . . . It is absolutely impracticable to make [artillery] battery commanders or commanders of engineer companies out of the available colored material."[24]

Meanwhile, two African-American infantry divisions, the 92nd and 93rd—composed of draftees, National Guardsmen, and volunteers—prepared for combat duty in France. The 92nd was in place at Camp Funston, Kansas, where, early in 1918, their commander, Major General George Baillou, issued an order that would raise a wave of protest within the black community.

> It should be well known to all colored officers and men that no useful purpose is served by such acts as will cause the "color question" to be raised. It is not a question of legal rights, but a question of policy, and any policy that tends to bring about its resulting animosities, is prejudicial to the military interest of the 92nd Division, and therefore prejudicial to an important interest of the colored race. . . . White men made the Division and they can break it just as easily if it becomes a troublemaker. Avoid every situation that can give rise to racial ill-will. Attend quietly and faithfully to your duties, and don't go where your presence is not desired.[25]

The response of George Frazier, chairman of the National Association for the Advancement of Colored Men, to Baillou's bulletin typified the tone of

23

General Pershing inspects the 92nd Division in France during World War I.

meetings held by African-Americans around the nation. "You cannot expect the Negro to cringe before the white people and at the same time expect them to go overseas and fight the German people in the trenches of France."[26]

The racist inclinations and near-total insensitivity to the deepest feelings of black Americans implicit in Baillou's order foreshadowed worse to come from the American high command.

The 92nd Division, made up of the 365th, 366th, 367th, and 368th Regiments and with artillery, signal, engineer, and machine gun components; and the 93rd, composed of the 369th, 370th, 371st, and 372nd Regiments, joined the American Expeditionary Force in France in late 1917 and early 1918. Both of these regiments were composed of conscripts. The 93rd was transferred to French command, where its men were incorporated with tens of thousands of Africans already serving in the Army of France. This action was taken over the objections of the AEF's commander, General John J. Pershing, who wished to employ the members of the combat-ready unit as uniformed laborers. The 92nd remained under AEF command.

The AEF's leadership made a serious effort to inculcate the French military and civilian populations with American-style racial biases and stereotypes. An extraordinary document entitled "Secret Information Concerning Black American Troops," unearthed at this time by Dr. W. E. B. Du Bois, editor of the NAACP journal *Crisis*, casts a bright light on this immoral and counterproductive policy. Though the document was couched in language that made it appear to originate from French military sources, Du Bois established that it was, in actuality, prepared at AEF headquarters:

. . . We French are not in our province if we undertake to discuss what some call "prejudice." American opinion is unanimous on the "color question" and does not admit any discussion.

The increasing number of Negroes in the United States would create for the white race in the Republic a menace of degeneracy were it not for the impassable gulf that has been made between them. . . .

The indulgence and familiarity [with which the French are accustomed to treating blacks] are matters of grievous concern to the Americans. They consider them an affront to national policy. They are afraid that contact with the French will inspire in black Americans aspirations which to the whites are intolerable. . . .

Although a citizen of the United States, the black man is regarded by the white American as an inferior being. . . . The black is constantly being censured for his tendency toward undue familiarity. The vices of the Negro are a constant menace to the American who has to repress them strongly. . . . We must prevent the rise of any pronounced degree of intimacy between French officers and black officers. We must not eat with them or seek to talk with them outside of the arrangements of military service.

We must not commend too highly the black American troops, particularly in the presence of white Americans. [We must] make a point of keeping the population from "spoiling" the Negroes. White Americans become greatly incensed at any public expression of intimacy between white women with black men. Military authorities cannot intervene directly on this question, but it can through the civil authorities exercise some influence on the population.[27]

It would be difficult to find a clearer expression of prevailing white attitudes during the Woodrow Wilson era. It should be remembered that during this

Virginia-born intellectual's two terms in the White House, at the helm of an administration notoriously reactionary on matters black, 441 African-Americans were lynched in the United States.

The French war ministry, on learning that the document was being distributed to local officials throughout the country, ordered all copies confiscated and burned.

Comparing the two divisions' experiences in France is instructive. The 93rd's service with the French was characterized by severe logistic, material, and communications problems. Yet despite these difficulties, the division's success in combat was, by any standards, remarkable. The 371st and 372nd Regiments played vital roles in the defense of the Meuse-Argonne region. The 369th performed admirably in the fighting north of the Oise-Ardennes canal. It would be awarded more citations than any other regiment in the AEF. The first American unit to reach the Rhine River, the 369th fought for 191 consecutive days "without losing a trench, giving an inch or surrendering a prisoner." No other American unit served as long a span of nonstop combat. It was an accomplishment that would be rivaled in the next war by the 761st Tank Battalion. The people of France awarded the 369th as a unit and 170 individual members its highest military honor, the Croix de Guerre. The 370th and 371st would receive the Croix as well.

The 92nd's Division star did not shine so brilliantly. Remaining under AEF control, its men saw little action, although the 1st Battalion of the 367th Regiment was the recipient of a Croix de Guerre. The division did, however, fight capably in the war's final battle, the decisive American assault on the Hindenburg line. It is clear that the uninspiring overall performance of the 92nd did not stem from any shortcomings inherent in the African-American fighting man. It was, rather, the result of a racist philosophy that pervaded the psyches of the military establishment. The 92nd had a high quotient of draftees in its ranks, unlike the 93rd, three quarters of whose members were National Guardsmen. The 93rd had high-ranking black officers; the officers of the 92nd were mainly Southern whites. These commanders, furious over their assignment to a black unit, constantly and vehemently reviled their men as badly motivated cowards who were a detriment to overall morale.

Six months after the Armistice, the War Department received a document written by a black civilian, Charles Holston Williams, that catalogued the complaints voiced by the 92nd Division's African-American officers and enlisted

Colored doughboy in training during World War I.

men. In a memorandum to the chief of staff, Colonel W. P. Clark commented on its contents: "This report criticizes every white officer . . . mentioned by name and is, in effect, an attack on the social system that draws lines of racial distinction both in and out of the Army. As such it is considered that a reply, other than an acknowledgment, is neither necessary nor desirable."[28]

The 369th Regiment came home to Harlem and a celebration rarely rivaled in the black capital's history. They paraded up Fifth Avenue to the beat of their renowned regimental band, under the baton of James Reese Europe, an important but little remembered composer and musical innovator. The "Fighting 369th," respectfully dubbed the "Hellfighters" by their German foes, acknowledged the accolades—louder than "Big Bertha's" cannon barrages—of hundreds of thousands of African-Americans, glorying in the heroism of their doughboys.

W. E. B. Du Bois, usually a tough-minded realist, was moved by the spectacle to write: "We stand again to look America squarely in the face. It lynches . . . it disenfranchises . . . it insults us. We return fighting. Make way for democracy! We saved it in France and we will save it in the U.S.A."[29] Du Bois's words undoubtedly reflect African America's emotions of the moment. Making America safe for democracy, however, would prove no less chimerical than fighting a war to end all wars.

With the end of hostilities in Europe, the War Department launched an extensive but extremely self-serving review of the performance of its African-American outfits. MacGregor and Nalty summarize the results:

> The War Department concluded that it had made some errors in the employment of black troops, although its basic wartime plan was sound. The failures lay in discipline and training, not in the segregated conditions in which the Negro had served nor in the other forms of discrimination to which he was subjected.[30]

An appraisal submitted by Lieutenant Colonel Allen Greer, who served with the 92nd Division, is representative of responses to the department's survey:

> Taken on average, their [black officers'] ignorance was colossal. Practically every [patrol] report had to be checked up on by a white officer. This check nearly always showed a total ignorance on the part of the Negro leader and usually a disregard for the truth. Nearly every Negro officer had the same attitude, so far as veracity was concerned, as the Negro soldier. To both it was an unknown quantity. . . . Generally speaking, only about fifty percent of the Negroes have the characteristics to make good combat soldiers. . . . The Negroes make excellent teamsters, better in fact than white soldiers do. They also make excellent chauffeurs.[31]

On November 11, 1991, United Press International reported:

> A black soldier who single-handedly turned back a German raid will be finally honored by his fellow Americans nearly 75 years after his heroic deeds. Sgt. Henry Johnson of the 369th Infantry Regiment received the Croix de Guerre for his World War I heroics but he never received so much as a Purple Heart from the United States. In stopping the raid by 24 enemy soldiers, Johnson killed at least four Germans and saved a wounded comrade's life, getting shot twice and

having his leg shattered in the process. He died a penniless alcoholic and is believed to be buried in a pauper's cemetery in Albany, New York. [Some historians contend, however, that Johnson is buried in Washington, D.C.]

Today a monument to Johnson is being unveiled in the city's Washington Park. The Veterans Day Parade is marching in his honor and the main street of Albany's largely black Arbor Hill neighborhood will be renamed Henry Johnson Boulevard.[32]

The years between the two world wars would see no major changes in the army's policies toward blacks. Though the African-American leadership and press would periodically call attention to the service's discriminatory policies and its insistence on segregated units and facilities, the status quo prevailed. In the wake of the stock market crash of 1929 and the subsequent near collapse of the nation's economic system, black leaders had more pressing matters to address.

CHAPTER 2

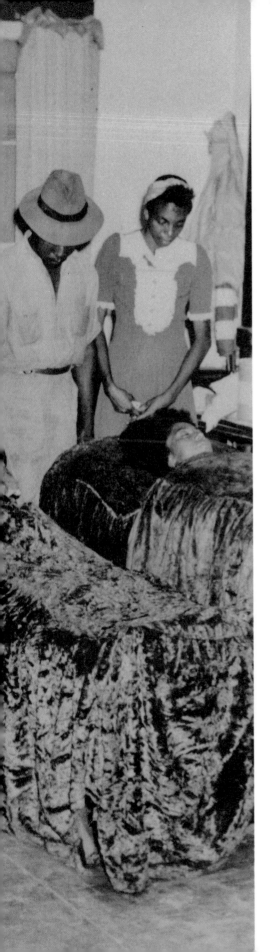

I wish the rent

Was Heaven sent.

Langston Hughes

Lynch victims at a funeral parlor.

On a warm June night in 1938, seventy thousand fight fans gather in the Bronx for perhaps the most symbolic event in sporting history. In homes, taverns, and workplaces throughout the nation, tens of millions of Americans sit anxiously by their radios. Five thousand miles away, the sun has not yet risen. Nonetheless, lights glow in German houses as the citizens of the Reich eagerly await the contest. In one corner of the ring stands the great Aryan hope, Max Schmeling. He has been dispatched to America by Adolf Hitler, who has announced that Schmeling will prove, once and for all, the innate superiority of Nazi manhood. Facing him is a tall, well-muscled African-American, Joe Louis, the heavyweight champion of the world, born twenty-four years earlier in a sharecropper's shack in Chambers County, Alabama. Two years before, in this same ring, the "Brown Bomber" had suffered his only professional defeat, a twelve-round knockout at the hands of the German champion. But on this night there is more at stake for Joe Louis than mere personal revenge. Like Jesse Owens in the Berlin Olympics of 1936, he is standing in for his nation and for democracy. He bears this immense pressure with grace and dignity. At the sound of the bell, Louis swiftly emerges from his corner and with controlled ferocity speedily demolishes his opponent. It is over in barely a minute. Latecomers to Yankee Stadium and tardy listeners at home have missed the match. For this night, at least, the Führer's braggadocio has rung hollow. Across the river from the stadium, shouts of jubilation reverberate through the streets of Harlem. "Our Joe" has once again done the home folks proud.

World heavyweight champion Joe Louis.

The exploits of black superstars like Joe Louis, probably the greatest folk hero that American blacks had ever known, provided a measure of psychological and emotional sustenance for African America during the bleak and bitter Depression years of the 1930s. The country as a whole was confronting an economic collapse, coupled with a crisis of the collective will; its citizens of color were among those who suffered the most. Uptown's poet laureate, Langston Hughes, succinctly summed up the plight of the black masses: "When downtown catches cold," he wrote, "Harlem gets pneumonia." Through that terrible decade, the affliction was nearly terminal.

The situation in Harlem mirrored conditions in urban black communities across the land. By the mid-thirties, Harlem's population density rivaled Calcutta's. Two hundred thirty-three persons lived on each acre of its turf; one hundred fewer people occupied the average acre in the rest of the Manhattan cityscape. Harlemites were spending forty to fifty percent of their meager incomes on rent, while white New Yorkers were allocating only half that amount for their housing accommodations. The poorer half of the city's black residents survived on an income that was fifty percent less than that of the poorer half of the white population. Harlem's infant mortality rate doubled that of the city as a whole; twice as many black women died in childbirth.

Employment discrimination reached staggering levels: Consolidated Gas had a work force of 10,000; 213 were black. New York Edison also had a payroll of 10,000; 65 of its workers—all porters—were African-American. The IRT subway system was relatively liberal by comparison: of its 10,000 workers, 580 were persons of color.

The corner of 167th Street and Jerome Avenue in the Bronx was the scene of the "domestic slave market." Each day, hundreds of black women gathered in search of work in the homes of the petite bourgeoisie; prospective employers drove up and took their pick. Twenty cents an hour topped the wage scale, and for those women not hired, their bodies, rather than their labor, often became the articles of trade.

It was inevitable that the Dickensian conditions endured by most of Harlem's 400,000 residents would eventually result in a violent expression of their rage and frustration; the community was a tinderbox lacking a spark. On March 19, 1935, a young boy was caught stealing a ten-cent penknife from a store on 125th Street; other black shoppers attacked the lad's white captors. False word flew through the neighborhood that the youth had been beaten to death. Within the hour, mobs were rampaging through the streets. One thousand policemen—

on foot, on horseback, and in squad cars—were dispatched to confront thousands of rioters, who were targeting white-owned businesses, many of whose owners were perceived—not inaccurately—as exploiters of the African-American community. A Chinese laundryman ran out to the street and hurriedly posted a sign on his window: "Me colored too." During the course of events, two hundred stores were looted. Thirty-eight blacks were hospitalized with bullet wounds and other life-threatening injuries. Two hundred more were treated for less serious physical damage. Three blacks lost their lives in the riot.

The press and the municipal authorities blamed the outburst solely on Communist agitation. The observations of YMCA Field Secretary Channing Tobias, a respected community leader, were much more to the point. "It is erroneous," he wrote, "to rush to the easy conclusions of the District Attorney and the Hearst newspapers that the whole thing was a communist plot. It is true there were communists in the picture. But what gave them their opportunity? The fact that there were and still are thousands of Negroes standing in enforced idleness on the street corners of Harlem with no prospect of employment while their favored Negro neighbors are compelled to spend their money with business houses directed by white absentee owners who employ white workers imported from every other part of New York City."[1]

Much has been written about the role and influence of the Communist party in the African-American community. In many cases, these analyses have been somewhat flawed by their authors' dogmatic and adversarial stances—giving the extreme left either too much or too little credit for its contributions to the struggle for racial justice. Mark Naison, however, in his exhaustive study, *Communists in Harlem during the Depression*, provides an extremely well documented account.

Harlem, he writes, had been targeted by the Party's leadership as the "concentration point of its strategy to win influence in black America." It dispatched its best black organizers, from all parts of the nation, to African America's capital city. By 1938, Naison states, "the Harlem Communist Party had close to a thousand black members and activated many thousands more through its work with trade unions [and other organizations]. No Socialist organization before or since has touched the life of an African-American community so profoundly."[2]

The Party's platform, emphasizing a commitment to a free and racially integrated society with economic opportunity for all, could not fail but strike a responsive chord within African-Americans. Its tenacious battle to save the lives of the "Scottsboro Boys," nine black youths ages twelve to twenty-one—all but the youngest one sentenced to death by a white Alabama judge and jury for the alleged rape of two young white women—in the most celebrated civil rights case of the decade, gave more than a few blacks the impression that the Communist party was willing and able to back up its words with action.

The Party did face considerable opposition in Harlem—primarily because it was white-led—from black nationalist groups that had split away from Marcus Garvey's United Negro Improvement Association. Before its charismatic leader's imprisonment in 1924 on fraud charges, the UNIA had boasted a nationwide membership of more than one million blacks (a large percentage of them immigrants—like Garvey—from the West Indies). Garvey's philosophy advocated a fervent racial pride, self-help through business enterprises, and the eventual repatriation of America's blacks—under the UNIA's aegis—to Mother Africa. His nationalistic discourse, a precursor in many ways to the "cultural nationalism" of the 1970s and today's Afrocentric movement, reflected a worldview that has long had significant impact upon the thought, actions, and life-styles of many blacks in the American diaspora.

Despite the opposition, the Communist party, according to Naison, was able to attract many of Harlem's workers and intellectuals as sympathizers, if not members. By the mid-thirties, such previously vocal anti-Communists as labor leader A. Philip Randolph and Lester Granger of the Urban League were advocating a "united front" against discrimination. In May 1935, Father Divine's newspaper, *The Spoken Word*, editorialized: "The Communists are the only outstanding organization or party with enough courage to stand flatly for social equality or equal opportunity, regardless of race, creed or color."[3]

During the thirties, several new leaders appeared on the Harlem scene. None excited the community more than a young Baptist minister, the scion of one of the district's most distinguished families. Adam Clayton Powell, Jr., tall, handsome, and a rousing orator, was fresh out of Columbia University when he assumed the leadership of relief efforts at his father's pastorate, Abyssinian Baptist Church, at the time the largest black congregation in America. The elder Powell, in marked contrast to most Harlem ministers—who were much more concerned with their followers' welfare in the hereafter than in the here and now—was an outspoken proponent of the social gospel. In 1930, he had challenged his reluctant fellow clergymen to either aid the growing army of the unemployed or step down from their pulpits. Those who turned their backs on the people's misery were, he said, unfit to lead their congregations. Young Powell put his

Congressman Adam Clayton Powell (center)
at a fund-raiser for the war effort.

father's philosophy into practice. In the first four months of his supervision of Abyssinian's aid program, 29,000 free meals and thousands of garments were distributed to Harlem's needy.

By the time of the Harlem riot, Powell had succeeded his father as Abyssinian's pastor and had established himself as a militant spokesman for Harlem's masses, a man who believed in using direct action in the battle against discrimination and segregation. While still in graduate school at Columbia, Powell had led a successful campaign to integrate Harlem Hospital's all-white medical staff. At one point during the drive, six thousand Harlemites followed him to City Hall for a mass demonstration against the hospital's biased practices. In the wake of the riot, Powell organized the Coordinating Committee for Employment, a seemingly unlikely coalition of ministers, professionals, Communist party members, and black nationalists. Over the next five years, under Powell's leadership, and with the motto "Don't buy where you can't work," the committee sponsored successful boycotts of New York Bell Telephone, Consolidated Edison, the New York World's Fair, the city's mass transit system, and the white-owned businesses that refused to employ black workers along 125th Street, Harlem's main stem.

During the Depression decade, another charismatic religious figure made Harlem his home. Unlike Powell, Georgia-born George Baker, aka Father Divine, was short, stocky, and verbose, a rather ungrammatical orator whose past was a secret to all but himself. Still, his fifty thousand followers believed him to be Jehovah incarnate. Divine shared—at least in public—their conviction. "Read my messages with an open heart and mind," he wrote, "and you will learn of Me and receive Truths such as man has never given. You are not dealing with Man, but with God."[4] Naturally, this message was not well received by Harlem's more orthodox religious leaders. In 1936, Powell bitterly characterized Divine as "the colossal fraud of the Twentieth Century" and termed his followers "truly a lost generation."[5]

However, as Divine's biographer Robert Weisbrot points out, "Divine's ministry to the needy helped fill a void in clerical activity and in so doing, he rapidly became one of the ghetto's most influential figures."[6] A strong advocate of

Father Divine and his "angels" at the Brigantine Hotel in Atlantic City.

"self-help," Divine encouraged his followers—a racially integrated band, rare for the period—to open businesses as a means of providing both employment for themselves and reasonably priced goods and services for the community as a whole. These enterprises included meat markets, groceries, clothing and jewelry stores, dry cleaners, barber shops and shoe repair shops, as well as tailoring, paperhanging, painting, and trucking businesses. Restaurants in the Divine Peace Missions offered quality meals to all for ten and fifteen cents. His workers, or "angels," surrendered their worldly assets upon joining Father's family and were rechristened with names like "Heavenly Love" and "Precious Blessing." They were fed, clothed, housed (in quarters segregated by sex), and provided with medical care by Divine's organization.

Unlike most other African-American cults of the era, Father Divine's paid close attention to political and racial issues. During the mid-thirties, Divine organized the Righteous Government Movement. Its platform called for equal treatment of all races and demanded an end to every form of segregation and discrimination in the nation's economic, educational, and political systems.

To many African-Americans living below the Cotton Curtain, the mere formulation of such idealistic demands would have seemed an extraordinary exercise in futility. The 1930s had extended and exacerbated the disastrous economic circumstances endured by a large majority of rural Southern blacks since the end of the Reconstruction era. The drop in demand for their produce—cotton in particular—had sharply reduced a standard of living that for the half-million sharecroppers and tenant farming families had, in the best of times, seldom exceeded subsistence level. The situation was little better for the 175,000 black families fortunate enough to own and work their own land.

Politically, the ten million African-Americans living in the South did not exist. In 1940, only five percent of the nearly four million blacks old enough to vote were registered. This massive disenfranchisement, resulting from exorbitant poll taxes, rigged literacy tests, "grandfather clauses," and the time-tested tactics of physical and economic intimidation, effectively prevented the bulk of the black population from exercising an appreciable degree of control over their individual and collective destinies. The absence of political leverage enabled the Southern states to limit the benefits their African-American citizens were entitled to receive under various New Deal programs. The denial of suffrage rights was also responsible for the disproportionate allocation of monies for public services. In 1939, for example, the states of the old Confederacy were spending

A family of sharecroppers.

Three young field-workers.

less than twenty dollars on each black pupil in their public school system while disbursing nearly sixty dollars on the education of every white child.

Racial discrimination was the custom and the law throughout the region. The term "Southern justice" was, therefore, an oxymoron. Since blacks' names did not appear on voting rolls, they could not be called for jury service—a catch-22 that made worthless the fundamental constitutional right to trial by a jury of one's peers. The legal system was, like most of the South's institutions, racist and corrupt. Black defendants received longer and harsher sentences than whites for similar offenses. The word of black witnesses received little or no credence in the courtroom. A black man who slapped a white neighbor could look for-

Two lynch victims, Marion, Indiana, 1930.

ward to a hard stretch on the chain gang; a white who murdered an African-American in cold blood stood a much better than even chance of walking out of the courtroom free and clear. Southern policemen were notorious for their adherence to a "shoot first, ask questions later" philosophy of criminology. And if the local citizenry harbored some doubt that "justice" might be served, they retained the option of playing judge, jury, and executioner themselves; during the 1930s, 119 African-Americans were known to have been lynched.

The day-to-day struggle to survive in a society dedicated to the proposition that one is somehow not quite human was too much for many African-Americans to endure. Between the two world wars, over a million and a half blacks

Preparing for an antilynching rally in Harlem, 1942.

bade farewell to their Southern homeland. They decamped for the industrial cities of the North and the promise, often unfulfilled, of a more humane and less constricted way of life.

A s one of the most somber decades in the nation's history came to a close, Americans, still preoccupied with their own economic troubles, were casting a more than anxious eye across the Atlantic. Though large isolationist factions, vocal and powerful, among press, politicians, and public were still advancing the view that Europe's agony was not America's affair, each day's dispatches from the war zone made the "America First" position less and less tenable. A continuing stream of refugees arriving on our shores bore tragic firsthand testimony to the racial, religious, and political persecution, of unprecedented magnitude, within Nazi Germany and its rapidly expanding continental empire.

With the possibility of United States military involvement in the struggle against fascism increasing, the leadership of the African-American community voiced its determination to prevent a repetition of the unequal and demeaning treatment accorded black servicemen during World War I. As early as 1937, the NAACP's special counsel, Charles Houston, brought the issue to President Roosevelt's attention:

> . . . Our Negro population is the most loyal element in the country, and as ten percent of the total population, its loyalty and support are indispensable to the United States in any major war. During the World War the patriotism and devotion of the Negroes in the armed forces was sorely tried by all the devilish insults and discriminations which prejudice could devise. We pray that the Negro population will always remain loyal, but it will not again silently endorse the insults and discriminations imposed on its soldiers and sailors in the course of the last war.
>
> We respectfully ask you then as Commander-in-Chief of the Armed Forces to issue whatever orders may be necessary to remove race discrimination in all branches of the armed forces on land, sea and in the air, and to give Negro citizens the same right to serve their country as any other citizen and on the same basis.[7]

Houston's appeal would be repeated in the next years by other concerned leaders and on the editorial pages of black periodicals across the nation. These calls for preemptive action by the White House and the military high command were met at best with platitudes, at worst with silence.

In the summer of 1940, Congress, after bitter debate, passed into law the Selective Training and Service Act. The legislation provided that "every male citizen of the United States . . . between the ages of twenty-one and thirty-six . . . shall be liable for training and service in the land and naval forces of the United States. . . . In the selection and training of men under this act, there shall be no discrimination against any person on account of race and color."

The letter of the law seemed clear enough, but the question of how it would be interpreted by the traditionally racist military establishment that was charged with carrying out its provisions deeply disturbed leaders of the African-American community. On September 27, Walter White, Executive Secretary of the NAACP, T. Arnold Hill, former Industrial Secretary of the Urban League, and A. Philip Randolph, President of the Brotherhood of Sleeping Car Porters, met with FDR in the White House to voice their concerns.

The black delegation specifically opposed the establishment of any new segregated units in the armed forces. They demanded integration of all existing units, acceptance of African-Americans into the all-white Army Air Corps, expanded training of black officers in all service branches, integration of the navy, and assignment of black sailors to positions "other than the menial ones to which they are now restricted." White, Hill, and Randolph also called upon the President to ensure the nonsegregated deployment of African-American women as army, navy, and Red Cross nurses and to issue orders providing for the "equitable participation of Negroes" in all defense-related industries.[8]

The response to these requests by the man who had received nearly eighty percent of all the votes cast by American blacks in the 1936 election can best be judged by a bold headline in the October 9, 1940, edition of *Crisis:*

WHITE HOUSE BLESSES JIM CROW

The magazine reported that two days after the meeting, the White House issued a statement which, while noting that "the services of Negroes would be utilized on a fair and equitable basis," went on to reveal a design for maintaining ironclad segregation in the armed forces. "It is the policy of the War Department," the White House release continued, "not to intermingle colored and white enlisted personnel in the same regimental organizations. This policy has proven satisfactory over a long number of years."

The three African-American participants in the meeting were further angered by the implication, made to the press by Roosevelt's aide Stephen Early, that they had acquiesced to the administration's plan. *Crisis* called for immediate action, urging its readers to "write President Roosevelt opposing segregation in the army, especially an army that is supposed to be fighting for democracy; write the President and General George C. Marshall, chief of staff, protesting against the restrictions for Negro officers and demand more of them. Write Major General H. H. Arnold, chief of the army air corps, and demand the enlistment and training of Negroes in the air corps; write to Commissioner Sidney Hillman of the Council of National Defense and urge the wiping out of the color line in plants having contracts for national defense."[9]

For A. Philip Randolph, the most prominent African-American in the trade union movement, letter-writing campaigns were, given the temper of the times and the importance of the issues, too mild a form of protest; a more dynamic expression of discontent was demanded. One hundred thousand blacks must, he concluded, march on the nation's capital.

Born in 1889 in Crescent City, Florida, to a family headed by an itinerant Methodist minister, Randolph developed an early hatred of social injustice. His mother refused to let her children ride on segregated streetcars; it was better to walk, she told her youngsters, than to submit to indignity and disrespect. Randolph migrated to New York as a young man and, almost immediately, joined ranks with the Socialist party, headed by Eugene V. Debs. With fellow radical Chandler Owen, he edited and published *The Messenger*, a black publication that advocated "scientific socialism." In its pages in 1917, Randolph, then a pacifist, declared his opposition to America's participation in World War I. For this principled dissent, he served a short term in prison. In 1925, Randolph organized the Brotherhood of Sleeping Car Porters, and after years of struggle against both the railroads and racist elements within the American Federation of Labor, he saw his union become the black workers' strongest and most uncompromising voice. Throughout his life, Randolph's first concern was justice and fairness for the working class; in his view, the struggle for the rights of the workingman was a holy crusade, "since Jesus was a carpenter and all his disciples laborers." Randolph's courtly manner and eloquent turns of phrase disguised an indomitable will, as Franklin D. Roosevelt would learn.

Randolph selected the defense industry as the demonstration's primary target. It was an excellent choice. Seventy-five percent of defense contractors refused to hire African-American workers in any capacity. Fifteen percent employed blacks only in menial positions. The exclusion of skilled black artisans was institutionalized: state employment services, according to Lester Granger of the Urban League, "refused to register skilled Negro workers at their trades or failed

Miami Beach employment office advertising
jobs by skin color, 1939.

to refer them to jobs when they were registered or referred them only when
employers clearly expressed a preference for Negroes." In addition, many craft
unions under the jurisdiction of the American Federation of Labor—which was
extremely reactionary on racial matters—barred African-Americans from ad-
mission to their local chapters. Though the National Defense Training Act, designed to prepare workers for war-matériel production jobs, contained an
antidiscrimination clause, as of March 1, 1941, only 4,600 of the 175,000 train-
ees in the program were African-American.

Randolph's plan was indeed audacious. During the 1930s, blacks in Northern cities had effectively used the picket line as a means for expressing their

Billiard hall for blacks on Beale Street, Memphis, Tennessee, 1939.

grievances. Never before, though, had anyone conceived of—or had the organizational ability and wherewithall to execute—such a massive public protest. That battalions of black Americans would exercise their First Amendment rights on the broad avenues of Washington—one of the nation's most rigidly segregated cities—was an extraordinary and unprecedented proposition. And it was to be an African-American expression: Randolph was firm in the conviction that no whites, no matter how committed they might be to the cause, should join the march. "There are some things," he wrote in the *New York Age* (a major African-American newspaper), "that Negroes must do alone."[10]

Walter White placed the NAACP's manpower and resources at Randolph's disposal. A date was set for the demonstration—July 1, 1941. Roosevelt and his advisers now realized that the March on Washington was no pipe dream and would, indeed, transpire. It most certainly did not fit into the administration's agenda of the moment. Such staunch advocates of the cause of racial justice as First Lady Eleanor Roosevelt and Interior Secretary Harold Ickes attempted, unsuccessfully, to dissuade the black leaders from their chosen course of action. With time running out, the march organizers were summoned to the White House on the morning of June 25 for a showdown meeting with the President and key members of his cabinet and staff.

Roosevelt opened the session by characterizing the march as a "bad and unintelligent" tactic. The problems of discrimination that Negroes suffer, he said, must be dealt with by methods that are well thought out and planned—a very good description, actually, of the upcoming demonstration. The President opined that a march on Washington would give the impression to the American people that Negroes were seeking to exercise force to compel the government to do certain things. Such an attitude, he stated, would do more harm than good.[11]

Randolph replied that a wave of bitterness, disillusionment, and desperation was sweeping through the black community. Its source was the discrimination rampant in the defense industry, the military, and the various departments of the federal government. An executive order was necessary, he said, that had teeth in it to compel the defense industries to give Negroes employment opportunities equal to those afforded their white fellow citizens. The meeting continued with the President fervently reiterating his opposition to the march. It is a grave mistake, he told his audience, one that may well lead to serious trouble and violence. In any event, replied Randolph, the march would go on. Franklin D. Roosevelt blinked. Later that day, Executive Order 8802 was issued:

Beale Street in Memphis, Tennessee, 1939.

It is the duty of employers and labor organizations to provide for the full and equitable participation of all workers in the defense industries without discrimination. . . . All departments and agencies of the Government of the United States concerned with vocational and training programs for defense production shall take special measures appropriate to assure that such programs are administered without discrimination. All contracting agencies of the Government of the United States shall include in all defense contracts hereafter negotiated by them a provision obligating the contractor not to discriminate against any worker. There is established in the office of Production Management a committee on fair employment practices, which shall consist of a chairman and four other members to be appointed by the President.

The march was canceled. Executive Order 8802 represented a milestone victory in black America's arduous and bitter struggle for equal opportunities and justice. The tactic of mass direct action and/or the threat of same proved its viability. Twenty-two years later, on August 23, 1963, three hundred thousand African-Americans and their nonblack supporters were challenged by Dr. Martin Luther King, Jr.'s utopian vision of America as a blessed society and did march on Washington. The leading signatory on the call to convene that extraordinary moment in this republic's history was a militant septuagenarian idealist by the name of Asa Philip Randolph.

The country's mobilization effort moved millions of Americans from the relief agencies' welfare rolls to the payrolls of defense industries. A war economy was bringing down the curtain on the Great Depression. Executive Order 8802 had a salutary effect on the employment prospects of the African-American working class; a year after Roosevelt's edict had gone into effect, the number of blacks employed in shipyards, aircraft factories, and munitions plants had increased significantly.

During the summer of 1941, the national pastime held the nation's sports-minded citizens in thrall. In the still segregated major leagues, all eyes were riveted on Boston Red Sox slugger Ted Williams's bid to join the rarefied ranks of .400 hitters and on the Yankee Clipper, Joe DiMaggio, as his batting streak reached fifty-six games. African-American fans also followed the fortunes of their own diamond heroes in the Negro National and American leagues. Only in

Leroy "Satchel" Paige.

postseason "barnstorming" tours would black and white players compete against one another. On July 27, fifty thousand people jammed Chicago's Comiskey Park to watch the black leagues' East All Stars defeat their Western counterparts, eight to three. In the lineup were future Hall of Famers Roy Campanella and the legendary Leroy "Satchel" Paige.

Gridiron enthusiasts eagerly anticipated the professional debut of All-American Jackie Robinson with the Los Angeles Bulldogs. The only four-letter man in the history of the University of California at Los Angeles, Robinson was considered by many to be the finest all-round athlete ever to compete in the collegiate ranks.

In boxing, Joe Louis continued his domination of the heavyweight division. During the course of the year he defended his title seven times—all against white challengers—scoring six knockouts and winning one bout on a disqualification. The pages of black newspapers, meanwhile, breathlessly chronicled each new episode in the long-running soap opera of the Brown Bomber's stormy marriage to Marva Trotter.

From left: unknown, Joe Louis, Marian Anderson, Bill Robinson, Paul Robeson, unknown, and Olivia De Havilland at a USO gathering.

On Armistice Day, Reverend Adam Clayton Powell, Jr., was elected to New York's City Council—with strong support from the Communist party and its allies—by a landslide margin. He was the first African-American to take a seat in the city's legislative chamber.

Nine days later at a banquet in New York, the noted black educator and civil rights champion Mary McLeod Bethune told an assembly of the extremely conservative Daughters of the American Revolution that Negroes "feel that the fight against fascism is their fight too." They realize, she said, "that their persecution would be even worse under Hitler." During the war years, Dr. Bethune would be a tireless advocate for the rights and welfare of African-American servicemen. Her very close friendship with Eleanor Roosevelt assured her access to the highest levels of the political power structure.

During the first week of December, Lionel Hampton's new band was the headliner at Harlem's Apollo Theater. Billie Holiday appeared on the bill as an "extra added attraction." On that showplace's screen, Dorothy Dandridge and Mantan Moreland were starring in the premiere presentation of *Four Must Die.* A few blocks away, at Minton's Playhouse on 118th Street, jazz aficionados were listening to (and being baffled by) the startling sounds of bebop, as performed by the new music's innovators, Charlie Parker, Dizzy Gillespie, Charlie Christian, Kenny Clarke, and Thelonious Monk.

Harlemites were already preparing to jitterbug Christmas Eve away to the music of Jimmie Lunceford's swing band at the Renaissance Casino's annual ball.

African-Americans were making their presence felt on the classical stage as well. Marian Anderson, Dorothy Maynor, and Paul Robeson were all listed among the year's highest-paid concert artists. On December 4, tenor Roland Hayes appeared with the New York Symphony Orchestra at Carnegie Hall.

Also that first week of December, Bluebird Records announced the release of a new single by Clarence Williams: "Uncle Sam, Here I Am."

Dawn was breaking over the Hawaiian Islands on December 7 when the catastrophic event needed to propel this country into history's most horrific conflict finally came to pass. As the bombs rained down on Pearl Harbor, a twenty-two-year-old messman serving on the U.S.S. *West Virginia* became the first African-American hero of World War II.

Dorie Miller, born into a family of Texas sharecroppers, was nearing the end of his first enlistment in the navy, a service that restricted its African-American members to the most menial duties. During the onslaught, Miller moved his gravely wounded captain from the battleship's bridge, then returned and took his place at a machine gun in an unmanned battle station. Although he had never received weapons training, the former star high school halfback blasted two Japanese war planes from the skies.

World War II hero Dorie Miller, 1941.

51

For his heroism, Miller was awarded the Navy Cross by Admiral Chester W. Nimitz, commander of the Pacific fleet. The citation extolled the young man's "distinguished devotion to duty, extreme courage and disregard for his own personal safety during attack." The War Department brought him back to the mainland for a national personal appearance tour to encourage enlistments. In December 1943, Dorie Miller—still a messman—was killed in action aboard the U.S.S. *Liscome Bay*, somewhere in the South Pacific.

The overwhelming majority of black Americans shared their white countrymen's outrage at what was perceived as a perfidious attack by the Japanese. But as is usually the case, they put their own interpretative spin on the events of the hour. The *New York Age*, in a December 26 editorial, reflected the opinion of much of the African-American community: "This is America's supreme hour of peril. . . . Because of this fact, the Negro as the largest single minority group in this country has an opportunity unsurpassed in history. We can play our part in this war so well that even the prophets of Nordic superiority will be forced to change their opinions of the Negro. Future generations will judge whether we took full advantage of this opportunity."

In the same issue of the *Age*, A. Philip Randolph wrote: "If we fail to fight to make the democratic process work in America, while we fight to beat down Japan and Hitler, we will be traitors to democracy and liberty and to the liberation of the Negro people."[12]

Father Divine, whose organization's byword was "Peace, it's truly wonderful," encouraged his followers to seek conscientious objector status but refused to prohibit them from serving in the armed forces. His biographer Robert Weisbrot writes: "Father Divine increasingly identified his interests with a strong and aggressive America, which he saw as a bulwark against the growing menace of totalitarian states. In particular he viewed Germany, with its anti-democratic racist dogmas and expansionist policies, as the antithesis of his own values. This resentment deepened in 1941 when a fascist journal editorialized that America had fatally weakened itself through racial integration and cited Divine's movement as an example."[13]

Divine himself warned, in his peace mission's publication, that "the democracies are put to a hard test because they reflect to some degree, even to a great degree, the evils present among the aggressor nations."[14]

Three men who would cast long shadows in black America's postwar struggle for equal rights and justice openly dissented from the patriotic fervor of the day. They were James Farmer, founder of the Congress of Racial Equality; Bayard Rustin, architect of the 1963 March on Washington and Randolph's chief organizer in the 1941 effort; and Elijah Poole Muhammad, leader of the Nation of Islam.

Farmer, a Texas-born graduate of Howard University's School of Religion, had declined ordination as a Methodist clergyman because he would not serve in a still segregated ministry. Early in 1942, he sought Selective Service classification as a conscientious objector for religious and humanitarian reasons. Farmer's request was denied—over his strong objections—and he was deferred from the draft on the grounds that he held a divinity school degree. Later in his life, Farmer wrote: "I believed that opposition to all war and all killing was not only mandated by a Supreme Being but also by my conscience. Were I not opposed to all war on principle, there was simply no way I could, in conscience, enter the United States' racially segregated armed forces to fight for freedom, liberty and equality in other parts of the globe."[15]

Bayard Rustin, a former organizer for the Young Communist League, who left the Party in 1941, was active in two pacifist organizations—the War Resisters League and the Fellowship of Reconciliation—when the United States entered the conflict. While in California on a mission to help save the property of Japanese-Americans who had been unconstitutionally detained in concentration camps, Rustin was arrested and sentenced to prison for Selective Service Law violations. He served two and a half years in the Ashland Correctional Institution for his antiwar beliefs. "Being a follower of Mahatma Gandhi," he would write, "I am an opponent of war and war preparations and an opponent of universal military training. I hold that segregation in any part of the body politic is an act of slavery and an act of war."[16]

To his legion of dedicated followers, Elijah Muhammad was a Messenger sent by Allah to the "lost-found nation" of Black America; to his army of detractors he was a power-mad charlatan. Many people called him many things, but "pacifist" was never among them. Muhammad's case, therefore, differs in the extreme from Rustin's and Farmer's.

Born in Sandersville, Georgia, in 1897, he was one of Wali and Marie Poole's thirteen children. Muhammad's father was a Baptist preacher; both of his parents had been slaves.

In 1923, according to C. Eric Lincoln's classic study, *The Black Muslims in America*, Elijah Poole migrated to Detroit, where he associated himself with W. D. Fard, an individual whose mission was the conversion of black Americans to the Islamic faith.[17] Fard was a man so mysterious that neither his race nor

The Honorable Elijah Muhammad.

his nationality can be absolutely authenticated. "I come from the Holy City of Mecca," he told his flock. "More about myself I will not tell you yet for the time has not yet come. I am your brother. You have not yet seen me in my royal robes."[18]

On the periphery of Fard's movement was an equally shadowy Japanese national, known as Major Takahashi, who tried to convince the Muslims to swear allegiance to the Mikado and, according to Lincoln, succeeded in splitting off some members.

Shortly before Fard's still unexplained disappearance in 1934, he appointed Muhammad as chief minister to the congregation. Soon after his mentor vanished, Muhammad moved to Chicago, where he continued his proselytizing activities with some degree of success.

On September 22, 1942, the *Chicago Tribune* reported:

> The arrest of more than eighty Negroes, members and leaders of three organizations, on charges of sedition, conspiracy and violation of draft laws, was announced by the F.B.I. . . . They were charged with conspiracy to promote the success of the enemy, making false statements to those about to be inducted into the armed services, disrupting morale and causing mutiny. The three organizations are known as the Peace Movement of Ethiopia, the Brotherhood of Liberty for Black People in America, and the Temple of Islam. . . . Elijah Poole, who calls himself Elijah Muhammad, was among those arrested.

The head of the Chicago office of the FBI told the press that "no definite connection had been found between Negro organizations and Japanese activity in this country." Nonetheless, a federal grand jury handed down indictments alleging that the three groups had "taught Negroes that they are akin to the Japanese." Muhammad, for his part, asserted that "the [white] Devil" cooked up the charges: "I have been tried and imprisoned for teaching my people about themselves."[19] He was convicted on two counts of violating Selective Service laws and sentenced to a five-year term at the federal prison in Milan, Michigan, where he apparently was able to direct his movement's activities from his cell. An unrepentant Elijah Muhammad was released in 1946.

C. Eric Lincoln states:

> He taught that the white man is and has been since his creation the oppressor of all who are not white; and he asserted that all who are not white are, by the white man's own social definition, black. Consequently, he reasoned, it made little sense for black people in this country to fight against the Japanese, who are equally victims of the white man's hatred and color prejudice. World War II was not a battle in which American blacks ought to have been forced to participate. The black man's war is "the battle of Armageddon in the wilderness of North America: a battle for freedom, justice and equality—to success or to death."[20]

As the positions espoused by Muhammad, Rustin, and Farmer demonstrate, African-American support for the war effort was not monolithic in nature; but, unquestionably, the vast majority of America's citizens of color committed themselves in mind and body to the struggle against the Axis powers. The *Pittsburgh Courier*, the largest and most influential of the nation's 210 black newspapers, caught the mood and allegiance of the masses with its "Double V" campaign: Victory over fascism abroad. Victory over racism here at home.

CHAPTER 3

To be a black soldier in the South in those days was one of the worst things that could happen to you. If you go to town, you would have to get off the sidewalk if a white person came by. If you went into the wrong neighborhood wearing your uniform, you got beat up. If you stumbled over a brick, you was drunk and got beat up. If off-post you was hungry and couldn't find a black restaurant or a black home you know, you know what? You would starve. And you were a soldier . . . out there wearing the uniform of your country, and you're getting treated like a dog! That happened all over the South.

Johnnie Stevens
761st Tank Battalion

Soldiers boarding a troop train.

Camp Claiborne was situated in central Louisiana's Rapides Parish, midway between Shreveport and Baton Rouge, a locale noted for its moccasin-infested swamps and an implacable tradition of intolerance and segregation, enforced through intimidation and Ku Klux Klan–inspired violence. In 1941, the news that an all-black tank battalion would be stationed in their backyard was greeted with less than patriotic joy by an indigenous white population already exercised by the presence of several thousand African-American servicemen at Camp Claiborne and other nearby bases. The sight of an elite corps of proud black soldiers roaring down the region's roads in their machines of war did nothing to ease the white community's anger and resentment. Organized, armed African-Americans had long inhabited the racists' worst nightmares. The reality of blacks in M41A tanks was, therefore, an abomination unto the myth of black inferiority/white supremacy that they and their ancestors had cherished for four hundred years.

Though most of the men of the 758th Tank Battalion (the unit would be redesignated the 761st in April 1942) had sampled the Southern way of life during their basic and/or specialized armored training at Fort Knox, the extraordinarily hostile Louisiana environment made their Kentucky experience most strongly resemble, in retrospect, a several-month sojourn in summer camp. Fort Knox and the surrounding communities—including the city of Louisville—were segregated, but Kentucky's racial atmosphere was considerably less oppressive than Louisiana's. Some black soldiers from the Northern states would receive their first taste of Southern reality on troop trains carrying them to bases below the Cotton Curtain. E. G. McConnell of the 761st remembers his journey from Long Island's Camp Upton to Fort Knox well: "The cars were not integrated at all, and they put all the black cars at the front part of the train. As it was slowly climbing the hills in Kentucky, they came through our cars and ordered us to pull our shades down. I couldn't understand this. My curiosity got the best of me, so I went between the cars to see exactly what was happening, why we had to pull the shades down. I saw a bunch of hillbillies out there—this was real hillbilly, redneck country. And they were waiting alongside the tracks with rifles. I later found out that several troop trains were fired on. So they were ordering us to pull the shades down for our own safety. Yeah, and we were going to fight for the *whole* United States, not just for Harlem."

For the man at Camp Claiborne, a visit to the nearby town of Alexandria could assume the characteristics of a field problem set in a well-planted minefield. McConnell says: "When we went to town on the bus, we had to get in

Bus station in Durham, North Carolina, May 1940.

the back, and if the bus was full—I mean full of whites—we had to wait until the next bus came. I've seen them just completely push the black soldiers off. We'd wait in line for hours and hours."

Those tankers "fortunate" enough to make it into Alexandria would find most of the community off limits. They could neither shop in the downtown stores, eat in the downtown restaurants, nor drink in the downtown bars. They could move freely only in an impoverished "colored section," known as Little Harlem, which was devoid of any recreational facilities beyond a movie theater and the shabby and sometimes dangerous jook joints. Black soldiers in general and the tankers in particular—who, in their stylishly cut uniforms, stood out from the other GI's—were subject to near constant verbal and physical harassment from whites—civilians and soldiers alike. The African-American tankers were also special targets for the Klan Klavern, some of whose members had exchanged their traditional bed sheets for peace officers' uniforms. The military police on patrol in Little Harlem were seldom more circumspect in their dealings with the tankers than their club-wielding civilian counterparts. For the black servicemen these confrontations became almost routine, just another trial

Water fountain for "coloreds," Halifax, North Carolina, 1938.

to be endured. The NAACP's influential magazine, *Crisis*, in a February 1942 editorial, succinctly summarized the situation:

> Our boys found that their behavior off-post was supervised by white military police and that even after some details of Negro military police were established, these latter were not armed and [were] restricted in their authority. Worst of all our troops discovered to their dismay that the United States Army, mightiest force in the land, had meekly surrendered control over its Negro troops to any white constable, sheriff or mayor in Dixie who wanted to take over.

Even within the perimeter of their base, the men had little respite from the demeaning and demoralizing realities of racism. Though they constituted an elite unit, the tankers' pigmentation remained the determining factor in their treatment. Handpicked by reason of their above-average intelligence and resourcefulness, the men lived and trained within a separate and unequal bubble.

60

Nonetheless, their presumed special status remained a bone of envy and contention not only for the majority of the forty thousand white troops stationed at Camp Claiborne but for more than a few of the battalion's own white noncommissioned and commissioned officers as well. This white-over-black command structure did not arise by accident. It was in fact the result of a long-standing army policy, which decreed, in essence, that white men from the South, by virtue of their life experiences, best knew how to handle Negroes.

Though civil rights organizations—together with the black press—had campaigned long and strenuously for the intensified training of black officers, at the time the 758th was activated, only one third of one percent of the more than two hundred thousand African-Americans then under arms held ranks above that of sergeant. In a revealing memorandum submitted to General Dwight D. Eisenhower in April 1942, Brigadier General R. W. Crawford of the War Department's general staff declared:

> Probably the most important consideration that confronts the War Department in the employment of the colored officer is that of leadership qualifications. Although in certain instances colored officers have been excellent leaders, enlisted men generally function more efficiently under white officers. Officers experienced with colored troops lay this to the lack of confidence on the part of the colored enlisted men in the colored officer.

This view, held by a white high command residing in the Pentagon's rarefied atmosphere, was most certainly not shared by the African-American enlisted men laboring and suffering in the field.

On their part, the black tankers regarded many of their white officers with suspicion. They noted the alacrity with which white lieutenants and captains leaped at any opportunity to transfer to all-white units. Harold B. Gary, a black first lieutenant from Abilene, Kansas, who served with the 761st, holds an opinion on the subject that is shared by his former comrades. "Most of the white officers in black outfits were incompetent," Gary says. "That was why they were there. A lot of the men in the 761st were a lot sharper than their officers."

There were, however, notable exceptions to the general rule, among them David Williams, who says: "I got my commission in February of '42. A major came down to the 12th Armored Division, and he interviewed every second lieutenant on the post. His question was: Would I be willing to serve with black

Tourist cabins in South Carolina, 1939.

tankers? I thought it over for a minute or two, and I thought, Maybe I am well qualified because I don't have the prejudices that a lot of whites have and I've been around blacks in Texas all my life and had a very good relationship with them and maybe I could serve my country there better than anyone else. So I said yes. Sometime later—I'd more or less forgotten about the incident—I got orders transferring me to the Fifth Tank Group. And I was told—I quote exactly—'That's the bunch of niggers down at Camp Claiborne.' And that's how I wound up being in the 761st Tank Battalion."

The Northern-born tankers, raised in comparatively benign racial climates, found the rigidly segregated conditions and unbridled hostility of whites—on-post and off—a constant source of anger and frustration. They directed their bitterness at both the daily injustices perpetrated against their dignity and manhood and their powerlessness to meaningfully confront their adversaries.

Preston McNeil reports: "My comrades did not understand about segregation, so I explained to them about segregation because I was raised under segregation. They couldn't understand the sign that says, 'Colored,' 'White.' I said, 'Well, I'm used to all this, and this is what y'all will have to get used to as long as you are in the Southern states.' I preached to them every night. Some it sinked in, but a lot of them refused to listen, and they went to town and got in a little trouble."

In November 1940, Secretary of War Henry L. Stimson appointed Judge William H. Hastie, the distinguished dean of Howard University's School of Law, as his "civilian aide" and adviser on race relations. The position had not been created in response to the department's recognition of a potentially serious

Greyhound bus rest stop near Louisville, Kentucky, 1943.

Dr. Mary McLeod Bethune (center) at
a segregated USO facility.

problem that required black perspective and input for its solution; it was, in
fact, a reaction to intense pressure directed at the War Department by civil
rights organizations, the black press, and the White House in the person of First
Lady Eleanor Roosevelt. Dr. Mary McLeod Bethune was particularly active in
lobbying for Hastie's appointment.

Why would a liberal President—regarded by many blacks as a savior—generally take positive action against racial prejudice in the armed forces only when
placed under intense pressure, in which his wife frequently joined? A disproportionate number of Southern whites held high positions in both the uniformed
and the civilian segments of the military establishment. Roosevelt, always a
political pragmatist, believed, in all probability, that he could not afford to an-
tagonize these officers, bureaucrats, and their powerful allies in Congress by

spontaneously taking measures that would be perceived by them as gratuitous attacks on the South's hallowed white supremacist traditions.

Judge Hastie, a thirty-six-year-old native of Knoxville, Tennessee, came to his new office bearing a most impressive résumé. A Phi Beta Kappa graduate of Amherst College and the holder of L.L.B. and J.D.S. degrees from Harvard's School of Law, he had previously served the Roosevelt administration as assistant solicitor in the Department of the Interior and as judge of the United States District Court in the Virgin Islands. Hastie's tenure at the War Department would, however, be marked by increasing frustration at his inability to sensitize, to any significant degree, the segregationist mentality long ossified within the psyches of most members of the military establishment. Secretary Stimson, a leading member of the New York establishment who had served as a colonel in World War I, as secretary of war under President William Howard Taft, and as secretary of state in the Hoover administration, boasted the racial outlook of an "old

Judge William Hastie.

school" Southerner. He made little effort to camouflage his contempt for his African-American countrymen and those persons—white or black—who sought to advance the race's position in American society. "We must not place too much responsibility," he would write, "on a race which is not showing initiative. Mrs. Roosevelt engages in impulsive and impudent folly in her criticism of our policies. The foolish leaders of the colored race are seeking, at bottom, social equality."[1]

Few issues better symbolized the military's racial mind-set than its decision—made in concert with the American Red Cross—to segregate its blood supplies. In a 1941 memorandum to John J. McCloy, assistant secretary of war, the army's surgeon general, James C. Magee, commented: "For reasons not biologically convincing but which are commonly recognized as psychologically important in America, it is not deemed advisable to collect and mix caucasian and negro blood for later administration to members of the military forces." Ironically, the scientist most responsible for establishing the feasibility of storing blood plasma and maintaining blood banks was Dr. Charles Drew, an African-American professor at Howard University's medical school.

Despite angry protests from black organizations and the press, this policy—based on the rather dubious scenario of wounded white GI's refusing blood on the battlefield because it may have been donated by a black—remained in force throughout the war.

Hastie's uniformed counterpart was Brigadier General Benjamin O. Davis, who had enlisted in the army in 1899. Commissioned two years later, he worked his way up through the ranks and, in 1930, was awarded a full colonel's eagle. His elevation to star rank—he was the first black to achieve it—came with his assumption of new duties as the high command's troubleshooter and point man on racial issues. His son, Major B. O. Davis, Jr., would serve with great distinction in Europe as the commander of the Army Air Corps' all-black 99th Pursuit Squadron—the so-called Tuskegee Flyers.

The contrast between the general and the judge could not have been clearer. Hastie was an activist by nature. Davis, for obvious reasons, had early on in his career adopted the philosophy that the best way for a black man to get along in the U.S. Army was to go along with its program. His ultimate superior, chief of staff General George C. Marshall, though less acerbic than Secretary Stimson, left no doubt about his priorities. "Segregation," he believed, "is a vexing social problem that has perplexed the American people throughout the history of this nation. The settlement of vexing social problems cannot be permitted to complicate the tremendous task of the War Department and thereby jeopardize dis-

Lena Horne and Brigadier General Benjamin O. Davis, Sr.

cipline and morale."[2] The military's ostrichlike attitude toward its institutionalized racism would, however, prove to have a most deleterious effect on morale and discipline.

The army's policies of racial separation held for servicewomen as well as servicemen. Four thousand black women—120 of them officers—served in World War II in the Women's Army Corps. They were trained in segregated units and, as Bernard C. Nalty reports, while white WAC's worked in offices, African-American women were more likely to be assigned positions as cleaners, laundry workers, and kitchen help.[3] Only one unit of black women—a postal battalion—was assigned overseas and that did not occur until 1945. Of the 50,000 women in the army's nursing corps, only 500 were black.

A contingent was sent to England to tend to the black wounded. However, since only a minimal number of African-American troops were in the hospital, the nurses were assigned to care for German prisoners of war. They were offended by this action and their protests reached the office of the chief surgeon of the European Theater of Operations. Policies were changed, and thereafter, black nurses were assigned to treat Americans without regard to the color of the patient's skin.

The navy was even more recalcitrant in its policies toward women of color. Not until October 1944 were African-Americans permitted to serve in the WAVES (Women Accepted for Volunteer Emergency Service). The decision to admit black women came only after Governor Thomas E. Dewey made their barring an issue in his presidential campaign against Franklin D. Roosevelt. In the end, however, only seventy-four African-American women served with the WAVES before the war's conclusion. Of the eleven thousand nurses employed by the navy during World War II, four of these women were black.

In April 1941, the body of Private Felix Hall was discovered in a remote area of the sprawling base at Fort Benning, Georgia. This first casualty in the war within a war that raged stateside until post–VJ Day (demobilization) was found—hands bound behind his back—hanging from a tree. Following the best traditions of Southern justice, military authorities at first implied that the victim had taken his own life. Though this contention, absurd on its face, was later retracted, no person or persons were ever charged with the crime. The slipshod investigatory practices followed in the Hall case were a harbinger of the extraordinary carelessness and mendacity that characterized the inquiries—military and civilian—into the many racially motivated conflicts that would plague the armed forces over the next four years.

Though the savagery of the Hall lynching was unusual, it was not unique. Paul Parks, who was on maneuvers in rural Louisiana in 1942 as a member of the 183rd Battalion of Combat Engineers has bitter memories: "Two of us were told by officers to go into a little town and pick up supplies. I got out of the truck and went into the store, and I was ordering. I started out, and the storekeeper said, 'Don't go back there!' I crowded under the porch, and I saw my comrade being dragged up and down the street until he died. It was about four o'clock, so I stayed under the porch until after dark, and then they took me out and back to camp. There was a big upheaval about it, and they moved us black troops out of the area immediately."

In the months following the murder of Felix Hall, disturbances erupted on military reservations and adjacent communities throughout the South. At Fort Jackson, near Columbia, South Carolina, members of the 48th Quartermaster Corps were attacked on the base by elements of the white 30th Infantry Division following an earlier dispute between the black soldiers and members of a Civilian Conservation Corps unit. Shots were fired before authorities could calm the situation. In July, two black soldiers were shot down in Tampa, Florida, in a fracas with military and civilian policemen.

Several weeks later, a white MP and a black soldier were shot dead in a gun battle in Fayetteville, North Carolina, which broke out following a dispute over seats on a bus bound for nearby Fort Bragg. Two other white MP's and three African-American enlisted men were wounded. In the aftermath, hundreds of black soldiers—the overwhelming majority of whom had been nowhere near the scene of the conflict—were herded into the base stockade, where many were beaten by their guards.

On August 11, five days after the Fayetteville shootings, three hundred black troops from the 94th Engineer Battalion—stationed at Fort Custer, Michigan, but at the time on maneuvers with the Second Army—fell victim to mob attacks near the small community of Gurdon, Arkansas.

After exchanging some harsh words with townsfolk, the men had returned to their bivouac area. A few hours later, they were confronted by a force of state troopers and armed, newly sworn deputy marshals from the town, who were still furious over the earlier confrontation. The soldiers were verbally harassed and some were severely beaten by their antagonists. Meantime, another contingent of black troops was attacked outside the nearby town of Prescott; in this instance, white officers were beaten along with the black enlisted men. Many of the engineers were so terrified by the ferocity of their attackers and the army's inability or unwillingness to protect them that they left the maneuvers immediately and, on their own, hitchhiked back to Michigan.

In the wake of the Fort Bragg disturbances, Judge Hastie undertook a major fact-finding mission that carried him to installations around the country. His lengthy report, submitted to Secretary Stimson on September 22, 1941, is a document remarkable for its insight and its prescience.

> Superficially, the morale of the Negro soldier is good, but beneath the surface is widespread discontent. Most white persons are unable to appreciate the rancor and bitterness which the Negro, as a matter of self-preservation, has learned to hide beneath a smile or joke or merely an impassive face. . . . It is true that probably half of the Negro selectees had so little chance in civilian life and so few creature comforts that a decent place to sleep, good meals and generally wholesome environment leave them fairly well satisfied. But the intelligent, well educated Negro soldier from the North stationed in the South and often in other sections as well, carries within himself a bitterness and dissatisfaction that is deep seated and keenly felt.

Among the key issues addressed by Hastie in his report were those concerning the problems existing between African-American enlisted men and military

Klan march on Washington, D.C.

White House protest, 1942.

and civilian law-enforcement personnel. "Probably no single factor," he wrote, "has contributed so greatly to the lowering of morale of the colored soldier as his relationship to the Military Policeman. Bullying, abuse and physical violence on the part of white Military Policemen are a continuing source of complaints. The recent killings at Fort Bragg appear . . . to have been the result of extreme tension between colored troops and bullying and abusive white Military Policemen." He noted that blacks were rarely used as regular MP's, and "at many posts the policy is not to use them at all." Hastie called for a revamping of selection and training policies and the placing of the military police under a central command. His call for the establishment of black MP units was implemented one month later.

Citing the Gurdon, Arkansas, clash as "the single most serious manifestation of continuing friction between colored soldiers and elements of the civilian population of the South," Hastie stated that "if soldiers are not to take the law into their own hands, the Army must make it clear by its actions that every effort is being made to protect the soldier against civilian violence. . . . The problem will not be solved," he continued, "by reminding the colored soldier that he is in the South and to behave accordingly. Responsible officials of local government and the lawless elements of the civilian population must be reminded that they are in America and to behave accordingly." The judge

71

appealed to Stimson to call publicly on the governors of those states where substantial numbers of black troops were stationed to exert "the full influence of their office to the end that local governments accord to Negro soldiers the respect and consideration due all soldiers who have placed their lives and their services at the disposal of the nation for its defense." Not surprisingly, Hastie's plea fell on deaf ears. The Roosevelt administration—dependent as it was on the Democratic party's hegemony in the so-called Solid South—was hardly prepared to openly chastise Dixie's leaders over an issue that spoke to the very essence of the plantation ethos.

It was, in fact, the army's meek, unchallenging acceptance and adoption of "the traditional mores of the South as the basis of policy and practice in matters relating to the Negro soldier" that Hastie accurately perceived as the root cause of the service's continuing racial turmoil:

> In the Army the Negro is taught to be a man, a fighting man; in brief a soldier. It is impossible to create a dual personality which will be on one hand a fighting man toward a foreign enemy, and on the other, a craven who will accept treatment as less than a man at home. One

A group of schoolchildren preparing for a minstrel show.

hears with increasing frequency from colored soldiers the sentiment that since they have been called to fight, they might just as well do their fighting here and now.

Sixty days after Judge Hastie's detailed and eloquent report reached Secretary Stimson, General Davis would submit a three-paragraph memorandum on the same subject to General Marshall. He noted great improvement in morale and allowed that the "first colored selectees inducted into the new Army were subjected to a radical propaganda spread before them prior to induction. This is no longer true and much of this dissatisfaction seems to have disappeared." For the general, the causes of unrest were not embedded in an abhorrent and degrading system but emanated from the subversive pipe dreams of troublemaking civil rights advocates and the African-American and white liberal press.

Had Camp Claiborne been on Davis's inspection itinerary, the general's Panglossian optimism might have been somewhat tempered. From the moment of their arrival in Rapides Parish, the men of the 758th found themselves in near ceaseless conflict with white soldiers and townsfolk. Not surprisingly, thoughts of retaliation occasionally crossed their minds.

Employment protest, Chicago, 1941.

The new year of 1942 was but a few days old when local police in Alexandria, in an unprovoked assault, severely beat several tankers in town on a weekend pass. No action was taken against the offending officers. Several days later, a black female civilian worker was threatened and struck by a white soldier in the base's post exchange. Word quickly spread to the barracks, and within minutes, the PX was surrounded by an angry crowd of black enlisted men, who

Agricultural workers' Farm Security Administration
camp in Bridgeton, New Jersey, 1942.

threatened to burn the building down. The tankers' tempers were slow to calm, and only after impassioned pleas from their white officers did the men return to their quarters. On the night of January 10, however, tensions that had long been building surfaced with a vengeance.

The conflict began outside a movie theater in Alexandria's Little Harlem, with the attempted arrest of an African-American soldier by a white military policeman. Incensed by the MP's strong-arm tactics, a group of soldiers moved to free his prisoner by force. As the scene on the street grew uglier, several tankers quickly returned to Claiborne to alert their fellow soldiers to the situation. Chester Higgins, Sr., who was in the barracks at the time, recalls the reaction. "The guys went nuts. This was the final straw." The men dashed out to their tanks, loaded the vehicles' guns with live ammunition, and prepared to attack Alexandria, where, by now, a pitched battle was raging in the streets.

African-American soldiers and civilians hurled rocks, bottles, and whatever other missiles they could find at a hastily augmented force of military policemen, local officers, and Louisiana state troopers. The lawmen, in return, lobbed volleys of tear gas grenades. When this tactic failed to quiet the angry crowd—estimated at some six thousand blacks, roughly half of them soldiers—the whites opened fire with revolvers, automatic pistols, and shotguns.

Camp Claiborne, meantime, was in utter turmoil as the tankers continued to declare their intention of waging war on the white citizenry of Louisiana. Floodlights blazed on the tanks and their battle-suited crews. White troops, armed with light weaponry that would have been useless against an armored assault, surrounded the area. Other soldiers hastily erected log barriers across the camp's gates. The base's officers quickly realized that persuasion, not firepower, offered the only way out of their potentially deadly dilemma. After a tense hour of shouted negotiation, the bitter men of the 758th climbed reluctantly from their vehicles and returned to the barracks. The crisis had been defused, but the depth of these soldiers' discontent could not go unrecognized.

In Little Harlem, black and white folks fought each other for more than two hours. When quiet finally came, twenty-eight African-American enlisted men lay wounded—many by the peace officers' bullets, others by their clubs. Four of those shot were in serious condition. One civilian black woman and one state trooper were also hospitalized for injuries.

All the black troops at Camp Claiborne and nearby Camp Livingston were confined to their base for a week. None of these men were brought before courts-martial, but many, alleged by the army to be troublemakers, were quickly transferred to other military installations. The army would announce that almost all of the African-American troops involved in the Alexandria disturbance "were from the Northern States, principally New York, Pennsylvania and Illinois." The march of events had confirmed, as it would many times, the prophetic qualities of William H. Hastie, the civilian aide.

It must be noted that the military's racial problems were not confined to the continental United States. In 1942, black supply and labor units were among the first American troops to land in the United Kingdom, where they were warmly welcomed by the British people. Soon, however, despite stringent wartime censorship, word began to leak back home of serious clashes—some of near riot proportions—between white and black GI's in England and Northern Ireland. Mrs. Roosevelt would be moved to write Secretary Stimson:

> I have heard that the young Southerners were very indignant to find
> that the Negro soldiers were not looked upon with terror by the girls

in England and Ireland. I think we will have to do a little education among our Southern white men and officers, explaining the fact that every effort should be made to prevent marriage during this period, but that normal relationships with groups of people who do not have the same feeling about the Negro that they do cannot be prevented and that it is important for them to recognize that in different parts of the world, certain situations differ and have to be treated differently.[4]

The army high command shared the First Lady's concern. In addition to reports of confrontations sparked by African-Americans' socializing with white women, white troops were said to be attempting to compel pub and restaurant owners and the proprietors of other amusement places either to refuse the patronage of black soldiers or to find ways to segregate them. These efforts were deeply resented by many Britons, and fierce fights between English civilians and white GI's over the Americans' racist attitudes were common occurrences. Questions were raised in Parliament; Prime Minister Winston Churchill responded that he was "hopeful that without any action on my part, the points of view of all will be respected."[5] In September, General Davis arrived in England to investigate the situation.

On his return to the States, Davis told reporters that he had found "no serious friction" between white and African-American troops. Davis's old nemeses, the black and white liberal press, roundly condemned the general's denials. In his official report to the inspector general, however, Davis told quite a different story.

> The colored troops were profuse in their praise of the treatment accorded them by the British people and the British soldiers. . . . They greatly regret the attitude shown by certain white United States soldiers. A certain soldier of many years service stated that the men were somewhat bewildered. The actions of some of our white soldiers were causing some of the men to say: "Who are we over here to fight, the Germans or our own white soldiers?"[6]

Davis placed the bulk of the blame on the "inefficiency of small unit commanders in controlling their men. They tended to rely on noncommissioned officers to assume their own responsibilities. It is imperative," he observed, "that

A. Philip Randolph and Eleanor Roosevelt
in New York City, 1943.

steps be taken to bring about better racial relations in our Army at home in
order that troops may be better prepared for service where there are no discrim-
inations against colored troops or colored people." Davis also called on the army
to "assign its most experienced and able officers to colored units."

Though the general, rather remarkably, called for crash courses in African-
American history for white troops, his other recommendations were typically
conservative. He defended segregated military facilities and clubs abroad. And
in concluding his report, Davis offered an extraordinary reason for white GI's to
be tolerant toward their black comrades in arms:

> During the period 1861–1865, many of the slave owners left their
> families in the care of slaves to go forth to fight for a cause they
> believed was right. There is no record of these slaves having violated
> this confidence imposed on them by their owners. Many of the col-
> ored men wearing the uniform of the United States are the descen-
> dants of these slaves. It is right and honorable that the white soldiers,
> descendants of the slave owners, accord the descendants of those slaves
> fair play and the rights and privileges of citizenship earned by the
> fidelity of their ancestors.

Black troops returning from a practice hike near Bovington, England, 1942.

The Davis report had little impact on policy or practice. Jim Crow had crossed the Atlantic. As we shall see when we examine the 761st Tank Battalion's service abroad, many white Americans would carry both their rifles and their prejudices into battle.

The 758th, meanwhile, continued to master the strategic, tactical, and technical mechanics of armored warfare at Camp Claiborne. By April 1942, when it was redesignated as the 761st, the battalion was composed of 27 officers and 313 enlisted men—slightly less than half its authorized strength. They were under the command of Major Edward Cruise, from Poughkeepsie, New York. One month later, 216 new tankers would be added to the roster.

In July, the unit received its first African-American officers—Second Lieutenants Charles Barbour, from Kansas; Ivan H. Harrison, of Michigan; and Samuel Brown, a South Carolina resident. Graduates of the Officers Candidate School of the Armored Forces at Fort Knox, the three men were assigned as tank platoon leaders in Companies B, C, and D.

The battalion's relationship with the white community did not mellow. On bases around the country, antagonisms between black soldiers and whites, civilian and military, likewise remained tense and uneasy. As 1942 drew near its close, an incident in Phoenix, Arizona, would receive considerable attention.

On Thanksgiving night, according to Ulysses P. Lee in his authoritative work, *The Employment of Negro Troops*, some one hundred members of the 364th Infantry Regiment fought a gun battle with a squad of black military policemen. Though this conflict was black on black in nature, it reflects the continuing problems between black servicemen and MP's regardless of their pigmentation. During the confrontation, one policeman, one enlisted man, and one civilian met their deaths. Twelve enlisted men were seriously wounded. Sixteen members of the regiment were sentenced to fifty-year prison terms by a general court-martial. Both the commanding and the executive officers of the 364th were replaced. "To overcome some of the basic causes of friction within the regiment," Lee states, "a new camp with improved facilities was provided. The new commander was certain that the regiment had returned to a normal state of discipline. The men of the unit, according to intelligence operatives, were equally certain that they had profited from the changes following the clashes."[7]

Walter White reviewing troops.

Father and daughter listen to a news broadcast
in Chicago, 1942.

During the year following Pearl Harbor, the Germans' quixotic Russian campaign ground to a humiliating halt in the waist-deep snow outside Stalingrad. It had fallen victim to the winter, the Red Army's tactics, the Führer's strategic stupidities, and the extraordinary resolve of the people of the Soviet Union. In North Africa, Hitler's most skilled combat commander, Field Marshal Erwin Rommel, was battling the British through Libya, Egypt, and Tunisia. On November 8, the Allies invaded the North African coast in Operation Torch. Commanding one of its three task forces was fifty-seven-year-old tank warfare specialist General George Smith Patton.

Black soldiers in the war zones—including those fully trained for combat—remained relegated to the menial, though not unimportant, role of uniformed laborers. The reluctance of the U.S. high command to commit African-Americans to battle replicated a policy—driven by the myth of black inferiority—that had already proved absurd in World War I. The NAACP's Walter White, after visiting the Second Cavalry Division in North Africa, said, according to Nalty, that "he had never seen more depressed troops."[8]

Meantime, the first rumors of the barbarities under way in Nazi prison camps were beginning to filter back to America, while the U.S. government pleaded ignorance. In January, Reinhard Heydrich, head of the SS intelligence division, convened a select group of Nazi officials in a villa in Berlin's lake district, Wannsee. They decided to implement the "Final Solution." By the end of the month, 230,000 Jews had been murdered in the Baltic region and White Russia. In October, in the Byelorussian capital of Minsk, 16,000 Jews were killed in one twenty-four-hour period. By now, Ben Bender, a Polish boy whose parents had preferred suicide to capture by the Nazis, had spent two years as an inmate of the Buchenwald death camp.

CHAPTER 4

I just wanted to be a patriot. And I wanted to get away from life in Jamaica [Queens] and see the world. I enlisted at Whitehall Street. It was in May 1942. My moms went with me . . . that embarrassed me so much. Moms had packed my clothes, and I didn't want to take any of the old knickerbocker britches. I only had one pair of long pants in my life up until that time. My moms packed all this mess and went on down there. I had taken my sister's eyebrow pencil and put a little smudge over my lip to make myself look a little older. And Moms went back talking to the recruiting sergeant, telling the sarge, "Take care of my boy." Good God, was I embarrassed! I wanted to break ranks and leave.

E. G. McConnell,
761st Tank Battalion

Inspection of segregated barracks,
Fort Huachuca, Arizona, 1942.

E. G. McConnell, sixteen when he enlisted, did not break ranks. The lad from Queens, New York, said good-bye to his father, a munitions worker; his mother, a dressmaker and a devoted Sunday school teacher; and his older sister. As a youth, E.G. had two great desires—to learn auto mechanics and to travel. Both of these wishes would be fulfilled during his four-year tour of duty with the 761st. He took basic training at Camp Upton in New York before heading to Fort Knox for advanced instruction in armored warfare. When he was assigned to the 761st at Camp Claiborne, he was reunited with his boyhood friend Leonard "Smitty" Smith.

Smitty joined the army at seventeen. He and E.G. had met at Allen A. M. E. Church in Queens, where both were students in Mrs. McConnell's Sunday school class. His father had died when Leonard was quite young, and he, two sisters, and a brother were raised by their mother. On entering the army, Smitty had tried to sign up with the Air Corps. When he was turned down because of his race, he decided to join an armored unit.

Smith remembers the training regimen at Claiborne and Camp Hood, Texas: "It was very intensive. We had so many seconds to get in and out of a tank. You had to learn each man's position . . . how to drive, how to be a bow gunner, how to load, how to shoot. We had to learn each other's position so well that in case anything happened, the bow gunner could drive or the driver could be a gunner or a loader. We had to learn how to take weapons apart almost blindfolded. We shot 111's, 45's, machine guns, all types of weapons. We went to the range practically every week. We kept our tanks clean—they shone almost like they were Simonized. When we came back from any trip, you better believe we cleaned those tanks before we ate. On maneuvers, we had combat

E. G. McConnell.

Leonard "Smitty" Smith.

New recruits in front of an army recruitment station, Tennessee.

simulations. We were shooting live ammunition. We stayed out in the rain, we bivouacked, we ate out as though we were in actual combat."

Johnny Holmes, a tanker from Chicago, vividly recalls the Louisiana swampland around Camp Claiborne. "They trained us in the backcountry, and it's like a jungle in there. You can see water moccasins sixteen feet long. This is the truth. And some of the biggest rattlesnakes I ever saw in my life was out there. There were seven-, eight-foot-long rattlers. Heads as big as tarantula spiders—good God! They were as big as your fist."

Paul Bates, the New Jersey–born commanding officer of the 761st—whose men affectionately nicknamed him "The Great White Father"—also reflects on the battalion's days in camp: "I've always lived with the point of view that the rest of my life is the most important thing in the world—I don't give a damn about what happened before. Let's go from here. And if you're gonna go from here, and you're gonna make it, we got to do it together. So I made a point of being with them as much as I could, for better or for worse. I always lived on the post where we were. And we just sort of came together, where if I told them to do something, they would do it. There were a lot of little things. One was: 'Hey, you guys are not supposed to be as clean as other people, and there's a

very simple answer to that: Make damn sure that you're cleaner than anybody else you ever saw in your life—particularly all those white bastards out there. I want your uniforms to look better, cleaner, than theirs do. I want your shoes and boots to shine better.' So they would set up their own tailor shops and everything, and man, we were the best-looking outfit you've ever seen."

But happily for the "Black Panthers" of the 761st, garrison life was not all spit and polish, water moccasins, and confrontations with military and civilian rednecks. As Walter Lewis, a Philadelphian, wrote in his unpublished memoir, "Diary of a Gunner":

> When we went to town—Alexandria, Opelousas, Oakdale, Lake Charles, New Orleans, or Houston—we were the choice of the ladies, particularly at Sam Houston and Prairie View [black] colleges. We were always GI sharp and were the vaunted 761st! We had been heard about! Once, when I was walking down Lee Street in Alexandria, I encountered a lady of the night. She threw her arms around me and said, "This is my meat." I replied, very casually, "Yeah, baby, how much am I worth to you?" "Who the hell do you think you are?" I said, "A tanker, baby . . . a tanker, that's all," and walked on.

Socialites in a fashion show for defense workers, Washington, D.C., 1942.

Black soldiers at a USO dance.

In Washington, meantime, Judge William Hastie was preparing to drop a bombshell. On January 5, 1943, the civilian aide to the secretary of war submitted an angry letter of resignation. Long frustrated by his inability to ameliorate the military's entrenched racist attitudes, Hastie announced that he would return to his position as dean of Howard University School of Law. The armed forces' anti-black attitudes, he wrote, "involve questions of the sincerity and the depth of our devotion to the basic issues of this war and thus have an important bearing, both on the fighting spirit of our own people and our ability as a nation to maintain leadership in the struggle for a free world. Segregation within Army theaters, the blood plasma issue and the unvarying pattern of separate Negro units are such matters."

In his letter to Secretary Stimson, Hastie stated that he had remained in his post as long as he had out of "an obligation of personal loyalty to my superiors" but that:

> recent compelling new considerations had now arisen. In one very important branch of the Army, the Air Forces, where the handling of racial issues had been reactionary and unsatisfactory from the outset, further retrogression is now so apparent and recent occurrences are so objectionable and inexcusable that I have no alternative but to resign in protest and to give public expression to my views. This ultimate decision has been forced on me by:
>
> (a) the announcement just made of the establishment of a segregated Officer Candidate School to train Negro ground officers for the Air Forces, to open at Jefferson Barracks, Missouri, on January 15, 1943; and
>
> (b) the humiliating and morale-shattering mistreatment which, with at least the tacit approval of the Air Command, continues to be imposed upon Negro military personnel at the Tuskegee [Alabama] Air Base, the principal training center of the Air Forces for Negro troops.[1]

To fully understand Judge Hastie's fury at the air force and its commander, General H. H. "Hap" Arnold, it is necessary to go back a bit in time.

During World War I, no blacks had served in the U.S. Air Service. However, one African-American expatriate, Eugene Jacques Bullard, who had gone to Europe to escape U.S. racism, joined the French Foreign Legion in 1914. Bullard suffered serious wounds in infantry combat, but upon his recovery, he volunteered for the nascent Aviation Corps. On completing his pilot training, he won a thousand-dollar bet from an American who believed that blacks were too stupid to learn to fly. Bullard—known as the "Black Swallow of Death"—flew many combat missions and is thought to have brought down two German warplanes in dogfights. His own aircraft was emblazoned with a personal emblem— a heart pierced by an arrow and the legend "All Blood Runs Red."

As the United States began to mobilize in 1940, it became clear that if General Arnold had his way, no African-Americans would occupy the cockpits of U.S. planes in the coming war.

Arnold, a West Point graduate born in a suburb of Philadelphia, had been taught to fly by Orville Wright in 1911. During World War I, he rose from the rank of captain to executive officer to the Air Services chief. During the years between the wars, Arnold gained prominence as an outspoken advocate of the highly controversial position that air power would render massed armies and navies obsolete. He became chief of the Air Corps in 1938 after his predecessor, General Oscar Westover, died in a plane crash.

In 1940, according to Morris J. MacGregor, Jr., in *Integration of the Armed Forces, 1940–1965*, Arnold had managed to prevent the Air Corps from being allotted African-American troops. "Black pilots could not be used," the general explained, " 'since this would result in having Negro officers serving over white enlisted men. This would create an impossible social problem.' "[2]

Tuskegee airman and World War II POW Alexander Jefferson.

The outright exclusion of African-Americans from what was considered the armed services' most prestigious branch drew the wrath of black leaders and the press. From his first days as civilian aide, Judge Hastie assailed the Air Corps's blatantly bigoted policies. The African-American community's anger was so great that Secretary Stimson felt compelled to reverse General Arnold. On July 10, 1941, the War Department announced that the "first class of ten colored aviation cadets would begin training at Tuskegee Air Force Base,"[3] for service with the newly activated all-black 99th Pursuit Squadron.

There was, however, much less to this announcement than met the eye. Since pilot training is—by definition—officer training, the air force was in clear violation of an army policy that called for nonsegregated officer candidate schools. Arnold's ability to so blatantly ignore army regulations testifies to the power he wielded within the high command. It may also reflect a belief that African-Americans would be so pleased at seeing black pilots flying fighter planes that they would not get too upset over the methods used to put them in the cockpits. So committed to American-style apartheid was Arnold's Air Corps that the Tuskegee base was constructed from scratch, at a cost of several million dollars, despite the fact that Maxwell Field—one of the service's largest and best-equipped facilities—was located a mere forty miles away. Hastie, of course, had fervently objected to this and to many subsequent instances of discrimination against the Tuskegee airmen. Referring, in his resignation letter, to the new segregated OCS facility at Jefferson Barracks, he summed up the Air Corps situation: "This latest development in the Air Forces officer training program must be considered in the whole setting of Negro personnel in the Army air program. It [must] be remembered that the policy of using Negro personnel in the Air Force at all was

Three black GI's manning a telephone switchboard, Columbus, Ohio, 1941.

Chief Cook R. Brown and his black assistants
at the U.S. Naval Academy, 1942.

imposed upon a command, reluctant from the outset. Resistance, bred of that reluctance, has been encountered repeatedly."[4]

The Pentagon's release of Hastie's letter sparked another storm of protest within a black community already inflamed by the facts that, two years into the war, African-American servicemen were yet to see combat and the overwhelming majority of black troops—as in World War I—were uniformed laborers. In response, the 99th Pursuit Squadron was dispatched to the Mediterranean, under the command of Colonel Benjamin O. Davis, Jr., four months after Judge Hastie's departure. The 99th's extraordinary performance in the skies over Europe will be discussed later in this volume.

Hastie, after returning to Howard University, continued to speak out forcefully and eloquently on issues of racial discrimination in both military and civilian sectors. After the war, he had a brilliant career in public service, as governor of the U.S. Virgin Islands, as a U.S. district court judge, and, finally, as the first African-American to serve as a chief judge of the United States Court of Appeals. He was succeeded as civilian aide by his deputy, thirty-one-year-old Truman K. Gibson, Jr., a Chicago attorney described most uncharitably by *Time* magazine as "a less insistent Negro."[5]

In 1943, a tidal wave of racial violence and turmoil struck military installations and cities throughout the nation. It was a grim and bloody period—the worst since the infamous "Red Summer of 1919," when seventy-eight African-

Dockworkers, Mobile, Alabama, 1943.

Americans were murdered by lynch mobs and scores more lost their lives in riots in Charleston, South Carolina; Longview, Texas; Elaine, Arkansas; Washington, D.C.; and Chicago, Illinois.

On May 25, 1943, violence erupted at the Atlanta Dry Dock and Shipbuilding Company in Mobile, Alabama, over the promotion of black workers. Police were able to quell the fight, but not before a dozen blacks were injured and Governor Chauncey Sparks had placed seven companies of National Guardsmen on alert.

Already, in April, 26,000 white employees had struck the Packard Motor Company in Detroit, protesting the promotion of three black coworkers. The NAACP's Walter White reported hearing one striker scream, "I'd rather see Hitler and Hirohito win the war than work beside a nigger on the assembly line!"[6] The United Auto Workers charged Ku Klux Klan elements with fomenting the wildcat walkout, and both the union and the NAACP accused some management personnel of encouraging the whites to protest the hiring and upgrading of African-Americans. The Packard episode—like the fierce street fighting that had erupted the year before when armed white mobs attempted, unsuccessfully, to block the integration of the federally funded Sojourner Truth Housing Project—was a preview of terrible things yet to come in the Motor City.

The bloody conflict that, during three hot days in June, would bring death to thirty-four citizens and paralyze an industrial complex crucial to the war effort was hardly unexpected; Detroit had never been celebrated for its peaceful racial atmosphere. In 1924, a Ku Klux Klan–sponsored candidate had narrowly lost the city's mayoral election. Charles Rowles received 107,000 write-in votes out of some 309,000 ballots cast in a three-man race.

Since the beginning of the war, both blacks and whites had been anticipating disaster. The Sojourner Truth riot took place, ironically, at a housing project named for one of the black heroines of the abolitionist movement. Of the seven hundred homes the federal government had built to house defense workers, two hundred were allocated to African-American families. Though some blacks had long resided in the immediate area in the city's northeast section, residents protested that the new homes would violate racially restrictive covenants on the site and lower their property values. Ku Klux Klan crosses were burned near the project.

On February 28, 1942, after the Federal Works Agency refused to

Women welders, New Britain, Connecticut, 1943.

change its policy, a mob of some 1,200 whites, which included known Klan members—many carrying weapons—blocked the first group of black families from entering their new homes. According to B. J. Widdick in *Detroit: City of Race and Class Violence*, the mob then attacked a group of some two hundred blacks who had gathered to protect the families. Despite the use of mounted police and tear gas, the fighting continued for several hours. Widdick writes: "Police bias showed itself in the record of arrests. Out of 104 persons arrested for rioting only two were whites, which caused a group of religious and union leaders to charge the police . . . with inciting the fighting in conspiracy with the KKK."[7] The black families finally moved into Sojourner Truth in the spring of 1943.

A secret study conducted by the Federal Office of Facts and Figures (predecessor of the Office of War Information) in the wake of the Sojourner Truth disturbances had concluded: "Unless some socially constructive steps are taken shortly, the tension that is developing is very likely to burst into active conflict." In August 1942, *Life* magazine had warned that "Detroit is Dynamite. Detroit can either blow up Hitler or it can blow up the United States."[8]

In June 1943, trouble began on Sunday the twentieth on Belle Isle. The unusually sultry day had drawn some 100,000 people—many, if not most, black—to the popular recreation spot in the Detroit River, accessible only by a narrow bridge and several small ferries. Widdick writes that the police had been deluged all day by complaints from both races of verbal and physical assaults.

By evening, according to Widdick, the friction had led to a "brawl between Negroes and whites and this turned into a general riot when over 200 sailors from a nearby armory rushed out and immediately joined the whites. For the sailors, this was a culmination of a series of brawls with Negroes in recent months."[9] Eventually an estimated five thousand white seamen would become involved in the fray. By late evening, as fighting continued on Belle Isle, false rumors had reached the black east side district known as Paradise Valley: Whites were said to have killed an African-American woman and her children and thrown their bodies off the Belle Isle bridge.

Enraged by this and other reports that would prove to be bogus, blacks began to loot white-owned neighborhood businesses and intimidate their proprietors, destroying over a hundred stores, while mobs of whites prepared to invade Paradise Valley. The *Detroit Tribune*, a black weekly, stated:

> Armed with beer and pop bottles, bricks and improvised weapons of scrap iron and table legs, white mobs gathered on the edge of the Negro district and brutally beat isolated Negro citizens, overturning automobiles in which Negroes were riding and setting the cars on fire. In retaliation, Negro mobs formed and stoned all whites who

were caught in the ghetto. Frantically trying to keep the mobs apart, the Detroit police whipped out tommy guns and tear gas, but almost always in the direction of Negroes.[10]

The overwhelmingly white police force was unable—or, as black leaders charged, unwilling—to contain or control the rioters. By morning the city's downtown business district was a bloody battleground. According to Widdick, "thousands of whites roamed the streets looking for victims." Their rage was fanned "by rumors, particularly the one that Negroes had killed seventeen whites overnight in Paradise Valley."[11] A widely heard radio report that carloads of armed blacks were on their way to town from Chicago did little to cool the white wrath.

After many hours of indecision, Governor Harry Kelly declared martial law. President Roosevelt authorized the dispatch of two thousand troops—all of them

Black man fleeing for his life with rioters in pursuit, Detroit, Michigan, 1943.

Police prevent rioters from further attacking a black victim in Detroit.

white—to bring the situation under control. The soldiers arrived on Monday night. By Wednesday the city had returned to a semblance of normalcy. But the federal government had intervened too late. More than six hundred people lay injured; over eighteen hundred were in jail. Twenty-five blacks and nine whites were dead or dying. Nineteen of the African-Americans had been slain by the police. None of the whites had fallen victim to officers of the law. Widdick quotes the commander of the federal forces, Brigadier General William E. Gunther, a former chief of the Denver police department: " 'They've been very handy with their guns and clubs and have been very harsh and brutal. . . . They have treated the Negroes terrible up here and I think they have gone altogether too far. . . . If they want everybody else to get back to normal, then the police will have to get back to normal themselves.' "[12]

Louis Martin editorialized in the weekly *Michigan Chronicle*:

> The race riot and all that has gone before have made my people more nationalistic and more chauvinistic and anti-white than ever before. Even those of us who were half-liberal and were willing to believe in

the possibilities of improving race relations have begun to have doubts—and worse, they have given up hope.[13]

On the afternoon of August 1, 1943, Private Robert J. Bandy, a black military policeman stationed in New Jersey, was in New York to have dinner with his mother and his fiancée. Mrs. Bandy, a Connecticut resident, was staying in the Braddock Hotel, at Eighth Avenue and 126th Street. As the three of them entered the hotel lobby, at about four o'clock, a white city policeman—James Collins—was arresting a disorderly black woman by the name of Margie Polite. Bandy, angered by the officer's rough manner, attempted to intervene. In the ensuing fight, the soldier allegedly knocked the patrolman to the floor. Collins then drew his revolver and shot a now-retreating Bandy in the left shoulder. The wound was not serious.

Walter White described the resulting chaos in the August 16 issue of the *New Republic*:

> Within a few minutes, the story spread like wildfire throughout Harlem that a Negro soldier had been shot in the back and killed by a policeman in the presence of his mother. Blind, unreasoning fury swept the community with the speed of lightning. The available symbols of the oppressor—as was the case in Detroit's East Side—were the shining plate glass windows of stores along 125th Street. At the beginning, there was no looting. Nothing but blind fury was expressed. Later, those from the more poverty-stricken areas of Harlem poured through the broken windows and began looting. Their acts were criminal and unforgivable. But let him who would criticize pause long enough to put himself in the place of the rioters. Still barred from many defense industries in the area because of color, with dark memories of the Depression, when seventy percent of Harlem was on relief . . . hemmed in a ghetto where they were forced to pay disproportionately high rents for rat- and vermin-infested apartments, the Bigger Thomases of New York passed like a cloud of locusts over the stores of Harlem.[14]

By sunrise, two thousand policemen saturated the area. Six blacks had been killed, three hundred injured, and five hundred alleged miscreants were behind bars. Thirty officers had been hurt.

White, speaking for the NAACP in a letter to Secretary Stimson, linked the summer's violent outbursts to the "fury born of repeated, unchecked and often rebuked shooting, maiming and insulting of Negro troops, particularly in the Southern states."[15]

The battles of Detroit and Harlem moved U.S. Attorney General Francis Biddle to call on President Roosevelt to ban blacks from leaving the South in search of work in the Northern defense industries. (In the three years since 1940, the number of blacks in Los Angeles, Chicago, and Detroit had risen, respectively, by thirty, twenty, and nineteen percent.) A continued increase in the African-American population in the industrial centers, he warned, would inevitably result in racial warfare. Biddle targeted Baltimore, Chicago, and Los Angeles as prime candidates for violent confrontation and predicted a renewal of clashes in Mobile and Detroit. After some deliberation, the President rejected his attorney general's counsel.

Over the summer, the violence on the Harlem and Paradise Valley streets was replicated on military bases and in nearby civilian communities across the country. These clashes pitted African-American troops against—separately or in varying combinations—MP's (white or black), white policemen, ordinary white citizens, and white GI's. Though most of the trouble spots were in the South, serious episodes had been reported during the spring in states as disparate in culture and attitude as Mississippi, California, and Pennsylvania.

In May, Benjamin O. Davis, Sr., now a general, arrived at Camp Stewart, Georgia—near Savannah—to investigate a deluge of complaints of ill-treatment submitted to the Pentagon by members of the 100th Anti-Aircraft Battalion. This unit, which Davis described as composed mainly of well-educated Northerners, had previously been stationed at Fort Brady, Michigan, where it was never involved in conflicts with either civilians or other military personnel.†

During his stay at Camp Stewart, Davis listened to a long litany of grievances, vigorously—and at times angrily—propounded by the men of the 100th,

---

†It should be emphasized that the authors are neither suggesting nor implying that all African-American GI's comported themselves at all times with dignity and aplomb. There were many instances where inappropriate behavior or criminal activity by black soldiers triggered confrontations with military or civilian authorities. However, in an extraordinary number of episodes, the troops involved were victims, not victimizers. Their persecution was the inevitable result of a philosophy of racial superiority that was pervasive throughout every aspect of American life: from sports and politics to the pulpit, from courts and cultural institutions to the combat zones.

a unit described by the camp's commanding officer—according to Ulysses P. Lee—as "the snappiest gun crews I have ever seen at this place."[16] They, along with members of other black units stationed at Stewart, told the general of inadequate recreation facilities and continual harassment by military and civilian police officers, whom they considered poorly trained and inexperienced.

Based on a report from Davis, General Virgil L. Peterson, inspector general of the army, submitted a series of proposals to the leadership at Camp Stewart, designed, Peterson said, to prevent the existing unrest from escalating to violence. These included improving recreational facilities, reducing overcrowding on buses, and stationing more black military policemen at bus stops.

However, before Peterson's recommendations could be carried out, a rumor —later proved false—flew through the barracks area. An African-American woman, so the story went, had been raped and murdered by white GI's after they killed her husband. Two recent incidents had already caused the blacks stationed at Stewart to be even more disaffected than usual. A few days earlier, machine-gun-wielding MP's had been used to break up a crowd of soldiers outside a dance held on the base. In another incident, a GI asking for a drink of water at an icehouse in a nearby town was badly beaten by white employees.

On June 9, over a hundred black soldiers—some carrying rifles—assembled in their sector of the camp. Military police dispersed them, but the GI's soon regrouped, their ranks swollen by men who had broken into supply rooms and armed themselves with rifles and submachine guns. At around ten o'clock, they began exchanging fire with detachments of MP's. The shooting continued for over two hours. After midnight, by which time one MP had been killed and four others wounded, two white battalions—in full battle dress and riding in armored vehicles—were ordered into the area, and the firing subsided.

Interestingly, Lee states, the one unit on the base with an all-black contingent of officers remained calm throughout the disturbance.

An army board of inquiry, while allowing that the black soldiers' stated reasons for their dissatisfaction with life at Camp Stewart might have some basis in fact, went on to echo the service's "party line" on racial conflict in its ranks. The board cited, as prime causes of the June 9 shootout, problems inherent in stationing Northern blacks in the South and "the average Negro soldier's meager education, superstition, imagination and excitability." These factors, the board's report continued, "make him easily misled" and "cause him to develop a mass state of mind."[17]

The Camp Stewart incident was quickly followed by disturbances—some involving gunplay—at Fort Bliss and Clark Field in Texas, Camp Van Dorn in Mississippi, Camp Breckenridge in Kentucky, March Field in California, and Fort Huachuca in Arizona. At the Shenango Replacement Depot in Pennsylvania, a pitched battle broke out between white and African-American GI's. During the course of the riot, black prisoners escaped from the guardhouse, stole weapons, and joined the fray. While suppressing the uprising, a racially mixed force of MP's killed one black soldier and wounded five others.

On July 3, General George Marshall stated, in a confidential memorandum to the commanders of the "Air Forces, Ground Forces and Service Forces," that:

> Disaffection among negro soldiers continues to constitute an immediately serious problem. . . . A study of detailed reports of many such cases indicated that there is general evidence of failure on the part of commanders of some echelons to appreciate the seriousness of the problem and their inherent responsibility. Under no circumstances can there be a command attitude which makes allowances for the improper conduct of either white or negro soldiers, among themselves or toward each other. Improper conduct cannot be justified on the basis of relative average intelligence. Discipline is not a matter of intelligence.
>
> Maintenance of discipline among soldiers and good order between soldiers and the civilian population is a definite command responsibility. Failure on the part of any commander to concern himself personally and vigorously with this problem will be considered as evidence of lack of capacity and cause for reclassification and removal from assignment.[18]

Such efforts by the high command to treat the symptoms while ignoring the underlying disease would continue until the end of the war—as would racial violence.

Two days after Marshall's memorandum, a group of black soldiers stationed at Camp McCain, Mississippi, angered by a series of altercations instigated by local civilians, picked up their rifles and went looking for revenge. They reached the town of Duck Hill and, firing some three hundred rounds of ammunition, struck several buildings, including the post office. Through luck or, possibly, design, no injuries were sustained during the attack.

Camp Claiborne—home of the 761st Tank Battalion—had a population of some 48,000 military personnel, 8,500 of them black. Lee reports that the facility had a reputation for poor morale and discipline. During the late spring and summer, he says, "there was a chain of disturbances . . . including mass raids on post exchanges involving loss of merchandise and damage to equipment; attempts by soldiers to overturn buses; and a near riot in a service club when an angry crowd, protesting the mistreatment of a black enlisted man by a white officer, dispersed only after tear gas was used."[19]

In nearby Alexandria—a scene of frequent racial incidents—Raymond Carr, a black military policeman, was shot and killed by a Louisiana state trooper. Civilian Aide Truman Gibson complained in a memorandum to General Davis that "the head of the Louisiana state police system refused to take any disciplinary action against the white state policeman although the deceased was unarmed and on active duty at the time."[20]

Though the tankers—whose morale and performance ratings were consistently excellent at Claiborne—managed to distance themselves from much of the turmoil on the base, off-post they were still subjected to hostility by white civilians and by military policemen of both races.

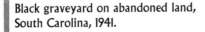

Black graveyard on abandoned land,
South Carolina, 1941.

Black MP's with their white commander, Columbus, Georgia, 1942.

Leonard "Smitty" Smith recalls one incident: "I was only seventeen and really didn't know too much about discrimination. I got into town and went through a field and got on the wrong side of town. I was in a store and going to buy some things that the man was going to sell me. Two white MP's came in and asked me what was I doing there and how did I get there. I explained to them, and they told me, 'Well, we're going to escort you back to your side of town.' I said, 'All right. Can I buy my things?' They said, 'No, no, you can't buy anything here.' So when we got back to my side of town, some black MP said, 'Well, what happened?' And the white guy said, 'Well, he just walked on the wrong side of town, and we just brought him back over here.' As soon as those white MP's got out of sight, the black ones whipped my butt and put me in jail."

In a poll of African-American troops stationed in the South and cited by Gibson in his memorandum to Davis, twenty-one percent of those questioned rated white MP's as fair in their treatment of them; the approval rate for black MP's, though considerably higher, was still a far-from-outstanding thirty-six percent.

In mid-September, the forty-two officers and six hundred one enlisted men of the 761st were transferred to Camp Hood, Texas, some two hundred miles southwest of Fort Worth, for advanced armored training. Those who might have harbored any ideas that this would be a more tolerant environment would soon discover their mistake.

Hood's black soldiers had long complained of their treatment. A year earlier, for example, Judge Hastie had received a letter from noncommissioned officers and enlisted men in the 826th Tank Destroyer Battalion:

> We were informed by the battalion commander, Lt. Col. Harvey Shelton, that if the Negro was more submissive and accepted the idea of white supremacy as a fait accompli, they would gain fuller rights. Company officers at official formations have repeatedly shown their hatred toward the Negro; for instance, 1st Lt. William C. Van Dyk has referred to soldiers as "Eight Ball" and has threatened to do bodily harm to enlisted men. At reveille, Friday, August 7, 1942, 1st Lt. Louis P. Beck stated that last year there were five Negro soldiers who refused to get off the sidewalk for Texas Rangers and in the melee [that followed] there were five Negro soldiers dead and the only witness was the coroner: "but I know that you *niggers* are courteous people." He further gave us the understanding that Negro soldiers have no rights or place in Texas; and if there be a misunderstanding, TEXAS RANGERS WILL FORM AS ONE AGAINST US. Due to this type of leadership, and also the section of the country where we are stationed, we have no protection whatever, even our very lives are at stake. . . . We are sure that you will see to it that corrective action be taken.[21]

Hastie forwarded this "very disturbing communication" to the adjutant general and requested an inspection of the unit. As far as can be determined, neither the adjutant general nor the inspector general followed up on the soldiers' appeal.

Walter Lewis, in "Diary of a Gunner," relates several anecdotes that capture the attitudes encountered by the tankers during their stay in the Lone Star State:

In Waco, I hailed a speeding taxi. I was dead tired. He slammed on the brakes and backed up just long enough to let me know that he "didn't ride no niggers." Another time in the Greyhound Bus Station in Belton, I was very hungry. I walked up to a greasy spoon lunch counter, where I expected to see a roach greet me any minute, and ordered a ham sandwich and a Royal Crown cola. When the man had served me and taken my money, he said, "Niggers eat in the back," pointing to the kitchen. I said, "Number one, you are the nigger, and number two, I am not eating in anybody's kitchen, now give me my money back." He said, "I don't know if I will or not." I said, "If you don't I will jump over that counter and make you wish you had." He threw the money at me. On the crowded bus, a white woman said to me, "Soldier, I heard what went on at that lunch counter. I am a Texan and I want you to know not all Texans are prejudiced. Please have my seat." I thanked her for her concern and remained standing.

Killeen, Texas, is just outside Camp Hood. We were greeted by a sign there as we returned from maneuvers. "Niggers have to leave this town by 9 P.M.!" Well, I don't have to tell you what the tankers did. We tore that sign down and integrated another southern town! First Sergeant Hubert H. House of Company A even took up residence there. When we went to Killeen we were treated courteously, with unnecessary awe, with respect!

Few army practices infuriated African-American GI's more than the preferential treatment accorded German and Italian prisoners of war detained on bases in this country. Enemy officers who died while interned were buried in their uniforms with full military honors—American rifle teams fired salutes over their graves. Their coffins were draped with the Nazi flag. At Camp Hood, where there was a large German POW camp, the unguarded prisoners were given work assignments cleaning up around the base. E. G. McConnell remembers them "walking around just like any other Tom, Dick, or Harry. We were in the camp too, but they didn't pick up in the black area. We had to do that ourselves. And these German prisoners of war, knowing how discrimination was in the States, used to smirk and look at us like we were crap. And here we were, first-class Americans, never been in prison, never been in war. Weren't prisoners of war or anything like that. And they would smirk at us, because they knew that they could go to any PX on the post and purchase whatever they wanted. We

Funeral with full honors for a German POW, Camp Chaffee, Arkansas, 1944.

Black soldiers handling laundry of German POW's.

couldn't. They weren't stepping back for no blacks like they did for the white American soldiers. Hell, they'd step *on* you!"

On August 14, 1944, at Fort Lawton, Washington, this resentment of the privileges afforded the POW's would find violent expression. Black soldiers on the base attacked an Italian POW service unit, and a full-scale riot ensued. The next day, the body of one of the prisoners was found hanging from a tree in a gully near the base. Forty-one soldiers were court-martialed on rioting charges, three of them charged with the murder; twenty-seven of the defendants were

Soldier and volunteer at a blacks-only canteen, Washington, D.C., 1943.

found guilty of riot. Those charged with homicide were acquitted but received prison sentences on the other counts ranging from twelve to twenty-five years.

Another bone of contention for black soldiers was the USO's policy of segregation. The United Service Organization was established to provide entertainment for soldiers, sailors, and marines on bases here and abroad. Like all else connected with the military during this period, the USO operated according to Jim Crow rules. The traveling troupes that put on the "camp shows" and included most of America's leading entertainers were segregated. So were their audiences.

Dick Campbell, a Harlem-based producer, was placed in charge of the African-American contingents. He recalled the temper of the times in an interview with William Miles and Nina Rosenblum:

"I had to fight in the beginning even to get the army and navy to accept USO camp shows. The shows existed for two years before they hired me to produce black USO camp shows to go and entertain black soldiers. [A big] problem was getting to and from those camps, particularly in the Southern part of the country. [For example,] I had one of my USO units playing at Camp Shelby in Mississippi. I got a long distance call in my office in New York saying, 'Mr. Campbell, they won't let us in to entertain the soldiers.' I got on the phone and I called Washington and I spoke to the commander in chief of the U.S. Armed Forces and I told him what the situation was. He says, 'Call me back in half an hour.' I did. He said, 'Mr. Campbell, if your unit is still there, tell them to go right on in.' So I called Camp Shelby, and they said, 'Mr. Campbell, we're already in here now. You don't have to worry.' I said, 'I imagined you were.' That not only happened once, it happened in many other cases where the armed forces were concerned."

As their training continued at Camp Hood, the 761st took part in massive maneuvers, which ranged far and wide across the Texas and Louisiana countryside. Their performance would catch the eye of the most celebrated and controversial of America's World War II commanders. Johnnie Stevens remembers his unit's first encounter with General George S. Patton. "He was inspecting troops on maneuvers, and he got a report that there was a black tank outfit that looked pretty good. When he saw us maneuvering tanks and firing guns and hitting targets, he said that he thought we were the finest tankers he had ever seen."

In several of these combat simulations, the Black Panthers fought together with the famed 100th Infantry Battalion, made up entirely of Japanese-

Americans. In 1945, elements of the two legendary units would meet again and participate in the liberation of the prisoners in the Dachau death camp.

As the 761st and the 100th were preparing for combat, inmates at Dachau—outside Munich—were being murdered by the thousands. Most were gassed, shot, or hanged; others had their lives taken in monstrous "scientific" experiments. One of these is described in a 1948 U.S. Army publication, *Dachau*:

> Jews were selected for this experiment. A truck, completely equipped, would roll up to between Barracks 3 and 5. The internee selected for this experiment was placed in a cylinder, and the air pressure lowered to a point which coincided with air pressure at an altitude of 5,000 to 8,000 meters. The air pressure was then brought back to normal sea level pressure at a terrific speed. These conditions simulated a parachutist dropping at a speed much greater than would be encountered in reality. The reactions of men undergoing these experiments were

Jewish deportees locked in cattle cars on the way to concentration camps.

observed and studied for future air force training. Not a single man was seen leaving this truck alive.[22]

Some 450 miles northeast of Dachau, the words "Jedem das Seine"—Everybody for Himself—are inscribed over Buchenwald's high iron gate. Inside the camp, Ben Bender and his brother Berick are among the 1,700 inmates who sleep, with not an inch of space between them, in a barracks built to accommodate one fourth that number. They are barely surviving on a daily ration of one slice of bread, one bowl of black coffee, and a portion of gray soup that is little more than plain lukewarm water, their diet occasionally augmented by scraps stolen from their captors' garbage. But the physical deprivations, according to Bender, paled beside the damage done to the spirit. "From the moment they came to this place," he remembers, "they were so degraded, so humiliated, they were already extinguished. There was no resistance. When you kill the soul, you destroy the body, and this is what the Germans did."

CHAPTER 5

When General Patton sent for us, he asked
for the best tank unit in the country. Hot
dog it, were we proud, proud! I was in a unit
I was damn proud of, and I knew that the
things we did would shape the future for my
children and grandchildren. We were so
proud and dedicated to the cause of
progress . . . going ahead so everyone would
be able to live like an American.

E. G. McConnell

Marines on leave, Harlem, 1943.

By June 1, 1944, 134,000 African-American soldiers were serving in the European Theater of Operations. Only one unit, however, the 99th Pursuit Squadron—under the command of Benjamin O. Davis, Jr.—was actually in combat. The Tuskegee Flyers—who had dubbed themselves the "Lonely Eagles" because they operated in a totally segregated environment—had already been awarded two Distinguished Unit Citations (the military's highest commendation) for their outstanding performance in aerial combat against the Luftwaffe during the invasion of Sicily and the Italian campaign. All other black soldiers were in service units, most of them working as laborers despite the fact that many, such as the 2nd Cavalry Division, the 24th Infantry Division, and several artillery battalions, had been fully trained for combat.

As early as July 1943, the War Department's Advisory Committee on Special Troop Policies (Negro Troops), chaired by Assistant Secretary John J. McCloy—who was regarded by many, including Civilian Aide Truman K. Gibson, Jr., as the black soldiers' only effective advocate among the department's upper echelons—was urging General Marshall to dispatch black combat troops "to an active theater of operations at an early date. In the opinion of the Committee such action would be the most effective means of reducing tension among Negro troops."[1]

In February 1944, New York Congressman Hamilton Fish, who had been an officer with the black 93rd Division in World War I, addressed the House of Representatives. Though an archconservative on most issues, Fish said that "fourteen millions of Americans have the right to expect that in a war for the advancement of the 'Four Freedoms' their sons be given the same right as any other American to serve and fight in combat units in defense of the United States in the greatest war in history."[2] Mrs. Roosevelt, likewise, was urging the Pentagon to see that "the colored people be given a chance to prove their mettle."[3]

On November 3, 1943, Gibson, looking ahead to the 1944 presidential election, had warned McCloy that blacks' dissatisfaction with the military might adversely affect FDR's reelection effort:

> There is, in fact, every present indication that the treatment of Negroes in the armed forces will constitute the most important issue in the general effort to capture the Negro vote. Undoubtedly much that will be said about the Army will be political in nature and thus essentially untrue. The essential fact is, however, that the present situation is such that the statements will be believed implicitly. There

have been many cases of violence against Negro personnel in the South about which nothing has been done. . . . Then too, no substantial number of Negro combat troops have been committed to action. Moreover, many combat organizations have been stripped of enlisted men who have been sent to Quartermaster Service Battalions. . . . The fact is that all incidents of this sort fit into the same general pattern.

Gibson went on to recommend sending black troops into battle: "I appreciate that this is no novel suggestion and I know your views on this matter. However, it is a fact that no large Negro units have seen action and most Negro soldiers feel that they will not be used as combat soldiers."[4]

One week later, in a memorandum to McCloy, General Davis shed his usual "go along" posture and took the offensive. It is a powerful document and merits quotation at length.

. . . there is still great dissatisfaction and discouragement on the part of the colored people and the soldiers. They feel that regardless of how much they strive to meet War Department requirements, there is no change in the attitude of the War Department. The colored officers and soldiers feel that they are denied the protections and rewards that ordinarily result from good behavior and proper performance of duty.

Davis voiced the deepest feelings of African-American soldiers and civilians as he castigated the War Department for its failure to send black units into combat, its conversion of trained fighting outfits into service companies, and its reluctance to assign highly trained black officers to unit commander posts.

The general then turned his attention to the adversities endured by African-American troops garrisoned within the United States:

The press news items and investigations show that there has been little change in the attitudes of civilian communities in Southern states. . . . The colored man in uniform is expected by the War Department to develop a high morale in a community that offers him nothing but humiliation and mistreatment. The War Department has failed to secure to the colored soldier protection against violence on the part of civilian police and to secure justice in the courts in communities nearby

A. Philip Randolph leading a demonstration, New York City, 1940.

to Southern stations. . . . On the training fields the development of morale does not take into consideration Jim Crow laws and customs. The "Four Freedoms" cannot be enjoyed under Jim Crow influences. Officers of the War Department General Staff have refused to attempt any remedial action to eliminate Jim Crow. In fact, the Army, by its directives and by actions of commanding officers, has introduced Jim Crow practices in areas, both at home and abroad, where they have not heretofore been practiced.

Davis continued with an attack on the McCloy Committee itself.

What, in over a year of existence, has the Advisory Committee on Special Troop Policies (Negro Troops) accomplished? The War Department appears to regard the colored soldiers as separate and distinct and, as such, sets them apart. Fraternization or any kind of comradely association with white troops is discouraged. The War Department is making no appreciable efforts to lessen the Jim Crow practices, which are by far the greatest factor in the morale of the colored soldier. Many colored units are kept in localities from which many of the families of these men left in order to escape Jim Crow practices. If the Department cannot change the attitude of these communities, it can refrain from locating colored units in communities hostile to them. Both colored and white soldiers are given the same intensive training, inculcated with the same desire to serve their country with honor—the privilege of every free citizen in any nation. It is the duty of the Department to demonstrate to the world the principle of tolerance to our own colored group.

I believe the problem is large enough to warrant that establishment of a bureau with General Staff representation to devote full time to the study of the conditions surrounding the colored soldier. This bureau should be large enough to enable its representatives to make personal inspections of colored troops and their surroundings. Some of this bureau should be colored. It is utterly impossible for any white man to appreciate what the colored officers and soldiers experience in trying to develop high morale under present conditions.[5]

General Davis's proposed bureau remained "proposed."

The army's official rationale for its policy of excluding African-American units from combat duty rested on the low scores of blacks—relative to whites—on the Army General Classification Test. Though most educational psychologists today recognize the fallacy of making broad generalizations and predictions based upon such test evidence, few in the 1940s challenged the accuracy of these examinations. Congressman Fish, however, in his February 1944 congressional speech, reviewed the sterling combat record of his 93rd Division. He then stated that given the improvement in the educational standards of African-Americans in the quarter century since World War I (the number of high school graduates among black recruits had risen by 1700 percent), it was absurd for Secretary Stimson to contend that black soldiers were incapable of mastering the weapons of modern warfare. General Patton—at least at one point in his life—shared the secretary's position. In a volume published posthumously in 1947, *War as I Knew It*, Patton states that blacks "cannot think fast enough to fight in armor."[6] Had he lived long enough to evaluate the 761st Tank Battalion's major contributions to his Third Army's success, the general might well have come to another conclusion.

Sharp criticism of the policy of combat exclusion—criticism from varied quarters, both within and outside the military—was, however, having some limited effect. In February 1944, the War Department issued, with General Marshall's imprimatur, a booklet entitled *Command of Negro Troops:*

Harlem boy hawking his newspapers, 1943.

It is alleged by some that the Negro cannot be reliable in battle because his race lacks the necessary qualities as a matter of heredity. Many Negroes, like many other people, do lack soldierly skills. But insofar as this belief assumes that there are mysterious inborn factors—such as courage, fear, or a fighting heart—whose presence or absence is a matter of racial inheritance, it is enough to say that there is no scientific evidence to support such a view. . . . All peoples seem to be endowed equally with whatever it takes to fight a good war, if they want to and have learned how. Among Negroes, as among white people, there is the widest range of individual abilities, and most of the less mentally alert in either race can be made to learn how to fight if properly led. . . . There is no place in the Army for the attitude, "these men are so limited in ability that there is no use trying to make good soldiers out of them." . . . The Germans have a theory that they are a race of supermen born to conquer all peoples of inferior blood. This is nonsense, the like of which has no place in the Army of the United States—the Army of a Nation which has become great through the common effort of all peoples. . . . The Negroes in our Army are Americans in both thought and behavior, but Americans of any color are not cut in a single pattern. . . . The Negro group is not unique in that many of its members have ideas of their own about what is proper and what is not, about what is insulting and what is just. Their history and the existing restrictions which limit their participation in the life of the community make it inevitable that most Negroes will differ somewhat from white people in their sensitivities, thoughts and actions.[7]

On February 29, the McCloy Committee recommended to Secretary Stimson that "as soon as possible colored Infantry, Field Artillery and other combat units be introduced into combat and that if present organizations or training schedules do not permit such prompt commitment, that steps be taken to reorganize any existing schedules so as to permit the introduction of qualified colored combat units as promptly as possible, into battle."[8]

The Pentagon, typically, was slow to act on these urgent recommendations. On June 6, 1944—three months after the committee's report—185,000 Allied

Tenants' meeting at the Ida B. Wells housing project, Chicago, 1942.

General George Smith Patton.

troops stormed the beaches of Normandy, in the largest amphibious invasion in military history. Only five hundred of these men were African-Americans. They were members of the 320th Barrage Balloon Battalion, who, according to John D. Silvera in *The Negro in World War II*, waded ashore in the early hours of D-day, struggling with their "flying beer bottles. . . . They brought their balloons to the shore line, dug in with the infantrymen of the 1st and 29th Divisions and proceeded under fierce enemy fire to erect a protective curtain of silver barrage balloons that proved highly effective in combating striking German aircraft."[9]

Three days after D-day, the 761st—still training at Camp Hood—was placed on an "alert" status for overseas duty. Soon after these orders were received, the unit was inspected by General Ben Lear, deputy commander of the European Theater of Operations. Though Lear had been fulsome in his praise—"all reports coming to Washington about you have been of superior nature and we are expecting great things of your battalion in combat"—many of the tankers remained skeptical about the probability of their outfit going into action. As tanker Walter Lewis writes: "I never believed we would ever see combat in tanks. I thought we would be used as morale builders and training units for white tank destroyer units in the rear echelons."

About this time, the battalion acquired a most unusual nickname: "Eleanor's Niggers and Patton's Pets." It would stay with them throughout the war and after, part of the 761st legend. According to the story, the battalion's assignment to combat duty came about through the collusive efforts of Eleanor Roosevelt and George Patton as they made an end run around the Pentagon brass. On the face of it, this tale reflects a certain logic; the First Lady certainly campaigned vigorously for the inclusion of blacks in the fighting forces, and Patton certainly needed the most effective combat units he could find. However, it seems to go aground on the shoals of the general's reputed racism. Nalty writes of a Patton "who had no good words for any black unit. Not even the 761st Tank Battalion could impress him, despite its accomplishments, for he was convinced that blacks lacked the reflexes for armored combat." Diligent efforts by the authors to substantiate the Roosevelt-Patton scenario have been unrewarding. It is indeed a good story, but like many such, it is probably untrue.

During those last months of training under the searing Texas sun, the men of the 761st remained preoccupied with the bitter realities of life in a Jim Crow army. Of all the dehumanizing aspects of serving in that army, few infuriated African-American soldiers stationed in the South more than the difficulties encountered in riding military and civilian buses back and forth from base to town. Intercity travel on private buses was even more problematic—bus drivers in the South were permitted to carry firearms.

In June 1943, in a memorandum to Assistant Secretary of War McCloy, Civilian Aide Gibson, citing a series of violent incidents involving transportation, noted that:

> Bus travel in the South for Negro soldiers and officers has become one of the most serious problems facing the Army. In practically no

state in the South is a Negro soldier or officer permitted to board an intrastate or interstate bus if there are any white passengers not provided for, despite the "reservation" of the *rear seat* for Negroes. Intercity travel is a source of constant peril or uncertainty. The Negro soldier may at any time be removed from a motor coach to "wait for another section" if there are white soldiers or civilians to ride. Bus service between camps and cities in the South is almost as bad. Buses usually start in the white areas of camps and are loaded before they pass through the Negro sections, which are usually remote and isolated. Negro soldiers are usually not permitted to board buses until after white soldiers have been picked up.

Gibson went on to recommend that "commanders in the field be instructed that Negro officers and soldiers in inter- and intrastate bus travel be furnished accommodations equal to those furnished whites and that the companies be specifically advised that the War Department does not look with favor on the continuation of the present system of permitting Negro soldiers to travel only after all white travellers have been accommodated."[10]

More than a year later—on July 8, 1944—the secretary of war directed all commanding generals, the army air forces, all service commands, and the Military District of Washington that "Buses, trucks or other transportation owned and operated by either the Government or by a governmental instrumentality will be available to all military personnel regardless of race. Restricting personnel to certain sections of such transportation will not be permitted either on or off a post, camp or station, regardless of civilian custom."[11] The timing of Stimson's order is, as we shall see, of more than a little interest.

In March 1944, one of several black officers newly posted to the 761st was a second lieutenant, and a national celebrity, named Jackie Robinson. Johnnie Stevens remembers him affectionately as a "real fireball." To E. G. McConnell and "Smitty" Smith, he was a guy they "had fun with," a guy who "kept us out of trouble." In an interview with William Miles, Commanding Officer Paul Bates fondly recalled Robinson, the future baseball Hall of Famer, writing that Bates "was one of the men he met in his life that was white both inside and out. He also wrote a very nice letter to my son about his father, which was a very special thing to do." Robinson, however, was a man who, throughout his life, inspired contradictory opinions among those who knew him. Harold B. Gary, for instance, a classmate of Robinson's at officer candidate school, a fellow officer

Black passengers heading for the back of the bus, Baltimore, 1943.

in the 761st, and one of the few African-Americans to hail from South Dakota, describes him as "probably the worst human being I ever met . . . and I knew him fairly well. That's all I'm going to say about him. Everybody thinks he's a great hero and he is, to a lot of people, so let's just leave it that way."

The term "American original" is more often than not misapplied; Jackie Robinson, though, fits firmly in that mold. He and his family—his mother, Mallie, and four older siblings—left Cairo, Georgia, in 1920 and settled in Pasadena, California. Jackie was eight months old when his father, Jerry Robinson, deserted the family, four months before they migrated.

In *Baseball's Great Experiment: Jackie Robinson and His Legacy*, Jules Tygiel writes that Robinson's mother toiled as a domestic and supplemented her meager income with public assistance payments. Jackie, early on, encountered the harsh realities of American race relations. "With the help of the welfare agency," Tygiel says, "Mallie Robinson purchased a house on Pepper Street in a white Pasadena community. The neighbors petitioned to have the Robinsons removed and, when this failed, they offered to buy out the black family. But Mallie was determined to keep her home. Residents subjected the Robinson family to abuse and harassment for several years, but the house on Pepper Street remained the physical and spiritual center for the close-knit Robinson clan."[12] Jackie Robinson recalled: "My brothers and I were in many a fight that started with a racial slur on the very street we lived on."[13]

During these years, most public facilities in Pasadena were segregated: movie theaters, the YMCA, swimming pools, etc. In 1936, according to Tygiel, "when a judge ordered Pasadena pools to allow blacks, the city government responded by purging all blacks from its payrolls. Among those fired was Jackie's older brother, Mack [a college graduate who could find work only as a janitor]. He had recently returned from the Berlin Olympic Games where he won a silver medal, finishing second to Jesse Owens in the 200-meter dash."[14]

In 1939, Jackie Robinson enrolled at the University of California at Los Angeles, where soon he established himself as the greatest athlete in that sports-oriented university's history. He was the school's first four-letter man—baseball, track, basketball (he led the Pacific Coast Conference in scoring for two straight years), and football. As an All-American halfback, he averaged

Lieutenant Jackie Robinson, former UCLA four-letter athlete and future baseball Hall of Famer.

an incredible eleven yards per carry in his junior year. He somehow managed to find time to win the Pacific Coast intercollegiate golf title and become a championship-caliber swimmer. As Tygiel notes: "It is probable that no other athlete, including Jim Thorpe, has ever competed as effectively in as broad a range of sports."[15]

Before being drafted into the army in 1942, Robinson and Nat Moreland, a pitcher in the Negro League, tried out for the still-all-white major leagues. Chicago White Sox manager Jimmy Dykes watched a limping Robinson in action and said, according to Tygiel: "I'd hate to see him on two good legs. He's worth $50,000 in anybody's money. He stole everything but my infielder's gloves."[16] Nevertheless, Dykes stood fast by organized baseball's racial principles and did not sign either player. Robinson would resoundingly shatter this color barrier in 1947, when he joined the Brooklyn Dodgers.

Jackie reported for duty at Fort Riley, Kansas, in April 1942 and applied for officer candidate school. Turned down, he attributed the rejection to racial prejudice. According to Tygiel, writing in *American Heritage* magazine, Robinson asked Joe Louis, who was stationed at Riley when he wasn't traveling the country on morale-building and recruitment tours, to intervene. The heavyweight champion brought the matter to the War Department's attention; Robinson and several other blacks on the base were subsequently admitted to OCS.

Fort Riley, like many posts, took pride in the quality of its athletic teams. The football squad was integrated, but the baseball team, following the tradition of the civilian national pastime, did not permit African-Americans to wear its uniform. Still, Robinson, who by now had probably decided that in the long run baseball offered him the best career prospects, sought a place on the Fort Riley nine. "Pistol" Pete Reiser, who would later be a fellow Dodger, was a member of that squad. He recalled: "One day a Negro lieutenant came out for the ball team. An officer told him he couldn't play. 'You have to play for the colored team,' the officer said. That was a joke. There was no colored team. The lieutenant stood there for a while, watching us work out. Then he turned and walked away. I didn't know who he was then, but that was the first time I saw Jackie Robinson. I can still remember him walking away by himself."[17]

Lieutenant Robinson was assigned to a cavalry unit as morale officer. After his protests over PX segregation led to a shouting match with Fort Riley's provost marshal, Robinson was transferred to the 761st, where he became morale officer for Company A.

On July 6, 1944—two days before Stimson's order to desegregate bus service to and from army installations—Jackie Robinson was scheduled for a physical examination to determine if an old ankle injury was serious enough for the army to waive responsibility should he go overseas with the 761st. He took a bus to the hospital, some thirty miles from Hood. Learning that there would be a long wait for the results, he decided to go back to camp and spend the time with his men. His bus trips to and from the hospital were uneventful.

Transportation problems were, at that moment, of even more concern than usual to black troops everywhere. Recent months had seen two highly publicized incidents involving bus travel. In the first, Joe Louis and Sugar Ray Robinson—who had just completed a tour of some ninety bases, during which they were cheered by more than 600,000 troops—clashed with MP's at Camp Siebert, Alabama, where they were stationed. Sugar Ray described the confrontation in his autobiography, *Sugar Ray*, written with Dave Anderson:

> One day Joe and I were waiting for a bus to town [Gadsen]. Getting a bus was a problem. There were two buses for white soldiers to every one bus for the Negro soldiers. . . . "No use standin' around here," Joe said, "I'm goin' to call a cab." He strolled over to where the white soldiers were waiting and disappeared into a phone booth. . . . When Joe came out an M.P., twirling a brown wooden billy club, sauntered over to us. . . . "Soldier," he snapped, "your color belongs in the other bus station." "What's my color got to do with it?" Joe said. "I'm wearing a uniform just like you." "Down here," the guard said in his 'Bama drawl, "you do as you're told." I never saw Joe so angry. His big body looked as if it would explode. But knowing Joe, I realized that he was trying to control himself. Then the M.P. made a mistake, he flicked the billy club and poked Joe in the ribs. "Don't touch me with that stick," Joe growled. "I'll do more than touch you," the M.P. snapped. He drew back the billy club as if to swing it at Joe. When I saw that, I leaped on the M.P. I was choking him, biting him, anything to keep him away from Joe. . . . A few more M.P.s ran up and separated us. The new M.P.s might really have roughed us up, but some of the soldiers were shouting, "That's Joe Louis, that's Joe Louis," and the M.P.s didn't know what to do then, so they lined us up.[18]

The two men were taken into custody and brought to the camp stockade. Word spread rapidly through Siebert that they had been badly beaten. Robinson was questioned by a lieutenant colonel, who, after hearing the boxer's story,

Standing, from left: Corporal Joe Louis, unidentified,
Lieutenant Jackie Robinson, and unidentified.

berated the arresting officer for his actions. Louis and Robinson were freed and
then driven through the camp in an open car to demonstrate to the angry troops
that they had not been physically harmed.

If two of black America's greatest heroes could suffer such disrespect and
come so close to being brutalized, what, the average African-American GI must
have thought, can happen to me?

In the second travel-related incident, Tygiel tells of a driver in Durham,
North Carolina, who had shot one of those average black soldiers to death for
the offense of refusing to sit in the back of his bus. The driver went to trial and
was acquitted by an all-white jury.

Jackie Robinson, before leaving Hood to return to the hospital for his test
results on July 6, stopped in at the black officers' club, where, witnesses stated,
he did not consume any alcohol. There he encountered a friend, Virginia Jones,
the wife of another lieutenant in the 761st. Mrs. Jones has been described as
being light enough in complexion to pass for white. Since she was going home
on the same bus line as Robinson, they decided to travel together. In a sworn
deposition taken on July 19, Mrs. Jones states:

> We left the colored officers club and caught a bus in front. . . . I got
> on the bus first and sat down, and Lt. Robinson got on and came and
> sat down beside me. I sat in the fourth seat from the rear of the bus,

which I have always considered the rear of the bus. The bus driver looked back at us and then asked Lt. Robinson to move. Lt. Robinson told the bus driver to go on and drive the bus. The bus driver told Lt. Robinson to move again, and Lt. Robinson said, "I'm not moving," so the bus driver stopped the bus, came back and balled his fist and said, "Will you move to the back?" Lt. Robinson said, "I'm not moving," so the bus driver stood there and glared a minute and said, "Well just sit there until we get down to the bus station."[19]

Upon reaching the depot—where both Robinson and Mrs. Jones were to change buses—the driver, Milton N. Reneger, demanded to see the lieutenant's pass. Robinson, who was in uniform, objected vigorously but, according to Mrs. Jones, did so without saying "anything vile and vulgar." At this point, a white female passenger berated Robinson for not obeying the driver's command to move farther back in the bus. She threatened to "report" him. As a crowd gathered, Reneger left and quickly returned, accompanied by the dispatcher and two other drivers. "Is this the nigger who's been causing you trouble?" the dispatcher asked his driver. Robinson then shook his finger in Reneger's face, demanding that he "stop fucking with me!" At this point, ten white MP's, apparently summoned immediately after the bus's arrival, appeared on the scene. The lieutenant was taken to their headquarters for questioning. What transpired inside became the central point of contention in the legal proceedings that followed.

In depositions and in court, Captain Gerald M. Bear, Camp Hood's assistant provost marshal, stated that he gave Robinson "a direct order to remain in the receiving room, that I would talk to him later. In an effort to try to be facetious, Lt. Robinson bowed with several sloppy salutes, repeating several times, 'OK, sir, OK, sir,' on each occasion. I gave him another direct order to remain in the receiving room. . . . Later on I found Lt. Robinson outside the building talking to the 761st Tank Battalion OD's [Officer of the Day] jeep driver. Lt. Robinson's attitude was in general disrespectful and impertinent to his superior officers and very unbecoming to an officer in the presence of enlisted men."[20]

Captain Edward L. Hamilton, the camp's prison officer, buttressed Bear's account and added: "During his statement, while referring to a PFC who had called him a nigger, Lt. Robinson turned to Captain [Peelor] Wiggington and stated that 'if you, Captain,' and pointed to me and Lt. [George] Cribari, 'or you, or you, should call me a nigger, I would break you in two.' This threat . . . was very unbecoming and his manner of conversation was very unbecoming to an officer of the United States Army."[21]

The PFC in question was one Ben W. Mucklerath, who had met Robinson and the MP's when they arrived at headquarters. Mucklerath had asked the policemen whether they had a "nigger lieutenant" in their car.

Robinson's explanations of the evening's events were not accepted, and he was charged with insubordination, disturbing the peace, drunkenness, insulting a civilian woman (a stenographer who repeatedly interrupted his interrogation with her own contemptuous questions), refusing to obey the commands of a superior officer, and conduct unbecoming an officer and a gentleman.

Lieutenant Colonel Bates of the 761st, a staunch Robinson supporter, refused to give his consent—as military law required—to the indictment. Robinson was swiftly transferred to another unit, whose commander acquiesced to the wishes of Hood's top brass for an immediate court-martial.

The army's prosecution of Jackie Robinson had two phases. In the first, a three-judge court would decide on the merits of the specific charges. Bates remembered well that hearing, where he testified in Robinson's behalf. He told William Miles:

I got about five of my guys and told them, "I want you to look your best." We went to the Court. I said [to the judges], "Look at 'em. See what kind of soldiers they are. Talk to them if you want to." And here are these guys, with polished boots and what not and they all stand up at attention and salute. I said, "These guys are ready to fight and die for their country, why should they have to work all day and then walk ten miles at night?"[22]

The judges dropped all but the two insubordination counts.

The second phase, the actual trial on the remaining charges, was held on August 2. The credibility of the army's

Lieutenant Colonel Paul L. Bates, commander of the 761st Tank Battalion.

witnesses was repeatedly and effectively challenged. Bates testified that the reputation of the accused was "excellent," as were his abilities as a soldier. "Would you be satisfied," he was asked, "to go into combat with this officer under your command?" "I would," he unequivocally replied. Robinson's counsel painted a picture of a defendant persecuted for being "uppity," for having, in Robinson's words, "the audacity to exercise rights that belonged to him as an American and a soldier."

During the proceedings, Jackie Robinson was asked to define a "nigger." "I looked it up once," he told the court, "but my grandmother gave me a good definition. She was a slave, and she said the definition of the word was a low and uncouth person . . . but I don't consider that I am low and uncouth. . . . I do not consider myself a nigger at all. I am a Negro but not a nigger."[23]

The nine judges declared Robinson innocent of all charges. Though he made it known that he wished to return to the 761st, the army had other plans. Robinson was transferred to Camp Breckenridge, Kentucky, where he served as a sports instructor until November, when he was honorably discharged.

Had Jackie Robinson been convicted, the minimum penalty would have been a dishonorable discharge, which, as Tygiel acutely observes, would certainly have barred him from the courageous, historic role he soon would play in the struggle of African-Americans for equality and justice.

Robinson later wrote that the defiant acts of the Brown Bomber and Sugar Ray at Fort Siebert had partly inspired his behavior that evening at Camp Hood. The South's segregated public-transit policies were to all African-Americans—civilian and military—one of the most hated manifestations of an altogether heinous system. It was, therefore, no accident that the modern civil rights movement was galvanized into being by the refusal of an African-American seamstress, Rosa Parks, to surrender her seat to a white man on a Montgomery, Alabama, bus on the first of December, 1955.

On July 17, 1944—while the Black Panthers were preparing for whatever fate awaited them—the worst home-front disaster of World War II occurred at Port Chicago, California, a small town on the Sacramento River not far from San Francisco. Two Liberty ships—the *E. A. Bryan* and the *Quinault Victory*—exploded as they were being loaded with tons of bombs and other ammunition. Three hundred twenty sailors—202 of whom were African-Americans—were blown to pieces by the blast. Ninety percent of the white dead were members of the crews of the two vessels.

It should be noted that throughout the war, the navy continued its long-standing policy of relegating the overwhelming majority of black recruits to the most menial assignments; not until March 1944 were thirteen black officers commissioned, and then only after strong representations by both the President and Mrs. Roosevelt. Port duty—which was also engaged in by soldiers—certainly fell in the menial category.

As early as March 1943, P. L. Prattis, executive editor of the black newspaper the *Pittsburgh Courier*, had warned Civilian Aide Gibson in a letter:

> I am afraid that if you do not attempt to persuade the proper officials in the War Department to take some action in respect to the so-called Port Battalions there is going to be an ugly climax that none of us will enjoy seeing. These Port Battalions are stevedore outfits. They are doing the same type of work into which Negroes were herded during the last war. The memory of this past experience is still bitter with Negroes. They don't mind doing their fair share of this work but it is easy for them to be persuaded that they are doing more than their fair share.[24]

The ammunition-loading facility at Port Chicago had been in operation since December 1942. As historian Robert L. Allen writes in his definitive study, *The Port Chicago Mutiny:* "From the outset the new naval magazine was beset with difficulties." These included problems both of design and of personnel. Neither the fourteen hundred black enlisted men assigned to the stevedoring operation nor their white officers had received specialized training in munitions handling. According to Allen, "during the weeks before the explosion, the longshoremen's union repeatedly warned the Navy that there would be a disaster"[25] if untrained personnel continued to load ammunition.

The sailors were not hesitant in expressing their dissatisfaction about conditions at Port Chicago—among themselves, to their officers, and in a letter to the NAACP. They were angered over segregation on the base, its lack of recreational facilities for blacks, perceived discrimination in promotions, and, above all, the fact that no whites were detailed to loading the munitions ships. Allen writes that the commanding officer, Captain Nelson Goss, "complained that the 'black recruits arrived with a chip on their shoulder, if not, indeed, one on each shoulder.' He suspected that they were under subversive influence because they 'insisted they had volunteered for combat duty and did definitely resent

The disastrous aftermath of the Port Chicago explosion that devastated the small town near San Francisco on July 17, 1944.

being assigned to what they called "laborers' work." ' "[26] The fact that the sailors were being paid a fraction of what civilians would receive for performing the same arduous and life-threatening job also took a toll on their morale.

There were 860,000 pounds of fragmentation and incendiary bombs on the loading pier and in the two ships' holds at 10:18 P.M. on July 17. The area was illuminated to near noontime levels by high-powered floodlights. The terrible explosion, later estimated as approximating the force of the Hiroshima A-bomb, rocked the entire San Francisco Bay Area. Bits of bodies flew like bullets through the air, severed heads floated with the river's current. The base and its immediate environs were left in shambles; the *E. A. Bryan* was virtually atomized, the *Quinault Victory* blown into many small pieces.

Four days later, judicial proceedings that would evoke harsh memories of the Brownsville Raid and the Houston Riot prosecutions began. The first stage involved a naval court of inquiry charged with determining the cause or causes of the tragedy. Only five African-American seamen were among the 125 witnesses—officers, survivors, and experts—who testified during the month-long investigation. In its findings, the court, for the most part, followed the arguments of the judge advocate (the military equivalent of a district attorney) that "colored enlisted personnel are neither temperamentally nor intellectually capable of handling high explosives. . . . These men, it is testified, could not understand the orders which were given to them."[27] Despite strong evidence of generally lax safety procedures stemming from the officers' failure to enforce standard navy regulations, the court—while declining to pinpoint any one specific cause—implied that the black sailor/stevedores bore most of the responsibility, though there was not enough evidence to make specific charges and, of course, the putative defendants were already dead.

The surviving black sailors, traumatized by the loss of so many comrades and their own narrow escapes, were reassigned to the Ryder Street Naval Barracks, in nearby Vallejo. A mere two weeks after the cataclysm, they were ordered to resume loading bombs and shells. The navy's decision is worth considering. If, as was stated before the court of inquiry, these African-Americans were truly believed to be mentally defective, why would the service return them to jobs in which they could conceivably perpetrate another disaster? Certainly there were commodities other than high explosives that needed loading.

On August 9, the sailors declined to return to the docks. Despite the entreaties of officers and the base chaplain, the men—convinced that negligence on the part of their superiors was responsible for the explosion—adamantly refused to

| Aid to victims of the explosion.

handle munitions. Robert L. Allen writes that they were individually interrogated and threatened with prison terms. Only seventy of the 328 black seamen backed down.

The remaining strikers were confined for seventy-two hours on a barge, where, in a brief meeting, they agreed to hold their ground. This solidarity dissolved the following day when Admiral Carleton H. Wright, commandant of the Twelfth Naval District, told them they were looking at death sentences for the crime of mutiny. "The hazards of facing a firing squad," he said, "are far greater than the hazards of handling ammunition."[28] The admiral's threat achieved its goal; all but fifty of the strikers returned to work.

Their trial began on September 11 at a naval facility on Yerba Buena (Treasure) Island, in San Francisco Bay. The defendants faced a seven-man panel of judges, senior officers appointed by Admiral Wright. They stood charged with conspiracy to commit mutiny in time of war. It was the largest mass court-martial in the history of the United States Navy. Defense efforts to have the charge thrown out, on the grounds that there had been no effort to unlawfully oppose, resist, or defy their officers with a "deliberate purpose" of seizing command, were overruled.

The court heard evidence for six weeks. On October 24, after but an hour and twenty minutes of deliberation, it found all fifty of the defendants guilty of mutiny as charged. They were sentenced to fifteen years in prison and dishonorably discharged from the United States Navy.

Thurgood Marshall, who observed the proceedings in his capacity as director of the NAACP Legal and Educational Defense Fund, wrote in the November issue of *Crisis* that the Port Chicago case represented "one of the worst 'frameups' we have come across in a long time. It was deliberately planned and staged by certain officers to discredit Negro seamen."[29]

Attorney Thurgood Marshall, a director of the NAACP.

Second Lieutenant Clarence I. Godbold, one of the first
black officers of the 761st, near Nancy, France, 1944.

Marshall appealed the decision, which had generated a wave of anger in the
black community. Mrs. Roosevelt also raised her voice in behalf of the accused.
Marshall told the Judge Advocate General's Office that "justice can be done in
this case only by a complete reversal of the charges." The appeal was denied.

In January 1946, with the war over and the military inching toward fairer
racial policies, the sentences of the "Port Chicago Fifty" were commuted and
the men released from prison. They were not pardoned, however, so the record
of their convictions and their dishonorable discharges stood. They were therefore denied all the benefits due veterans and their dependents.

In 1991, as a direct consequence of Robert L. Allen's book, two Bay Area
congressmen—George Miller and Ronald V. Dellums—introduced a measure in
the House of Representatives calling on the "Secretary of the Navy to carry out

without delay a thorough review of the Port Chicago cases . . . to determine . . . the extent, if any, to which racial prejudice or other improper factors now known may have tainted the original investigations and trials." Should the secretary make such a judgment, the measure calls on him to "rectify the error or injustice."[30] On November 19, 1991, the measure was admitted by a vote of 329 to 82. As of this writing, the navy has not reported its findings. Should these be favorable to the sailors, this will be another case of military justice coming much too late. According to Congressman Miller's office, only a dozen of the Port Chicago "mutineers" are still alive.

As the Port Chicago drama was unfolding in California, the Black Panthers were nearing peak efficiency at Camp Hood as they completed their final round of training before shipping out for Europe. Their orders were cut in July. A small advance party was scheduled to sail for England from New York later in the month, and the bulk of the troops were scheduled to follow shortly after.

On August 9, 1944, 701 members of the 761st Tank Battalion boarded a troop train at Camp Hood, Texas. They shed no tears as they departed a state that, like Louisiana before it, had been far from hospitable to African-American

Mass deportation of Jews to the concentration camps.

warriors who were preparing to fight—and possibly die—for so-called American values. Four days later, they arrived at Camp Shanks, New York. On August 27, they steamed out of New York harbor aboard a British troop transport, HMS *Esperance Bay.* They were on their way to join the "Big Show," leaving a homeland where, over the course of twenty generations, their people had survived both the physical genocide of the slave trade and the attempted spiritual and emotional destruction that—in the eighty years since Emancipation—had characterized their collective existence. The tankers were now to cross a deep and dangerous divide that their ancestors had traversed in chains. They would join a five-hundred-vessel convoy loaded with men and matériel consigned to the struggle against a malevolent foe called Nazism. They would fight a war in the name of freedoms that neither the men of the 761st nor their foreparents had ever truly enjoyed. As the *Esperance Bay* sounded its farewell whistle and steamed past Liberty's statue, that foe had refined the techniques of genocide and, in its German and Polish death camps, was mass-producing murder.

In Buchenwald, that summer of '44, Ben Bender could only gaze, in numbed horror, at the gray clouds billowing twenty-four hours a day from the crematorium's towering smokestacks. Yet somehow this boy, whom tragic experience had aged well beyond his fifteen years, never gave up his hope of liberation. "You will be lost," his brother Berick told him, "because you are a dreamer." But Ben felt, and still feels, differently. "There is a need for a dream in life," he says. "Otherwise, if we just accept the way it is, I think we are gone. We are gone."

CHAPTER 6

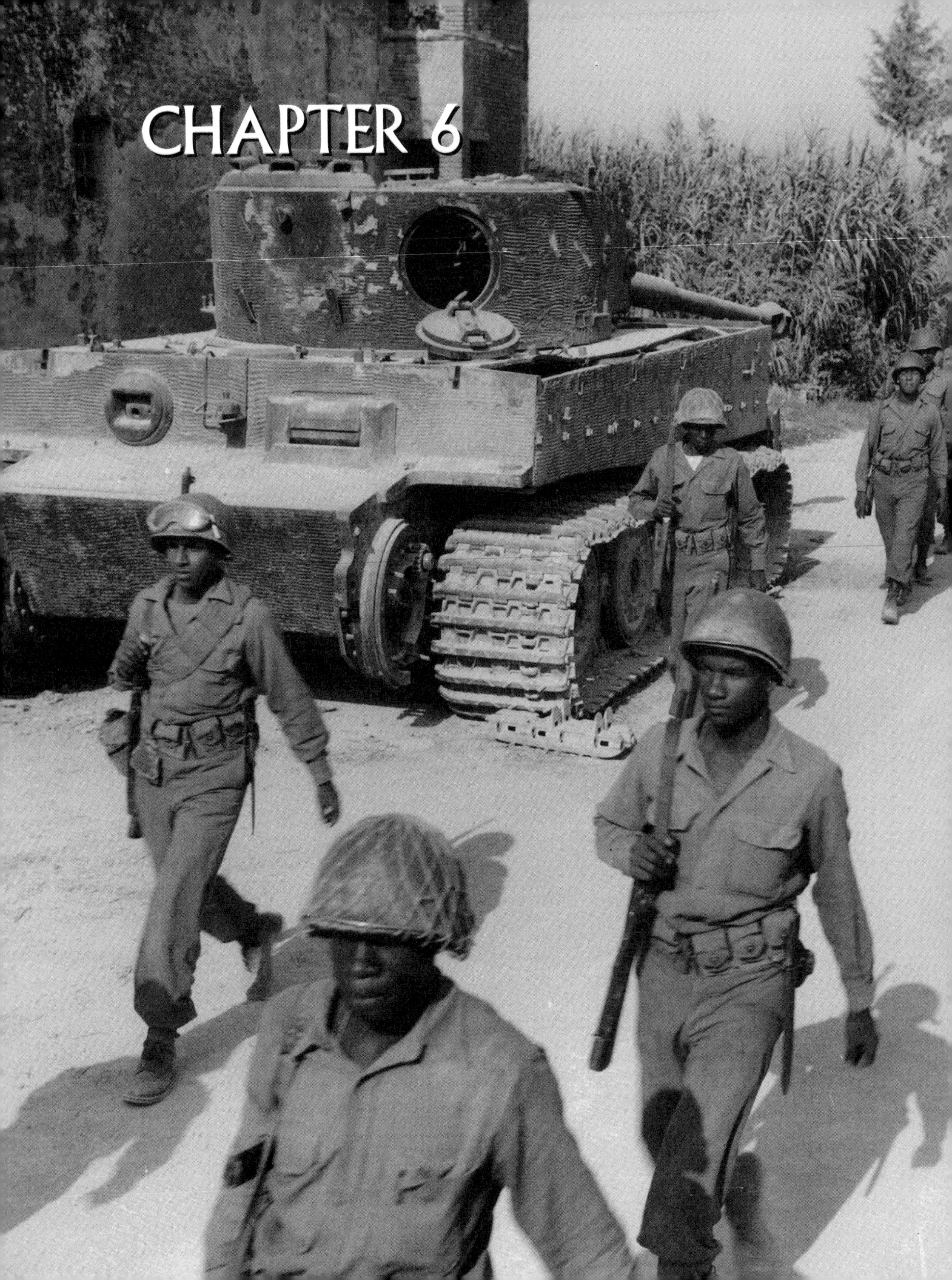

We were so curious when we saw land approaching. Omaha Beach. And we saw so many sunken ships and destroyed equipment—jeeps, trucks, tanks, gliders. I was so amazed. I couldn't believe what I saw. This was the first time I really saw American equipment that was destroyed. I had thought we were the superpower—that we were invincible. But that Omaha Beach kind of shook us up.

E. G. McConnell

Troops en route to the front lines, September, 1944.

The *Esperance Bay*'s North Atlantic crossing bore no resemblance to the prewar voyages of the great luxury liners that sailed a similar route. The memory of the journey still rankles the Black Panthers. They had been forced to ride in the back of Southern buses; now they were forced to ride in the bottom of the boat. White troops, by contrast, rode in bow and midship areas, where the stomach-churning effects of the huge swells that, according to E. G. McConnell, "tossed the ship every damn which way" were felt to a much lesser degree.

The food aboard the converted freighter was another source of great displeasure. "They [whites] tucked away all the good rations and gave us the garbage," McConnell recalls. "The bread they cooked on the ship was half raw. When we bit into a slice, we were eating dough. We didn't have any diet like we had eaten in the States. It was a sickening thing."

William McBurney dealt with the rations situation in his own way. "We couldn't eat the food," said the tanker from New York City, "so [my buddy and I] broke into the PX. We stole candy. And we ate Baby Ruths and Mary Janes and candies like that for twenty-one days in crossing the Atlantic Ocean."

As the eleven-mile-wide convoy slowly steamed a zigzag course to avoid the Nazi U-boats on constant patrol in the North Atlantic shipping lanes, other black combat units had joined the 99th Pursuit Squadron in the thick of the European fighting. The 92nd Infantry Division, which, recalling an earlier era, had been nicknamed the "Buffaloes," was in the midst of the Allies' bloody campaign in Italy. After only six months in combat, its foot soldiers had won 7 Legion of Merit awards, 65 Silver Stars, and 162 Bronze Stars. Altogether 7,000 of its members had been decorated, and 1,377 had received the Purple Heart for injuries sustained in battle. General Mark Clark, who commanded the Fifth Army's operations in Italy, would later say of them: "The 92nd jumped into La Spezia and with other Fifth Army units took Bologna. Then they moved to Genoa and took it, much to the surprise of the enemy and headquarters. I needed the 92nd and if anyone had tried to take it from me I would have protested loudly. . . . They were glorious." The 92nd earned such plaudits despite near-continual conflict between black enlisted men and some of their white officers. Bernard C. Nalty cites several such incidents: the stoning of a car in which officers were riding, a shovel-wielding assailant attacking an officer while he slept in his tent, the division's commander, General Edward M. Almond, being roundly jeered at an intramural baseball game.

Other African-American units performed with distinction during 1944–45. Among them were the 333rd Field Artillery Battalion, with Patton's Third Army

Black GI's on a troop ship, bunking "on the shelf" in the bottom of the boat.

in France, the 969th Field Artillery Battalion—the first black ground unit to receive the Presidential Distinguished Unit Citation—and the 614th Tank Destroyer Battalion, whose Third Platoon received the DUC for actions at Climbach, France. Its official commendation read, in part:

> Heedless of possible injury men continuously exposed themselves to the enemy to render first aid to the wounded. In the engagement, although the platoon suffered over fifty per cent casualties and lost considerable material, its valorous conduct in the face of overwhelming odds enabled the task force to capture its objective. The grim determination, the indomitable fighting spirit and the esprit de corps displayed by all members of the Third Platoon reflect the highest traditions of the Armed Forces of the United States.[1]

Black soldiers removing dead comrades near Malmédy, Belgium.

Many African-American service units, working in combat zones in capacities that far exceeded the expected roles of "uniformed laborer," were repeatedly commended for their courage and efficiency. Black Signal Corps construction battalions performed yeoman service laying communications lines, according to Silvera, "across France, Luxembourg, Belgium and deep into Germany in the face of heavy artillery fire, land mines and snipers." Black ordnance units, charged with keeping the troops at the front supplied with ammunition, were often involved in clashes with the enemy. The 56th Ordnance Company, for example, earned the title "Fighting 56th" when, in France, these "noncombatant" soldiers took on a detachment of Waffen SS troops—the cream of the German army—killing thirty-six of them, wounding three, and taking twelve prisoner.

Sixty-nine percent of the truckdrivers in the European Theater of Operations were black, many serving in the legendary Red Ball Express. Silvera writes that between late August and mid-November of 1944, the Red Ball's 132 companies hauled more than 400,000 tons of matériel from Normandy beaches and ports to the advancing First and Third Armies. Their trucks were on the road twenty-two hours a day—two hours were allotted for maintenance. The drivers stayed at the wheel, without sleep, for thirty-six-hour shifts. The extraordinary performance of these men was crucial to the army's success in the post D-day months. The acclaim accorded the Red Ball Express during the war and after was indeed well merited.

On the other side of the globe, in the Pacific Theater of Operations, some 200,000 African-American troops (a vast majority in service units) were engaged in the struggle against the Japanese. Blacks had gone into combat as early as May 1942, when the 24th Infantry Regiment landed in the New Georgia Islands. They were soon reorganized into a service unit, however, and worked as stevedores until 1944, when they went back into battle on Saipan Island in the Marianas. The inspector general of the army later commended these men for "exceptionally meritorious conduct" during that engagement, one of the most hard-fought of the Pacific war. Another black infantry regiment, the 25th, fought on the island of Bougainville with, as Nalty reports, "steadiness and even heroism."[2]

Troops wading across a river near the German front, 1944.

In Asia, as in Europe, African-American units performed arduous duties in an outstanding fashion. The work of the 45th Engineer General Service Regiment and the 823rd Engineer Aviation Battalion during the construction of the vital Ledo Road, linking India and China, deserves special mention. Work on this highway—later renamed the Stilwell Road, after General Joseph "Vinegar Joe" Stilwell, commander of the China-India-Burma Theater—began on December 15, 1942. Designed to serve as a combat support and supply route, it stretched for its first 271 miles through extraordinarily rugged and unsurveyed territory

Radiomen of the 903rd Air Base Security Battalion, South Pacific.

connecting Ledo in the Indian state of Assam with Shingbwiyang in Japanese-occupied Burma. Ulysses Lee describes this spectacular engineering feat:

> Rising as high as 4,500 feet, the road ran through five ranges of the Patkai [mountains]. For each mile between Ledo and Shingbwiyang, 100,000 cubic feet of earth had to be removed. Steep grades, hairpin curves and sheer drops for as much as 200 feet, all surrounded by thick rain forest jungle, characterized this first section. . . . Monsoons plagued the engineers. Landslides, washed out bridges and swollen streams hampered progress. [Nevertheless] on 27 December 1943, the lead bulldozer reached Shingbwiyang, three days ahead of schedule.[3]

Construction continued on to Kunming, China, with other African-American units, including the 330th General Service Regiment, the 76th Pontoon Company, the 45th Quartermaster Regiment, and the 849th and 1883rd Engineer Aviation Battalions, working tirelessly to complete this effort. For example, in July of 1944—the month when the turbulent, monsoon-swollen rivers were most dangerous—the 76th Pontoon Company, working harmoniously with the white 71st Pontoon Company, took only eleven hours to construct a 775-foot bridge over the Tawang River.

Much of the responsibility for waging the war in the Pacific fell on the United States Marine Corps—a service branch that had remained "racially pure" for one hundred sixty-seven years. Though administratively part of the Naval Department, the marines were perceived by most Americans as an independent organization. The corps' position on incorporating African-Americans into its midst was succinctly stated early in the war by its commandant, General Thomas Holcomb: "The negro race had every opportunity now to satisfy its aspirations for combat in the Army—a much larger organization than the Navy or Marine Corps—and their desire to enter the naval services is largely, I think, to break into a club that doesn't want them."[4]

Pressure from the NAACP and President Roosevelt eventually resulted in the marines grudgingly recruiting blacks. The first group of twelve hundred volunteers went into training late in 1942. They and the twenty thousand African-Americans who followed them into the corps were shipped to Asia. None were assigned to combat divisions or to the marines' air units. The corps did not commence training African-American officers until World War II was almost over.

Given the Leathernecks' historical disposition toward racial exclusion, it is not surprising that some white marines felt justified in expressing hostility toward black servicemen.

The Pacific island of Guam, a United States colony acquired as spoils in the Spanish-American War, had fallen to the Japanese in 1941. It was retaken in 1944.

Throughout that year, the military installations on the island were plagued by a series of incidents involving the harassment of African-American sailors by white members of the corps. So serious were these conflicts that in mid-December, Nalty states, "the island's commander, Marine Corps Major General Henry L. Larson . . . reminded his troops that 'the present war has called together men of many origins and various races and colors [all of whom] are entitled to the respect to which that common service is entitled.' "[5]

On Christmas Eve, these long-festering tensions erupted in gunplay. In the first incident of the evening, a white off-duty marine MP—apparently without provocation—shot at some black sailors but missed. Shortly thereafter, a white sailor shot and killed a black marine during an argument over a local woman. In the third clash, a black marine on sentry duty took the life of a white marine who had been badgering him with racial slurs. On Christmas Day, according to MacGregor, two truckloads of armed African-American sailors—inflamed by rumors that black seamen had been murdered by white marines—invaded a marine camp in the town of Agana. A riot ensued, and forty-three of the blacks were arrested.

They were tried on rioting charges by a marine court of inquiry, with the NAACP's Walter White, who had investigated conditions on Guam, as a leading witness for the defense. White recounted a litany of abuses suffered by African-Americans stationed on the island, citing, as well, numerous instances of inept leadership on the part of white officers in command of the naval supply depot where the accused worked as laborers. The defendants, however, were convicted and sentenced to four-year prison terms.

White did not let the matter rest. The NAACP appealed the decision through military channels and, ultimately, took their case to the White House. In the early part of 1946, the sailors were released from confinement in prisons in the United States, and the corps announced that the riot had resulted, in large part, from acts of provocation perpetrated by white marines.

———

144

Marines in a segregated mess hall,
Camp Lejeune, North Carolina,
1943.

The first black marines during
training, 1943.

Members of the 93rd Infantry Division, the first black ground troops in the South Pacific, 1944.

Though their voyage across the Atlantic had been less than salubrious, the tankers had taken the heavy seas and light rations in stride. The *Esperance Bay*'s commander, Captain Peter W. Jacoby, wrote Lieutenant Colonel Bates: "I commend your unit for its discipline, military courtesy, high morale, and soldierly conduct throughout the voyage. It has been by far one of the best disciplined units of its kind since the undersigned has been Transport Commander. My staff and I wish you Godspeed in your future missions, and the best of luck and success to final victory."[6]

When, on the morning of September 8, 1944, HMS *Esperance Bay* docked at Avonmouth, in the Bristol Channel, the Black Panthers disembarked on an island that was quite different from Guam: one where the climate was North Sea dreary rather than blue-lagoon tropical and the native population was not brown and Melanesian but white Anglo-Saxon. But if atmospherically and ethnically there were significant differences between Guam and Great Britain, the two places were linked by an American phenomenon that Walter White described as the "transplanting of racial emotions and patterns from the Mississippi to the [British] Midlands." (This was not a new tactic. We have noted the attempt by the expeditionary forces in World War I to convert the French into accepting white America's supremacist racial doctrines.)

From dockside, the tankers were conveyed across the country to barracks at Wimborne in Dorset, some twenty miles from the English Channel.

The British public had greeted the arrival of black GI's with equanimity. The celebrated author George Orwell wrote in 1943: "The general consensus of opinion seems to be that the only American soldiers with decent manners are the Negroes."[7] White troops had early on acquired quite unfavorable reputations. The joke of the time in England that the problem with white GI's was that "they're overfed, oversexed, and over here" was a rather accurate reflection of public opinion. The white Americans' persecution of their black comrades in arms did not endear them to the British. When they directed their racial hatred toward English blacks—most of whom were colonials from the West Indies— the population was outraged. Attacks on black Britons by white Americans were so numerous that in 1942, Harold Macmillan, the future prime minister, then serving as parliamentary under secretary for the colonies, lent his support to a proposal that the king's subjects of color wear badges to prevent confusion with African-Americans and thus be spared the white troops' wrath. Macmillan suggested that they also wear a Union Jack in their buttonholes.

By the time of the 761st's landing, two years after the inspection tour during which General Davis had been shocked by the depth of black resentment at their treatment by Caucasian comrades in arms, little had changed. The black troops stationed or in transit in Britain now totaled nearly 100,000, many of whom felt that they were existing at the sufferance of their fellow American GI's.

Two letters received by Mrs. Roosevelt—and quoted by Graham Smith in his meticulously researched monograph, *When Jim Crow Met John Bull*—speak with a rough eloquence to the situation in the British Isles. The first missive was originally sent to the renowned African-American classical tenor Roland Hayes while he was touring in England during 1943. In the course of the tour, Hayes spent a great deal of time visiting black troops. A corporal wrote to him, and the singer forwarded the letter to the First Lady:

> You cannot believe the lies [white GI's] had told about us. They try
> to keep us out of all the pubs and when they can't they fight us. The
> MPs lock us up and especially if they see us talking with any English

Two sailors on leave, separated by more than a bench, Chicago, 1943.

women. They go in gangs and beat you up and then if our boys have to cut some of them to keep from getting hurt, they say Negro soldiers are bad. . . . You [Hayes] are one of our leaders and if you want us to act proud you ought to tell some of the big shots about this.[8]

In November 1944, Mrs. Roosevelt received a cable from Private William Johnson, stationed in the United Kingdom:

This is a rather hard thing for me to do since it is my first time but I am very much sure that you have read many similar. We are, my unit, in a very tense situation and I am hoping you can help us in some way. We were told there was no segregation here in England, it isn't from the people, they are fine, only from our officers. . . . We are forbidden any recreation that might cause us to mix as a whole with the people. We are a Negro unit, I do hope you can help us in some way.[9]

Mrs. Roosevelt forwarded both epistles to Assistant Secretary of War McCloy and Lieutenant General Jacob L. Devers, chief deputy to General Dwight D. Eisenhower, supreme commander of the European Theater of Operations.

Devers, according to Smith, "refused to believe there was anything amiss in the ETO."[10] In his reply, the general told the First Lady that African-American GI's were not subjected to any discriminatory treatment. The facts, however, present a markedly different picture.

Clashes between white and black soldiers were frequent, bloody, and, quite often, deadly. They were usually sparked by segregation in public houses or by the whites' taking umbrage at the blacks' fraternizing with English women. On the latter issue, a white sergeant writing home—in a letter cited by Smith—voices an all-too-common attitude. "Every time," he writes, "we have seen a nigger with a white girl we have run him away. I would like to shoot the whole bunch of them."[11]

England, 1943.

Over the course of a three-month period in 1943–44, fifty-six racial incidents were catalogued by the inspector general's office. Though an appreciable number involved unwarranted and often vicious assaults on white soldiers by black GI's, much more of the color-based violence recorded in the British Isles during the war years was instigated by the actions of white American troops and/or British business people—particularly pub owners—who operated segregated establishments.

A few examples of the battles and skirmishes in this war within a war that shook the United Kingdom from 1942 until after VE Day:

Bamber Bridge, Lancashire. June 24, 1943. Four days after the Detroit riots, a group of African-American soldiers, members of the 1511th Quartermaster Truck Battalion, were involved in a nonracial disturbance at closing time, 10:00 P.M., at the Olde Hob Inn. MP's arrived. One fired his .45 automatic into the group. A soldier fell wounded to the ground.

Rumors raced through the truckers' barracks at their nearby base: several of their comrades had been murdered. They broke into weapons rooms, stole machine guns and rifles, commandeered vehicles, and rolled into the small town of Bamber Bridge, seeking revenge. They opened fire on any white army personnel whom they saw. "British civilians," Smith writes, "watched the activity with a mixture of awe and horror."[12] MP's shot one of the blacks to death and wounded two others. One white officer was shot. Twenty of the rebellious soldiers were court-martialed. They received sentences of up to twenty years, but these were soon commuted. Most were back on duty within the year.

Launceston, Cornwall. September 25, 1943. Black GI's from an ordnance outfit were refused service and ordered out of a pub where white soldiers were drinking. They returned, armed. In the ensuing fight, two MP's were wounded. Fourteen of the blacks were court-martialed and received long sentences.

Leicester, Leicestershire. September 26, 1943. Ever since their arrival, white paratroopers from the 82nd Airborne had been harassing mixed couples on the city's streets and in the pubs. Angered by this treatment, black soldiers banded together and attacked a contingent of troopers in the town. A riot resulted, during which one white MP was killed.

Bristol, Avon. July 15, 1944. In this bustling port city, where black troops were routinely confined by their officers to barracks as a means of preventing them from mingling with the civilian (read: female) population, tempers had been high for some time. As in Leicester, white paratroopers made clear their anger at the sight of black men and white women dating. There had been many confrontations. On the fifteenth, airborne soldiers attacked and badly beat several African-American members of an aviation truck battalion. Again there was a riot. One black GI was shot and killed by MP's, many more were wounded.

Few of the hundreds of racial clashes that occurred within the American ranks in Great Britain were reported by mainstream news organizations in the United States. Wartime regulations that often prohibited publishing the overseas location of certain units were in part responsible. But white male America's historical fear of miscegenation also came into play. In 1943, *Life* magazine published photographs of black GI's dancing with white women in London night spots. General Eisenhower, according to Graham Smith, was outraged. The photos, he believed, "unduly inflamed racial prejudices both abroad and in the United States." Reacting to the general's distress, the War Department banned the publication of any photographs "showing Negro soldiers in poses of intimacy with white women or conveying 'boyfriend-girlfriend' implications."[13]

Black newspapers in the States did their best to keep their readers informed of the serious problems their husbands, sons, and brothers were encountering

A tank unit in England making last-minute adjustments before departing from the Continent, 1944.

in England. The larger journals had correspondents or stringers on the scene, who duly chronicled—within the parameters of military censorship—many of the major incidents. This disturbed more than a few base commanders in Britain. Some went so far as to ban the sale on their installations of issues containing material they regarded as inflammatory.

In 1944, Walter White responded to stateside concerns about the treatment of black troops in the U.K. with an inspection trip. During this journey, he visited units stationed across England, interviewing British citizens as well as American officers and enlisted men. His subsequent report to Secretary Stimson echoed the conclusions reached two years earlier by General Davis. The NAACP leader noted that the morale of African-American troops had been so seriously damaged that white soldiers were now perceived by them as "the enemy." In the wake of White's findings, two assistant inspectors general were dispatched to Britain to investigate the situation. After a six-day stay, they reported to the Pentagon that there was "no evidence of discrimination against the colored troops."[14]

At the time of the 761st's disembarkation at Avonmouth, Britons were still discussing a case in which a black GI, Leroy Henry, had been accused of raping a housewife in Bath. The case had been given wide play in the nation's tabloids three months earlier, with the mass-circulation *Daily Mirror* taking a particularly sympathetic stand toward the defendant.

Henry was accused of sexually assaulting the purported victim at knifepoint on the night of May 5, 1944, on a street near her home. In a statement to military police, he admitted the crime.

Court-martial proceedings began three weeks later. The U.S. authorities had an agreement with the British government that GI's accused of crimes would be tried in military courts. Medical testimony as to whether the accuser had in fact been raped was, at best, inconclusive. On the witness stand, Henry testified that he had had sex with the woman on two previous occasions, for a fee of one pound. On the night in question, he continued, they had met at a local pub, where she responded to his propositions by doubling her price. He refused to pay and left the tavern. The thirty-year-old GI accused the MP's of beating his confession out of him and then proceeded to repudiate his admissions. They

Officers' mess, England, 1942.

were so vicious, Henry told the court, that he fainted during the long interrogation.

The tribunal, after extremely brief deliberations, returned its verdict: "We find you guilty and sentence you by unanimous vote of every member present to be hanged by the neck until dead." The decision elicited strong negative reaction from the press, the public, and members of Parliament. The NAACP wired a protest to General Eisenhower, calling for a stay of execution. Smith quotes the following excerpt from the private diary of the *Mirror's* political editor, Cecil King:

> This feeling is fairly common—that the negroes are nicer and better behaved than the ordinary Yank. So there is some indignation when negro soldiers are condemned to death for raping English girls. In the most recent case the evidence would surely have resulted in acquittal in an English court. In the far more numerous cases of rape or murder by white American soldiers, the punishment, if any, is of a wholly different order of severity.[15]

The chorus of protests had its desired effect. On June 19, Eisenhower, citing insufficient evidence, threw out the tribunal's guilty verdict. Leroy Henry returned to active duty.

During their four-week stay in Wimborne, the Black Panthers were fortunately spared the tribulations suffered by so many of their compatriots in the U.K. Their hassles with white soldiers were few and less momentous than many they had endured in Texas and Louisiana back home. They spent their free time dallying with the local ladies and searching for a decent meal. "The welcome was something," E. G. McConnell recalls. "And the girls were singing the songs . . . like 'Lay down and do it again.'"

William McBurney remembers the British as "treating us pretty fair in consideration to anyplace that we'd been in the South. I had no dislike for England. They treated us well. . . . The English girls had heard from white GI's that we had tails. They would come up and pat you on your butt to see if you got a tail. And some of the smarter brothers told them, 'Yes, I may have a tail.' 'Can't I see it?' 'Well, my tail doesn't come out till late at night.' Those girls were so curious that they would party with these brothers till late at night. And guess what? The tail would come out . . . the wrong end. So anyway, they loved us. They loved us. They loved us."

Satisfying their hunger was more difficult than satisfying their need for female companionship. In the PX, McConnell remembers, "They served you half a sandwich for half a penny. We couldn't understand it. Hell, in America we got a whole sandwich. Two full slices of bread."

Dorset is a rich farming area, and the tankers began to cook the local produce on the stoves in their barracks. McConnell recalls a culinary adventure undertaken to augment their half-sandwich diets. "We were so hungry, and we saw all these beautiful greens. So we decided, well, we got to wipe out those greens. And they only grew these greens to feed them to the hogs. We didn't know that. All we knew were greens. So myself and Smitty got one of our buddies and we went up [to a farm]. And we had our bayonets on and I said, 'We got to cut this crop down.' I remember Smitty cutting those greens like crazy. Next thing I know, I heard: 'Oh, hi, Yank.' The farmer and his family were there, and I'm laying on my stomach, cutting their greens. [The farmer] says, 'Do you have a cigarette?' I gave him some cigarettes. Then the kid says, 'Do you have chocolate?' I had none with me, so I gave him some chewing gum. So anyway, they took our cigarettes and our chewing gum and they allowed us to take their greens. Like I said, they only grew the greens to feed their animals, and when they realized *we* were going to eat them, they just laughed."

The tankers, though, had more on their minds than pretty girls and farm-fresh greens. France was their destination. They knew they were going to cross the Channel—not to be spear carriers in the background, as Walter Lewis had ruefully surmised back at Hood, but to be spearheaders. They were going to fight the Nazis, the first African-American armored unit to go to battle for their nation. On October 7, new tanks arrived from Liverpool, and the battalion departed Wimborne for the port of Weymouth. Two days later, they crowded into the landing craft, 36 officers—all but six of them black—and 676 enlisted men. The next morning, they landed on the Normandy coast at fabled Omaha Beach.

In October 1944, the tankers of the 761st, like most Americans, had little or no knowledge of the horrific events occurring within a realm that historian Lucy Dawidowicz so aptly termed "the kingdom of death."[16] The fact that now—a half century later—a chorus of misguided revisionists in Europe, Canada, and the United States vociferously dismiss the awful, awesome reality of the Holocaust sadly testifies to man's ability to marshal the bountiful resources of racism in the service of denying the undeniable.

During Hitler's reign, leaders of his allied adversaries did little to alert their populations to the pitiless, systematic extermination of millions of human beings

Machine gunner Corporal Carlton Chapman, Nancy, France, 1944.

Omaha Beach, 1944.

Implementing the "Final Solution."

in concentration camps scattered across Germany and Poland. This was not because Franklin Roosevelt, Winston Churchill, and their colleagues were unaware of the situation in Dachau, Buchenwald, Auschwitz, and elsewhere; rather it resulted from policy decisions that can only be described as shameful.

Two years before, in August 1942, the State Department had received a cable from the United States Embassy in Bern, Switzerland, quoting Eduard Schulte, a prominent industrialist within the Third Reich, to the effect that "there has been and is being considered in Hitler's headquarters a plan to exterminate all Jews from Germany and German-controlled areas in Europe after they have been concentrated in the east [presumably Poland]. The number involved is said to be between three and a half and four million, and the object is to permanently settle the Jewish question in Europe."

Under Secretary Sumner Welles's immediate response to this extraordinary information was to attempt to suppress it. His action continued a U.S. policy, established during the prewar years, of governmental indifference to the plight of Hitler's enemies (particularly those who were Jewish). As David Wyman has documented in his authoritative studies of official American attitudes during the period, the government erected "paper walls" of bureaucratic obfuscation that effectively denied entry to this country to hundreds of thousands of the persecuted.

After Pearl Harbor, the all-important concern of the Pentagon and the White House was, naturally, defeating the Germans and the Japanese and winning World War II. If the political and military leadership believed, as Leni Yahil surmises in *The Holocaust: 1932–1945*,[17] that the revelation of Nazi genocide would interfere with this crusade, clearly such information had to be withheld. It does not speak well of a people allegedly dedicated to the cause of human rights that its leadership believed that a significant number of their fellow citizens harbored anti-Semitic feelings of such intensity that they might react to the news of the massacres, at worst, with approval; at best, with disinterest. It should be noted that this perception was shared at the time by many members of the Jewish community. Though some prominent Jews, including Rabbi Stephen Wise, the recognized leader of the American Jewish community, finally revealed the terrible information, the fact is that during the Holocaust reports of this period had little effect upon the American consciousness. In any case, the blackout worked to a large degree. As late as December 1944, according to Yahil, polls showed that only four percent of Americans believed that millions of European Jews had been murdered.

Inmates of a concentration camp line up for morning roll call.

Bodies of murdered children in
a Budapest synagogue, 1944.

Less defensible is the military's decision to refrain from bombing the death
camps. Wyman, in *The Abandonment of the Jews*, devotes considerable attention to the War Department's refusal to sanction the bombing of Auschwitz,
the most efficient of the murder factories. Testifying at the Nuremberg war
crimes trials, camp commandant Rudolf Höss calmly described the operation:

> . . . I estimated that at least 2,500,000 victims were executed and
> exterminated there by gassing and burning, and at least another half
> million succumbed to starvation and disease . . . representing about
> seventy percent or eighty percent of all persons sent to Auschwitz as
> prisoners, the remaining having been selected and used for slave labor
> in the concentration camp industries. Included among the gassed and
> burnt were approximately 20,000 Russian prisoners of war. . . . The
> remainder of the total number of victims included about 100,000 Ger-
> man Jews and great numbers of citizens, mostly Jewish, from Hol-
> land, France, Belgium, Poland, Hungary, Czechoslovakia, Greece, and
> other countries. We executed about 400,000 Hungarian Jews alone at
> Auschwitz in the summer of 1944. . . .[18]

In April 1944, two Slovak prisoners, Rudolf Vrba and Alfred Wetzeler, escaped from Auschwitz. They made contact with the Slovakian Jewish under-

158

ground and dictated a thirty-page document that spelled out the macabre activities in the camp and meticulously pinpointed the location of gas chambers and crematoria. By late June, Wyman reports, their story had reached Allied governments and had been reported by some Western news organizations. Jewish leaders pressed the War Department to destroy the crematoria and the railroad lines to Poland, which continued to deliver thousands of soon-to-be-murdered victims to the camp. The Pentagon dismissed their pleas as impractical, for a bombing mission would require "the diversion of considerable air support essential to the success of our forces engaged in decisive operations." This response was, as Wyman makes clear, disingenuous to an extreme. The air force was, at that very moment, conducting raids on industrial targets in the vicinity of the death camp. Moreover, military officials in Washington had never discussed the bombing proposal with air force commanders in Europe. The Pentagon was, in fact, expressing a top-secret policy formulation that had gone into effect in February. "We must constantly bear in mind," an internal memorandum that elucidated the department's position stated, "that the most effective relief which can be given victims of enemy persecution is to ensure the speedy defeat of the Axis."

Wyman sums up the effects of this shockingly inhumane position:

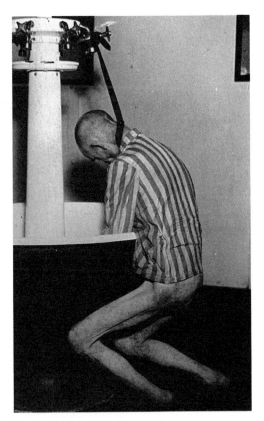

Dachau suicide.

If the earliest pleas for bombing the gas chambers . . . had drawn a positive and rapid response, the movement of the 437,000 Jews who were deported from Hungary to Auschwitz would most likely have been broken off and additional lives numbering in the hundreds of thousands might have been saved. More significant, though, than attempts to calculate particular numbers is the fact that no one could tell during the summer of 1944 how many hundreds of thousands more would die at Auschwitz before the Nazis ceased their mass murder.[19]

CHAPTER 7

Patton came down to Saint-Nicolas, France, to welcome us into the Third Army. We'd been there about two days. We could hear fighting at the front line, heavy artillery. We were in a state of nervousness. So Patton came down to greet us and said, "I don't care what color you are as long as you go up there and kill those Kraut sons of bitches! The whole world is looking at you. Your people are looking at you and I'm looking at you. So God damn it, don't let me down and don't let them down."

William McBurney

Soldiers searching out German snipers, France, 1944.

Lieutenant Harold B. Gary, as an officer, was privy to more information from Third Army headquarters than were the enlisted men. He recalled Patton's involvement with the 761st in an interview with William Miles: "We stayed in England for thirty days because there was some question about this black tank outfit and how they would perform in combat. Would they fight? And it was the opinion of many military people that they would not. . . . So then, finally, Patton said to his staff, 'If you give those niggers the best equipment you've got, give 'em good food, I'll take 'em.' That's a quote. 'Those niggers'—that's what he said. . . . Patton had a very high-pitched voice. He almost sounded like a woman. And that's why [he used] profanity, to make sure that he was heard and understood, and not perceived as a wimp. But he was a good general, you know. He was good."

After addressing the Panthers at Saint-Nicolas-du-Port, Patton climbed down from the half-track that served as his podium and walked over to E. G. McConnell's M4 Sherman tank. "He climbed up on top of my tank," McConnell recalls, "to inspect this new high-velocity gun we had on there. Then he climbed down on the commander's side and looked me straight in the eye and said: 'Listen, boy, I want you to shoot up every goddamn thing you see—church steeples, water towers, houses, old ladies, children, haystacks. Every goddamn thing you see. You hear me, boy?' I said, 'Yes, sir.' "

Almost to a man, the tankers have retained an overriding respect, even awe, for the legendary general. Johnny Holmes sums up their feelings: "He was

Members of General Patton's 761st Tank Battalion in France.

Sergeant William McBurney (standing in center)
with fellow tankers in Nancy, France, 1944.

straightforward, the type of man who would be right to the front. If he told you
he wanted something, you had the feeling that you had to follow him. I rank
him with Rommel and Wainwright and the great generals. Not the armchair
generals; the great frontline generals. That's who you have the real respect for.
I would have went to hell for him."

The annals of military history reveal few commanders as complex, contradictory, and successful as General George Smith Patton, Jr. He was a leader who
professed great respect and love for his troops, yet twice within a seven-day
period in August 1943, Patton physically assaulted soldiers being treated for
combat fatigue at military hospitals in Sicily. Patton's biographer Martin Blumenson (who was the Third Army's official historian and editor of the Patton
papers) details the second incident in *Patton: The Man Behind the Legend, 1885–
1945:*

Coming to a man shivering in bed, Patton asked what the trouble
was. "It's my nerves," the soldier said and started to cry. "Your nerves,
hell," Patton shouted. "You are just a goddamned coward, you yellow

son of a bitch. You're a disgrace to the Army and you're going to be sent back to the front to fight, though that's too good for you. You ought to be lined up against a wall and shot. In fact, I ought to shoot you myself right now, goddamn you." He pulled his pistol from the holster and waved it, then struck the man across the face with the gloves he held in his other hand. He started to leave the tent, turned, rushed back and hit the weeping soldier again.[1]

The unfortunate patient was saved from further battery by a doctor, who jumped between the two men. "Old Blood and Guts," however, had the final word: "I meant what I said about getting that coward out of here. I won't have these cowardly bastards crowding around our hospitals. We'll probably have to shoot them sometime anyway, or we'll raise a breed of morons."[2]

Patton had committed a court-martial offense of a very serious nature, and physician witnesses formally protested his conduct to General Eisenhower. The Allied commander, though he considered Patton's actions reprehensible, could ill afford to lose his best field commander. Ike convinced newsmen who had learned of the assaults to suppress the story for the sake of the war effort. In November, however, this embargo was broken by the influential columnist and broadcaster Drew Pearson. In the wake of Pearson's disclosures, Patton made a perfunctory public apology. While many Americans called for his dismissal, Secretary Stimson and General Marshall held fast in their support, and the furor soon blew over.[3]

The dichotomies that characterized Patton's personality were evident in his racial views. Two of his closest aides were Jewish, and he maintained a lifelong attachment to a Jewish soldier who had saved his life during World War I. Nonetheless, the general was capable—as we shall see later—of expressing his contempt for Jewish death camp inmates and displaced persons in terms that echoed Hitler and Goebbels, and he fiercely and publicly dissented from the Allies' intentions to denazify postwar German institutions. Regarding African-Americans, we earlier noted his opinion, as stated in his memoir, that they were genetically incapable of fighting effectively in armored units: "I expressed my belief . . . and have never found the necessity of changing it, that a colored soldier cannot think fast enough to fight in armor."[4] Reading these words, Walter Lewis felt "indeed disturbed and disappointed."

Ladislas Farago, in *The Last Days of Patton*, buttresses the argument that the general—though some of his "best friends" might have been black or Jew-

ish—harbored negative feelings about both peoples in the aggregate. He refused, Farago states, to respond to requests from blacks in the United States that he refute certain Southern senators' charges regarding the inferiority of African-American troops. Yet up until six months before the postwar crash that claimed his life, Patton's chauffeur had been a black man. "You have been the driver of my official car since 1940," he wrote Master Sergeant John L. Mims at the time of his discharge. "During that time you have safely driven me in many parts of the world under all conditions of dust and snow and ice and mud, of enemy fire and attack by enemy aircraft. At no time during these years of danger and difficulty have you so much as bumped a fender."[5] At Patton's side also, from 1940 on, was his personal orderly, Sergeant George Meeks, an African-American who, most sources agree, came as close as anyone to being Patton's true confidant.

Patton with his men.

George Patton, born to a wealthy California family in 1885, graduated from the United States Military Academy in the class of 1909. He first saw combat as an aide to General John J. Pershing in the army's unsuccessful 1916 foray into Mexico in search of Pancho Villa, the revolutionary. The following year, he accompanied Pershing to France as part of the American Expeditionary Force commander's staff; in the war's final months, he trained and then served in the newly formed tank corps. During the tankers' second battle, Patton sustained wounds severe enough to keep him out of action for the duration.

In July 1932, twelve thousand Depression-impoverished World War I veterans and their families descended on the nation's capital, camping on the Anacostia Flats. These so-called Bonus Marchers' demands on Congress and President Herbert Hoover for early payment of moneys promised them for their wartime service went unheeded. Hoover, who was locked in a bitter reelection campaign against Franklin Roosevelt, feared the marchers as harbingers of revolution and authorized an assault on their campgrounds. In the July 28 attack, Patton was operating under General Douglas MacArthur's command. Using gas, truncheons, and bayonets, soldiers overwhelmed the unarmed protesters and put their shacks and makeshift barracks to the torch. Scores of veterans and their family members were injured. Two were killed, one an eleven-week-old infant.

During the first years of World War II, Patton remained stateside, training armored units. In July 1942, he was given command of one of the three task forces committed to Operation Torch, the Anglo-American invasion of North Africa. Patton's men distinguished themselves during the ensuing advance across Morocco and Tunisia in pursuit of the forces of the legendary "Desert Fox," Field Marshal Erwin Rommel. He was rewarded for his efforts with command of the 90,000-man Seventh Army, then preparing for the July invasion of Sicily, code-named Operation Husky. The successful conclusion of the Sicilian campaign led to Patton's appointment, in January 1944, as commander of the newly activated Third Army. His new troops would not see their first action, in France, until August.

What is one to make of the enigmatic George Patton, that extraordinary warrior, that flawed human being? Historian Martin Blumenson, who has studied the general for nearly half a century, offers an interpretation:

> . . . His behavior was unpredictable and sometimes contradictory, flamboyant on one occasion, introspective on another. Hot tempered, sentimental, profane, humble before God, he was an exhibitionist who played to the gallery, with his pistols and polished appearance his props. Through the exterior of this exaggerated man, who was larger than life to his children and his colleagues, peeped a barely controlled hysteria. His extraordinary fluency with languages, his saucy wit, his unexpected turns of phrase covered his troubled interior, where his opposing inclinations battled for supremacy. Toward the end of his life, even he could barely distinguish his real self from the portrait he had deliberately faked.[6]

Fired by Patton's pep talk, the Black Panthers anticipated their first encounter with the German army. Lieutenant Harold B. Gary describes the battalion's state of readiness: "These guys were killers! These guys were good! They'd been trained since 1942. This is 1944. The average soldier didn't get that kind of training. . . . That's why they had this record . . . a small number of people killed. We had [a lot of] casualties, but we didn't have that many people killed. We were good; we knew what we were doing. We didn't do stupid things."

In early November 1944, the Black Panthers, in their state-of-the-art war machines, rolled eastward toward Athainville, the line of departure for the Third Army's campaign in the Saar basin. The operation's goal was to break through the Nazis' entrenched positions and carry the ground war into the German heartland. Here in northeastern France began the battalion's 183 days of nearly continual fighting across six countries, against some of the best units the German army had to offer. In the European Theater of Operations, the average American tank unit spent no more than a few weeks in combat before being sent back from the front for rest and recuperation. That these "tan tankers," as some called them, fought for six consecutive *months* without relief, against one of history's strongest and most dedicated armies, is a testament to training, endurance, discipline, and patriotism that can only be described as heroic.

Why did the 761st remain in battle so inordinately long? The easy answer— given the turbulent history of the military's relationship with African-Americans—is that the Third Army's command was following the philosophy of slavemasters at harvest time: work the blacks until they drop. Preston McNeil expressed the feelings of many of the tankers: "The white officers were against us because we were blacks and they said, 'Well, you're supposed to have been so good in the States so we're gonna keep you fighting.' . . . We weren't supposed to return. We were supposed to get demolished. Well, we returned; we survived."

Though one can certainly not discount conscious or unconscious racism as a factor, there are other possible factors: The battalion's "bastard" status would have made it difficult for Third Army headquarters to keep track of the daily whereabouts of its four companies; and the 761st's extremely high level of combat efficiency induced many infantry commanders to request the tankers to serve as their spearheads.

It should be noted that the present authors' account of the 761st's deeds in battle owes much to the reportage of Trezzvant W. Anderson, an African-American combat journalist assigned by the War Department to cover the battalion. A distinguished newsman, before and after the war, for the Afro-American newspaper chain and the Associated Negro Press agency, Anderson published an account of his four months with the Panthers, entitled *Come Out Fighting*. During 1945, his dispatches detailing the battalion's exploits were widely printed in black newspapers and ignored by the mainstream press.

War correspondent Trezzvant W. Anderson.

A poster advertising National Negro Newspaper Week.

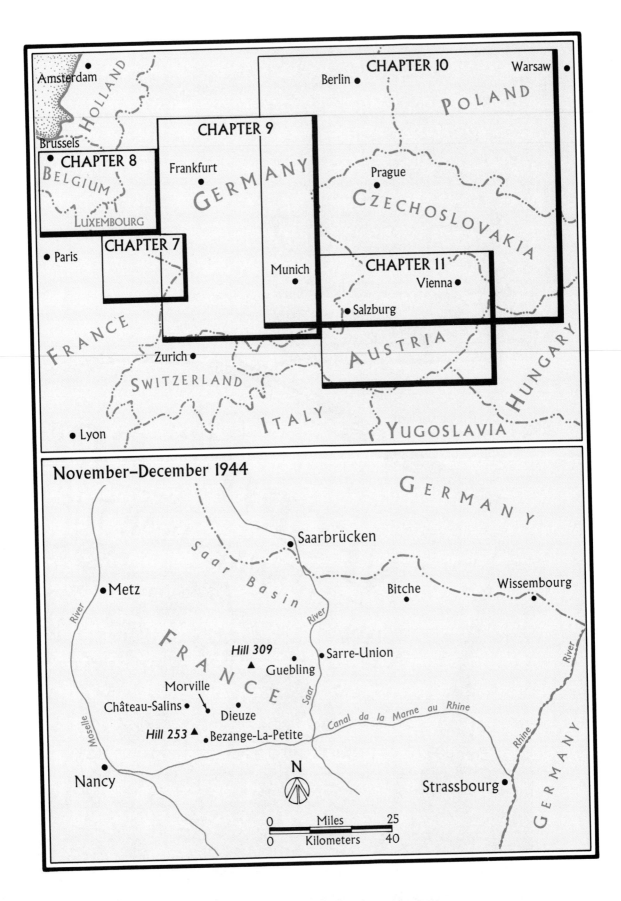

CHAPTER 8

CHAPTER 9

CHAPTER 10

CHAPTER 7

CHAPTER 11

Amsterdam

HOLLAND

Brussels

BELGIUM

LUXEMBOURG

Paris

FRANCE

Frankfurt

GERMANY

Berlin

Warsaw

POLAND

Prague

CZECHOSLOVAKIA

Munich

Vienna

Salzburg

AUSTRIA

HUNGARY

Zurich

SWITZERLAND

ITALY

YUGOSLAVIA

Lyon

November–December 1944

GERMANY

Saarbrücken

Metz

Saar Basin

River

Bitche

Wissembourg

River

FRANCE

Hill 309 ▲

Guebling

Sarre-Union

Morville

Château-Salins

Dieuze

Saar

Canal da la Marne au Rhine

Rhine River

Hill 253 ▲ Bezange-La-Petite

Moselle

N

Nancy

Strassbourg

GERMANY

Miles
0   25

Kilometers
0   40

November 7 was cold and rainy in Athainville. Many of the tankers were in church when they received the word to move out to the front. "We were singing a hymn," Walter Lewis wrote, "when the order came. Our service was interrupted, and we mounted our tanks and were off to meet the enemy."

They met the enemy on the road to Moyenvic, a town near Hill 253, a heavily fortified objective Patton had ordered the Panthers to take. The 761st was deployed—as it would be throughout the war—as a "bastard battalion," which would split up to spearhead different (and often widely dispersed) infantry units rather than fight as a unified force. On November 6, 1944, the tankers were attached to the 26th Infantry Division, A Company spearheading for the 101st and the 104th Regiments, C Company performing the same dangerous task for the 328th.

Training for war is one thing, imagining combat is another, but the reality of battle can be truly known only by those who have experienced its exhilarations and its terrors. "There's no such thing as any soldier not being scared," says Bronze Star winner Johnnie Stevens. "If any soldier tells you he wasn't afraid, he's a liar. But you do things; it's a job. At a time like that, you don't feel anything. You do what you've been trained to do, and you do it without thinking. You're concentrating on what's there, which takes your mind off being afraid or being brave. In combat, five minutes is like a year."

C Company led the 328th's successful assault on Hill 253 and the nearby town of Bezange-La-Petite. The area was defended by the German 11th Panzer Division, which had recently received a heavy infusion of men and matériel. This division belonged to the Waffen SS, a ground combat force with its own chain of command, independent of the Wehrmacht. Military historian Charles B. MacDonald in *A Time for Trumpets* describes these units as "a kind of Praetorian Guard of the Nazi Party."[7]

At Bezange-La-Petite, the 761st suffered its first fatalities. All five members of a tank crew commanded by Sergeant Harvey Woodard of Howard, Georgia, were killed under mysterious circumstances. As Trezzvant Anderson reports, after the fighting ceased and their unscathed tank was opened, "Not a single man had been hit by a shell fragment or touched by a machine gun bullet, and every man was sitting in his place of work . . . eyes staring, pupils dilated, but no fear showing on their faces, just a faint look of surprise."[8] The deaths were officially classified as having resulted from "concussion" caused by shock waves from high explosives landing in the immediate vicinity of the tank. But for

(Top): Overview of the areas covered by the 761st Tank Battalion, November 1944 through May 1945. (Bottom): The 761st spearheaded the Third Army's campaign through northeastern France and on into Germany.

Black soldiers at a religious service.

many of the Panthers, the deaths of Harvey Woodard and his crew fell under the category of unsolved mysteries.

Meanwhile, two of A Company's platoons were leading the 104th Regiment's assault on the riverside town of Vic-Sur-Seille. Walter Lewis writes of this, his first battle, in "Diary of a Gunner":

> As our tanks moved through Vic-Sur-Seille, Lieutenant [Joseph] Kahoe told me to stick my head out of the turret, he wanted to show me something. We were slowly moving upon a dead German soldier lying in the gutter. Blood was streaming from his mangled body and trickling down the street. Lt. Kahoe said to me, "You killed this man." This sight made me sick to my stomach and unnerved me to the extent [that] my senses were numb with fear and remorse. The gunner of a tank is not always able to see what he has hit. [Kahoe's words] were said, I suppose, to give me nerve, or to test my nerve. I don't know which, but it actually upset me and I have never forgotten it. Yet I realized I had to kill or be killed.

The victory at Vic-Sur-Seille owed much to the efforts of Staff Sergeant Rubin Rivers of Tecumseh, Oklahoma, who was awarded the battalion's first Silver Star for his heroism. Over two hundred German soldiers were killed by Rivers's crew. His medal citation reads as follows:

> During the daylight attack . . . Staff Sergeant Rivers, a tank platoon sergeant, was in the lead tank when a road block was encountered which held up the advance. With utter disregard for his personal safety, Staff Sergeant Rivers courageously dismounted from his tank in the face of directed enemy small arms fire, attached a cable to the road block and moved it off the road, thus permitting the combat team to proceed. His prompt action thus prevented a serious delay in the offensive action and was instrumental in the successful assault and capture of the town. His brilliant display of initiative, courage and devotion to duty reflect[s] the highest credit upon Staff Sergeant Rivers and the armed forces of the United States.

Company A crossing a bridge in Vic-Sur-Seille, France, November 1944.

Sergeant Rivers's medal was awarded posthumously. Twelve days after Vic-Sur-Seille, this brave young man was killed in action during the battle of Guebling.

On November 6, in their first encounter with the enemy, Company C's 3rd Platoon drove, ahead of the 101st Infantry Regiment, to Moyenvic and took the town after several hours of very hard fighting. The Panthers' commander, Lieutenant Colonel Paul Bates, was seriously wounded by machine gun fire during this action. (Bates had trained under George S. Patton in 1940 at Fort Benning, Georgia. Even now he attributes this event—rather tongue-in-cheek—to Patton's tactical philosophy: "One of the comments he made was that 'an armored unit is like a piece of spaghetti: You can't push it. You've got to get out in front and pull it, or it won't go anywhere.' And as a result, doing just that, I got my ass shot off.")

During the months that Bates was recuperating, the battalion had several commanding officers. The first of these, Major Charles M. Wingo, Jr., found little favor in the eyes of his men. Preston McNeil recalled that, "None of us cared for him because he was a redneck. He left us." E. G. McConnell's memory of Wingo's behavior still angers him:

"I didn't hate the man, I just disapproved of his ideas and the treatment that he gave us. Anytime he addressed us, it was usually, 'You boys,' something derogatory. There I was, a soldier in the United States Army, volunteered at sixteen in what I think was the greatest unit in World War II. We knew our business, and we knew our potential. And on the second day of combat, this man who had assumed the position of commander of our battalion turned around and deserted us when the closest shot came about three hundred yards from him. Hey! What kind of deal is this? We were on trial. Everyone was watching us. How would a headline look that said 'Black Tankers Cowards in Combat'? . . . I heard that this man has been buried in Arlington Cemetery. And some of our comrades who were killed, who lived in the South, couldn't even be buried in their hometown cemeteries because of segregation. They didn't allow blacks to be buried in the same graveyard as whites. Damn!"

Their tanks sloshing through the mud, the Panthers—followed by the 26th Infantry—now headed toward their next objective, Morville. En route, Company A, with the 104th Regiment, took the major town of Chateau-Salins, which would become XII Corps headquarters for the remainder of the campaign.

The battle of Morville was one of the rare occasions when three of the 761st's four companies fought in very close proximity. Company A advanced from the

| Company C on attack in France.

west; Company B came from the northwest; and Company C from the southeast. After sacking the town of Salival, Company D rolled north toward Morville.

As the units neared their objective, it began to snow, first lightly, then steadily deepening, giving cover to the Germans' dug-in machine gun positions. On November 9, at 9:00 A.M., the Americans launched their attack. It was met by round after round of heavy artillery fire. The tankers and the troopers continued to advance, but at a much slower pace. In this bloody encounter, ten Panthers—nine enlisted men and one officer—were killed.

The battle of Morville raged for two days. Though outmanned and outgunned, German defenders stopped the Americans in their tracks for twenty-four hours. Johnnie Stevens sums up the tankers' opinion of their Wehrmacht adversaries: "The German soldier was the most well-trained, most disciplined soldier in the world. He was the best. The only thing that defeated the German army was that they were fighting everybody. There was no one country in the world that, alone, could have defeated the German soldier, and any real combat soldier will tell you that."

On the second day, Company B's tanks crashed through the German defenses and entered the town. After hours of street fighting, in which both sides sustained heavy casualties, Morville fell to the black tankers of the 761st Battalion and the white infantrymen of the 26th Division. The victory had not been easily or cheaply earned. Trezzvant Anderson quoted a captured German officer who spoke of the Black Panthers' fighting prowess and their devotion to duty: "Never, except on the Russian front, have I seen such bravery."[9]

As American forces pursued the slowly withdrawing German units, every inch of ground was gained at a price. Land mines and booby traps, combined with heavy artillery and bazooka fire from camouflaged emplacements, took their toll on the GI's' ranks.

Johnnie Stevens (right) and Gerald Shorter.

On November 11, 1944, at 11:00 A.M., Sergeant Johnnie Stevens was commanding his tank in an assault on Hill 309, near the town of Wuisse. "After my tank got hit," he says, "I came out with three of my crew members—the other had been killed. We were laying in the field, and the Germans started dropping mortar fire. Because, you see, they want to kill tankers. Tankers kill too many people, and when you come out of those tanks, they're going to make sure they kill you. I had been hit pretty hard. My combat suit was all covered with blood, and I was laying in a ditch. A tall sergeant from the 26th Division calls out to me, 'Hey, Sarge, you hit?' I say, 'I'm hit hard as hell.' . . . He jumped over the other side of the embankment . . . and he took his arms and put them under me and he just shoved me over the embankment, where I was safe from the mortar fire. And before he could duck back down himself, a German raised up about fifteen yards away and with his burp gun, he cut that sergeant . . . in two. After I got out of the hospital, I tried to find out [the sergeant's] name. He should have been post-humously cited. But I never found out."

The white infantrymen of the 26th Division hailed mainly—as their unit's nickname, the "Yankee Division," implies—from the Northeastern states. Strong feelings of camaraderie developed between these foot soldiers and their spear-headers of the 761st. As Johnnie Stevens recalls, "When we were [transferred] to the 9th Division, the guys from the 26th, they didn't want to see us leave, because we never let them down."

But if the relationship between these two units seems to reinforce the World War II cliché that "there is no color line in combat," the many indignities suf-fered by the Panthers at the hands of other white Americans during their six months in battle call that romantic aphorism into question.

During the campaign in France, Sergeant E. G. McConnell's tank was hit by a high-explosive shell. Shrapnel pierced his helmet and entered his skull. At the field medical station, he remembers drifting in and out of consciousness. "This young white fellow from the 26th Infantry—who was much more seriously injured than I—he grabbed my helmet . . . which had all my letters in the lining, and held on to it, and here's this white soldier looking out for his black combat companion. This is sort of odd, you know."

The two men were evacuated by ambulance, with two other stretcher cases, to the 100th General Hospital, in Bardelieu. "This two-star general came through the hospital. I was the only black on the ward. He asked every soldier, 'What unit were you in, So-and-so? How do you feel today? What did you do?' These are the questions that he put to the white troops. He came all the way to me, and in the next bed was my buddy, a cast all the way up his body. The general looked over at me, and I had my head all wrapped up from being hit by the shrapnel. He said, 'What's wrong with you, boy? Got the clap?' God, did that sink a dagger into me! Did that sink a dagger! I was dumbfounded; I couldn't say anything. This kid in his cast looks up and says, 'If he got it, General, he got it from your mother, you motherfucker!' "

Later in the day, the general returned to the ward to hand out Purple Hearts. McConnell saw him coming: "I had a comic book. I didn't even read the damn things, but I put it up to my face, and he went through his ceremony and then handed it to me. I didn't even reach for it. Just let him put it down on the bed. Boy, I'm telling you. My country 'tis of thee, sweet land of bigotry. Things are changing, though. I've seen quite a change myself. I feel the lives lost out there were not lost in vain. I think America's coming out of it, but it's a slow process."

Captain Garland N. Adamson, unit surgeon for the 761st, Nancy, France.

Through freezing rain and snow, the American advance continued slowly but inexorably across the muddy pastures of Lorraine. Since Morville, the towns of Hampont, Obreck, Dedeline, and Chateau-Voue had all fallen to the tankers of the 761st and the Yankee Division's foot soldiers.

After seizing Wuisse, the 761st turned southeast toward Guebling. The town was attacked on the evening of November 18. Silver Star winner Rubin Rivers's tank was the first to crash through the Germans' positions and enter Guebling. The night was passed in hard and continuing combat. In the morning, two high-explosive shells struck the Oklahoman's tank. Rubin Rivers's war was over prematurely. So was that of his bow gunner, Ivy Hilliard of Houston, Texas.

The 761st did not want for other heroic men. For his actions at Guebling, Sergeant Walter Lewis was awarded the Bronze Star with oak-leaf cluster. The medal citation—reprinted in his memoir with little elaboration—describes his actions after his tank took a direct high-explosive hit:

> As Sergeant Lewis left the tank he heard the bow gunner [trapped under an 1,100-pound cannon] frantically calling for help. With utter disregard for his personal safety, he proceeded back through artillery fire, climbed into the tank, manipulated the mechanical devices that raised the cannon and released his fellow soldier. When it became apparent to Sergeant Lewis that the vehicle would have to be abandoned, he re-entered the tank a second time and removed the radio equipment to prevent it from falling into enemy hands. The prompt and courageous action taken by Sergeant Lewis saved his comrade from capture by the enemy, insured greater security for personnel in other tanks in the immediate area and reflects credit upon himself and the military service.

From Guebling, the Third Army fought on toward a major strategic and psychological objective, the legendary Maginot Line. Built by the French during the 1930s, the line, with its heavily fortified positions, stretched from Switzerland to Belgium, parallel to the German border. France's military commanders loudly proclaimed that the Maginot was impregnable. During May 1940, in a daring assault across the "impassable" Ardennes forest, German tanks and foot soldiers under the command of General Gerd von Rundstedt proved that the assumptions of the French high command were terribly and tragically wrong. Now, four and a half years later, the Maginot defended the German homeland rather than the French.

The road to the Maginot Line was not easily traveled. For the tankers, still spearheading for the 26th, there were difficult battles at Dieuze, Honskirch, and Sarre-Union. In combat at Dieuze, the 761st's mortar platoon had done such superior work softening up the defenders and covering the tankers' advance that, according to Anderson, the 26th's commander, Major General W. S. Paul, remarked that "he had never seen a better demonstration of firing weapons of that type." Anderson writes in *Come Out Fighting* that the army's newsmagazine, *Yank*, credited the white 4th Armored Division, which arrived only after Dieuze had fallen, with capturing the town.

The clash at Münster lasted fifty-one hours. German armored and infantry units attacked and counterattacked under the cover of constant heavy artillery barrages. Again the mortar platoon performed meritoriously; five of its members were wounded. Three tankers lost their lives at Honskirch, and the stalwart German defense momentarily halted the American advance.

On December 2, at Sarre-Union, the 11th and 13th SS Panzer Divisions caused heavy casualties among the attacking infantrymen of the 26th. In the early afternoon, the Panthers rolled into action against the German tankers on the town's eastern perimeter. For two hours, these two well-trained and dedicated bands of fighters went head-to-head, maneuvering through quagmire-like fields and pastures. Though the Germans' Tiger Royal tanks had much greater firepower and tougher armor than the 761st's Shermans, the American machines had better maneuverability, and in the end, the battalion carried the day, forcing the Panzers to retreat and setting the stage for Sarre-Union's capture by the infantry.

For his actions during the battalion's final days in France, A Company's commander, Captain David J. "D.J." Williams, received the Silver Star. The Pittsburgh native and Yale graduate—who was probably the most popular of the 761st's white officers—had, in the words of his medal citation, "from open ground subjected to artillery and machine gun fire, observed and directed the fire of his tanks and succeeded in silencing the enemy guns. He sustained injuries during this mission." The citation also commended Williams for heroic actions in two earlier battles.

Johnnie Stevens recalls: "Most of the white officers, they didn't want to go into combat with us, they skedaddled. But we didn't much care, because they just couldn't seem to get the trust of the men. We trusted D.J., which made him a good officer. He was a guy that we could depend on. And he never left us, either. After he came out of the hospital, he came right back to the outfit."

On December 9, the 761st approached the Maginot Line, their vehicles struggling in the mud. German gunners in the heavily fortified string of pillboxes that made up the line fired barrage after barrage at the slowly advancing tanks. P-47 fighter-bombers were called in to assist the assault. Walter Lewis described the aerial attacks:

We fired white phosphorus in the places we wanted the planes to hit. Minutes later the P-47s came in low, so low we thought they mistook

December 1944: the armies move on;
the ravages of war remain.

us for Jerry, as Jerry was also operating in captured Sherman tanks.
. . . We had radio contact with them, and when they were sure of
the places we wanted them to drop their load, they gained altitude
and swooped in low on the German tanks and pillboxes. We could
see their 500-pound block-busters being released from the planes. Their
bombs were set at delayed action, giving the planes time to take safe
altitude. Suddenly the earth trembled just as if there was an earth-
quake. The roar of explosions was ear-splitting. Everything became
black before us. Our thirty-two-ton tanks shook like tissue paper. We
were beyond the stage of being frightened. War had made us callous
and numb to feeling. It seemed like the whole world fell apart that
day, and I prayed.

The pilots did their job on the Maginot Line, reducing enough of the pill-boxes to rubble to allow Companies A and B to pierce the vaunted defenses near the towns of Aachen and Etting, while Company C punched through near Oermingen.

Two days later, the 26th Division was withdrawn from the front for rest and recuperation. The Yankees and the Panthers had fought courageously and harmoniously together. In a message to the battalion commander, Major John F. George,† General Paul of the 26th wrote that "your battalion has supported this division with great bravery under the most adverse weather and terrain conditions. You have my sincere wish that success may continue to follow you in all your endeavors."

The XII Corps commander, Major General Manton S. Eddy, also wrote Major George and described the Panthers' performance in glowing terms:

1. I consider the 761st Tank Battalion to have entered combat with such conspicuous success as to warrant special commendation.
2. The speed with which they adapted themselves to the front line under the most adverse weather conditions, the gallantry with which they faced some of Germany's finest troops, and the confident spirit with which they emerged from their recent engagements in the vicinity of Dieuze, Morville Les Vic and Guebling entitle them surely to consider themselves the veteran 761st.

With the 26th Division gone, the battalion was assigned to spearhead for their replacements, the 87th Infantry. Most of the 87th's personnel were from the South. The relationship between the two units was rocky from the start. William McBurney recalls that "when the shooting slowed down and we went behind the lines, they didn't even want to acknowledge who we were."

For E. G. McConnell, the memory of these "comrades" is still bitter: "A commander of the 87th Infantry—they were from the South—told that outfit, 'I don't want them niggers messin' with no white women, and don't you even socialize with them.' We were fighting for survival, and these were the words he brought out! And they were green, brand-new into combat. Green! And these bastards start talking all this kind of shit! But when it got hot and their lives

---

†Colonel Bates, recovering from his wounds, would not return to the unit until February.

were at stake, they forgot about the color. They didn't give a damn as long as they could jump inside our tanks. Before that they didn't even want to talk to us, but when the Germans were dropping all that shit on us, they begged us to let them get inside."

On December 14, the tankers rolled across the German border in the area between Wissembourg and Saarbrücken. But the Panthers did not linger long on Third Reich soil. Almost immediately, they received new orders. They were to move out for Belgium, where they would join one of history's most horrendous and pivotal clashes of arms, the Battle of the Bulge.

CHAPTER 8

They put us on flatcars in France and shipped us to Belgium, where the fighting was. We got off the flatcars, took our tanks off the flatcars, and went right into combat. But that Battle of the Bulge was something, I'm telling you! We never fell back. We never lost an inch of ground during the whole campaign. You can't find nothing in the record that says the 761st lost any of their ground. One of our tank crews that was knocked out, they got out of their tank and fought with machine guns—a captured German officer said he'd never seen anything like that before. Because we stood our ground up there, we really didn't give it up.

Johnnie Stevens

Soldiers survey the damage caused by the bombing of Bastogne, Belgium, on Christmas Eve, 1944.

In late autumn of 1944, Adolf Hitler, his forces on the eastern front battered by an advancing Red Army, mounted a last-ditch effort in the West. His troops, under the command of General Gerd von Rundstedt, would cross the Ardennes forest and move into the Low Countries, with Antwerp, the strategic Belgian port, their ultimate objective. This grandiose and daring scheme was opposed by the majority of the Wehrmacht's senior officers, including Rundstedt, its most respected commander. "When I received this plan, early in November," he stated after the war, "I was staggered. Hitler had not troubled to consult me. . . . It was obvious that the available forces were far too small for such an extremely ambitious plan."[1] As always, however, the Führer's will prevailed. The result was the Battle of the Bulge—a title derived from the convex shape of the battle lines—which ultimately involved more than one million Allied and German troops. Ironically, according to Charles B. MacDonald in *A Time for Trumpets*, the Allies' consistent misinterpretation of intelligence reports was in large part responsible for the German army's retention of the element of surprise and the initial success of its campaign. British cryptanalysts, beginning in September, had deciphered a series of German messages that indicated a major offensive was being planned. But the Allied Command could not believe that the Wehrmacht would strike in the Ardennes. Such a move, to their thinking, would be foolhardy to an extreme. They did not take into consideration the mentality of Adolf Hitler. "Allied intelligence," MacDonald writes, "had committed the most grievous sin of which [an intelligence operation] is capable. They had looked in a mirror for the enemy and seen there only the reflections of their own intentions."[2]

Early on the morning of December 16, the Germans attacked along their border with Belgium and Luxembourg. By nightfall, though not all of their first objectives—among them the capture of the town of Saint-Vit and a push to the Meuse River—had been reached, they considered Day One of the Ardennes campaign to have been a great success. The American defenders, members of the 12th Army Group, handicapped by ammunition shortages and thin manpower reserves, had fought with exceptional courage, sustaining heavy casualties in the process.

In the next days, the Germans continued their advance, breaking through the American lines at several points. On December 17, near the town of Malmédy, SS troops murdered, without provocation, eighty-six U.S. prisoners of war. These victims of the worst atrocity committed against American soldiers during the course of the war in Europe were members of the 285th Field Artillery Observer Battalion.

Preparing for Christmas dinner, 1944.

While one contingent of the 761st traveled by freight train, the bulk of the tank battalion were slogging their way through heavy snows toward the Belgian battlefields. On Christmas Day, they stopped at field kitchens for a traditional turkey dinner. Walter Lewis recalls in his "Diary of a Gunner" that before the food had finished cooking, "we received orders to move out, so hunks of hot half-done turkeys were savagely pulled apart and distributed as we mounted our tanks and were off."

During this journey, William McBurney remembers, "while we were on our way up to Bastogne, there were infantrymen walking along and saying, 'Where the hell are you niggers going with those tanks? You've got no business in them!' Just like that."

Johnnie Stevens was among those moved into the Bulge by rail, arriving several days ahead of the tankers traveling the highways. "Today is Xmas Day," he wrote in the combat journal he kept during the war, "but to us it's just another day. They are throwing everything at us but Hitler's dress suit and what makes it so bad, we are freezing like the devil."

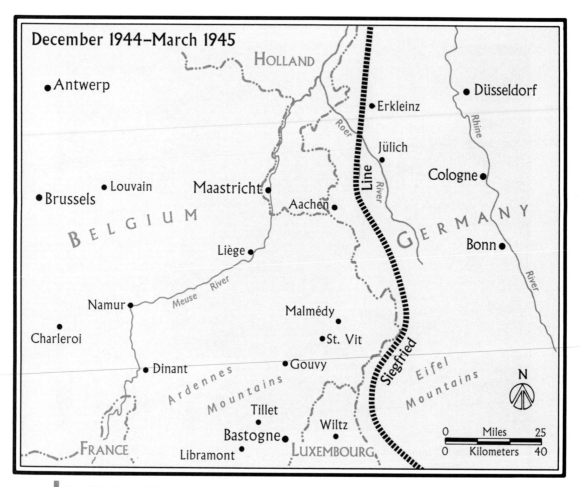

December 1944–March 1945

The 761st helped blunt the Ardennes campaign and fought in the Battle of the Bulge.

The men of the 761st approached the Bulge with some trepidation. "We heard about German atrocities," Lewis writes, "how they stripped [captured] tankers naked in groups and tied ropes around them [before] machine gunning them to death. At this point, Jerry was using American tanks, English-speaking soldiers, American uniforms and American guns. Some were able to infiltrate our lines before being captured, so we had to be exceptionally careful. It wasn't unusual in the Bulge to be attacked from the rear along a road you had just traveled hours before."

By New Year's Eve, all the tankers had reached their destination, Libramont, Belgium. The Panthers rang in 1945 spearheading for the 345th Infantry Regiment of the 87th Division. On January 1, they captured two towns—Rondue and Nimbermont—fifteen miles east of the city of Bastogne.

Bastogne was the headquarters of the First Army's VIII Corps and, for this reason, had been the battle's focal point since before Christmas. It was from

Bastogne—encircled by the enemy—that Brigadier General Anthony C. Mc-Auliffe, commander of the 101st Airborne Division, had given his legendary one-word answer to demands that he surrender: "Nuts!"

On December 26, units of the Third Army had broken through the German lines south of the city and relieved the siege. The German troops were now forced through a salient too narrow to be adequately defended. Rundstedt strongly advised Hitler to order his forces to withdraw. The Führer, however, refused to heed his commander's advice and ordered that the massive Ardennes offensive be resumed.

The all-black 183rd Battalion of combat engineers played a crucial role in the enormous effort to relieve the GI's trapped in Bastogne. A veteran sergeant of the 183rd, Dr. Leon Bass of Philadelphia retains vivid memories of the Battle of the Bulge: "We were told to go to a small town in Belgium: Martelange. It was small but very strategic, because there was a bridge there that had been blown apart by the enemy, and our responsibility was to rebuild it, because

Patton awarding the Distinguished Service Cross to Brigadier General Anthony C. McAuliffe in Bastogne, Belgium, 1944.

fifteen kilometers up the highway was Bastogne. And to rescue the Americans, they had to cross that bridge at Martelange. . . . We worked night and day. In spite of the weather, we worked. In spite of the strafing by the airplanes that would come down daily and machine-gun us. In spite of the shelling of the howitzers, we worked on that bridge. We finished it on time. And all the resources—the tanks, the guns, the men—went across that bridge and up to Bas-

Sergeant Leon Bass.

togne. And they rescued those men. And that was a glorious day. But my unit, the 183rd, paid a heck of a price for that glory. I know . . . because I stood in the snow and I looked at the grave-registration trucks on which the bodies of so many of my friends were placed."

The days and nights at Martelange set Bass to searchingly consider his role, as an African-American, in Uncle Sam's army: "It was the beginning of my saying, 'Leon, you weren't too smart to have joined this army. What are you doing here? You could end up that way. What are you fighting for? You can't get a drink of water at a fountain or a meal in a restaurant. They won't even let you have a seat on a bus, so what are you doing here and what are you fighting for?' I couldn't answer those questions. I was only nineteen. And I didn't know all the answers. All I knew was that I was angry. Deep down, I was an angry young black soldier. Angry at my country for using me. Putting me out there to fight and maybe even die to preserve the rights and privileges that they were telling me I wasn't good enough to enjoy back home. So I was angry."

Following the Third Army's breakthrough at Bastogne, the American forces had two aims: first, to prevent the Germans from reinforcing their positions in the area; and second, to push the enemy back. The 761st drew key assignments in this effort. En route to Tillet, their primary objective for the moment, B

Company killed one hundred fifty German infantrymen at Bonnerue, while at Remagen, C and D Companies, between them, knocked out eleven machine gun nests, killed thirty-one gunners, and took seventy German prisoners. These were but preliminaries, however; Tillet, where the Germans were well entrenched, was the main event.

The Americans were fighting both the weather and the Wehrmacht. Snow continued to fall, and when it slackened the skies remained, at first, too overcast for fighter-bombers to provide the ground forces with much-needed air support. The paths and hills in the region were so icy, trucks could not negotiate them; D Company's light tanks were pressed into service as supply vehicles.

During this period, Johnnie Stevens wrote: "Well I don't know what day it is because we have been so busy fighting, we have forgotten about day and time. A lot of my buddies have been killed here but, through the help of God, I am still here. We have taken a beating but these guys are still pitching and whoever said 'the colored soldier can't fight' is a damn liar. The guys in the infantry told us they'd rather have us with them than the white soldiers. We should pray to God in heaven because we are going through hell here."

In the four-foot-deep snow at Tillet, the Panthers again squared off against their adversaries, the 13th SS Panzer Division. "The Battle of the Bulge," Johnnie Stevens told interviewers Nina Rosenblum and William Miles, "was something, I'm telling you. It was one of the biggest tank battles that you could find. At Tillet, you could look through your field glasses and see nothing but tanks lining the snow. Ours and theirs.

"We had some advantages over them," Stevens continued. "Their 88-millimeter gun was so big and so heavy that it had to be manually turned, while our turret guns turned with a switch; they had gyrostabilizers and panoramic sights. You could turn them 360 degrees in less than two seconds. Their Mark IV's and Tiger Royals were so big that they were actually clumsy, whereas our M36's with those twin Ford motors in them could drive fifty miles an hour across a wet, snowy field. And our guys could turn them on a dime. So we could outmaneuver them, but they had so much armor, you could hardly knock them out. But we learned the vulnerable spots; we'd hit them on their tracks first and make them stop, and then there was nothing they could do. Because their gun turned slow, you could just go around them and fire in your shells."

The Sherman tank, though hardly approximating a Winnebago for creature comforts, was nonetheless a mobile home. "Four or five men in that tank," E. G. McConnell recollects, "they had a hell of a thing together. A togetherness that is hard to put into words, because it became automatic and systematic; everybody knew their job, and a guy would say 'Do this,' and before he's said it, it's already done. . . . We weren't taking baths because it was too cold up there to take a bath and we didn't have any damn place to take one. If we found some whiskey or some schnapps, we'd drink it. It was like a small family . . . better than a small family. That's why, I guess, after forty-seven years, some of these guys are still such friends."

"I wasn't gonna sleep outside," Leonard "Smitty" Smith says. "Me and this fellow Clark, we would put ten blankets down on top of the metal and ten blankets over our bodies, and you could still feel that cold coming through the metal, through those ten blankets. Some guys would go outside and sleep on the motor. The heat from its exhaust was so hot from running all day long that it would warm you up, like you're sleeping over a grate. We survived, and it was subzero out there."

The fighting began at Tillet on January 5 and raged throughout the area for five long, grueling days. The 13th SS Panzer Division mounted a formidable defense, absorbing, as Trezzvant Anderson writes, "everything the 761st had to offer and coming back for more."

The difficulties facing the Black Panthers were compounded by disorganization within the ranks of the 87th Infantry Division, for whom they were spearheading. "Smitty" Smith remembers that "they got so scared when the Germans came at them, they dropped their rifles and ran." From his vantage point, Johnnie Stevens recalls, "Man, those dudes were getting their hats. They were retreating. I said, 'I'm going to turn this tank gun right on you. You're gonna stay here!' If it wasn't for us, the Germans would have overrun Tillet, they'd have taken that place. . . . It wasn't that [the infantrymen] were cowards. It was just that the firing was too heavy and they were inexperienced. Young greenhorns, they didn't know what it was all about. Whereas we were well-seasoned combat troops."

Infantrymen would run up to the tanks, William McBurney remembers, "and they were begging us, they were hollering, 'Boy, let us in the tank!' Well, we had our prejudices too. We would say, 'Where you from, man?' And the guy would say, 'I'm out of Memphis.' 'Sorry, man,' we'd answer. 'We ain't got no room.' Two seconds later, somebody would knock on the tank and say, 'Hey, you guys got any room in there?' 'Where you from?' 'New Jersey.' 'Well, come on in!' So we had our prejudices too, but not to the extent that they did."

The battle for Tillet saw many instances of extreme bravery on the part of the 761st. One tank crew, commanded by Sergeant Henry H. Conway from Chi-

Capture of German soldiers during the Battle of the Bulge.

cago, single-handedly held off the advance of sixteen Mark IV's for an hour, before other members of the 761st could come to their aid. During those sixty minutes, Conway's men—though their tank was hit numerous times and its rear hatch was blown off—stopped the panzer platoon in its tracks.

On January 9, a tank carrying William McBurney, "Smitty" Smith, Theodore Windsor, and Willie Devore moved through a forest clearing under heavy fire. In one and the same moment, it struck a land mine and received a direct hit by an antitank shell. Devore was killed instantly. William McBurney recalls the incident:

"His head got almost taken off when the shell hit the tank. Smitty and I [and Windsor] got out, and we were getting fire from all over. The snow was about four feet deep, and we started doing the best we could to get into the woods. I was ready to stop. I was exhausted. I was shooting at anything I could see move. This American plane, a P-38, came out of nowhere and knocked out a tank that was attacking us. . . . And this clown, Smitty, he's hollering: 'Remember the Savoy!?' Hollering about what we used to do at the [ballroom in Harlem]. And here we were crawling on our knees and hands and fingers trying to get to the woods, to get out of the fire. We had on heavy winter clothing, and against the snow, you could see us from a thousand miles away. They were shooting at us while we were crawling. At some point Smitty jumped into a hole, and there was a dead German soldier in it. And he's scared to death of dead people, but he stayed and laid on top of that soldier until the firing stopped. But we finally made it to the wooded area, and we were fortunate enough to make it back to our lines. What I'm trying to say is that we were so young, we didn't realize that we were in hell at the time . . . and scared."

In fact, McBurney, Windsor, and Smith crawled in subzero temperatures, through deep snow and over thick ice, while exposed to mortar, artillery, and small arms fire, for more than three miles before they reached those woods.

Walter Lewis wrote:

I never thought of my tank as a death trap, since I had conditioned my mind to live in it. As long as I could keep my hands upon the cannon, with a round in the breech block, I wasn't worried; I thought my crew and I had an even chance of survival. One second's delay in firing this weapon sometimes spelled the difference between life and death. You had to get the enemy before he got you.

The Germans had a "bracketing" system that was most effective. If a round dropped in front of you and the second round dropped to your rear, the third round—if you stayed where you were—would hit the target. So the thing to do was to zigzag out of range as quick as possible, firing at them at the same time; trying to upset their equilibrium.

On January 4, in the attack on Remagen during the battalion's drive to Tillet, Walter Lewis's tank took a direct hit from an 88-millimeter delayed-action shell. It ricocheted behind driver Thomas Bragg's seat before exploding. Bragg, a private from Elizabeth, New Jersey, was killed instantly. Lewis and the other crewmen—Private James Jordan from Chicago and Private Charles Brooks from Charleston, West Virginia—were seriously injured. In his "Diary of a Gunner," Lewis wrote:

Transmission on our two-way radio was scrambled. The Germans were on our transmissions as well as Axis Sally, who was telling us about rioting in Cleveland, Ohio, and telling us to go home and doing all she could to break our morale . . . then [she] played Louis Arm-

strong's recording of "I Can't Give You Anything but Love, Baby."
. . . We did not move fifty yards before we were hit! It sounded like
heavy plate glass bursting into a million ear-splitting pieces. Concussion blew me out of the tank. Had my hatch not been open, all of us
would have been killed by the concussion alone. I got up and ran, for
I was in a state of hysteria. . . . My clothing was cut to shreds. [I
was] bleeding profusely. . . . The area was now drawing enemy fire.
I ran until I was exhausted. I remember stopping at a monastery. The
Germans began shelling this also, so I took off again. In my delirium,
I made my way to an aid station about three kilometers from the
scene of battle, running through wooded areas infested with German
snipers. . . . I collapsed. . . . When I came to my senses, I was on a
litter. I was evacuated at night in a convoy of ambulances which slowly
moved through mine fields and booby-trapped roads. I was operated
on the next day in a hospital in Sedan, France.

The fighting around Tillet was brutal. Charles A. Gates's Silver Star citation
hints at its ferocity:

Captain Gates, in command of a small force of ten tanks with sup-
porting infantry, after a personal forward reconnaissance, launched an
attack against an organized enemy defensive position which was supported by self-propelled anti-tank guns. Captain Gates gallantly led
and directed the attack on foot keeping his force going forward against
heavy opposition, inflicting heavy losses on the enemy and disregard-
ing his own safety until the objective was reached after five hours of
bitter fighting, up a long, gradually rising slope. When the objective
was reached only two of the tanks and a remnant of infantry remained of the original force.

Finally, the overcast skies above the Ardennes brightened. "We had just about
run out of gas and ammunition," Johnnie Stevens recalled. "We were in trouble.
But the skies opened up, and the C-47's dropped the stuff, so we were back in
business." On January 9, Tillet fell.

The following day, Stevens wrote in his journal: "Well, here I am in the
hospital again. I was not hit as bad as I was the first time, but I received my
Oak Leaf Cluster today and believe me, I earned it. The whole outfit has earned

a citation. They stayed on the line for 96 days without relief which is a darn good record for one tank battalion."

After taking Tillet ahead of the 87th Infantry, the Panthers were reassigned to the 17th Airborne Division, an elite combat unit operating north of Bastogne. Spearheading for these paratroopers, the 761st, at Wicourt, cut the Liège-Bastogne road, a vital German supply and retreat route.

Though the Wehrmacht's Ardennes campaign was now clearly a failure, the Germans were not about to lay down their arms and surrender. They waged a fighting withdrawal through the now swamplike fields. Throughout the region, the American forces kept the pressure on. The 761st and the 17th took the towns of Gouvy, Hautbillan, and, after overcoming bitter resistance, Watermall. At one point, Company C veered into Luxembourg, where they forced the Germans to retreat from Espeles and captured the town. Meantime, other elements of both units were moving eastward toward Saint-Vit. On this drive the Panthers cut two more major German relief routes, the Saint-Vit–Bastogne and the Saint-Vit–Trier roads. During the course of the Ardennes campaign, the 761st pushed back German armored, artillery, and infantry units a distance of some sixty miles.

Trezzvant Anderson describes the camaraderie between the white paratroops of the 17th and the black tankers of the 761st as "a beautiful thing, and they willingly risked death for each other on many occasions."[3] The commander of the 17th is reported to have remarked later that he "would prefer to have five tanks from the 761st to fifty from any other armored unit." E. G. McConnell would remember the Ardennes campaign in a verse written by Captain Philip W. Latimer:

> Black tankers and white paratroops,
> They made a lovely sight
> Unless you were German
> And then you'd best take flight.
> Black tankers and white paratroops,
> They all were color blind.
> They went into battle
> With winning on their mind.
> Black tankers and white paratroops
> Made Patton shout with glee,
> "They fight the way I want them to.

They're good enough for me."
Black tankers and white paratroops
Lie buried side by side.
They gave their life for country,
They gave it all with pride.
Black tankers and white paratroops,
Our memories take us back.
Since we've been in battle
There is no white or black.

The Battle of the Bulge brought heavy casualties on both sides. Of the 600,000 Americans engaged in the struggle, 19,000 were killed, 17,000 wounded, 15,000 captured. Five of the dead were members of the 761st. One fifth of the half-million-man German force were killed, wounded, or captured. During the brutal campaign in the Ardennes, the fortunes of war turned decisively in favor of the Allied cause.

The German advances during the first stage of the Bulge made clear a serious situation—a marked shortage of replacement foot soldiers—of which American commanders were already cognizant. By the end of December, U.S. forces in the European Theater were short some 23,000 riflemen. This shortfall was, in large part, a result of the effectiveness of the German submarine blockade in Europe's coastal waters. The U-boats had considerably slowed the arrival of troop ships from the States carrying replacement forces.

General Eisenhower and his staff at Supreme Headquarters finally decided to convert GI's in service units into combat soldiers. A side effect of this decision was a plan for racial integration, of which Morris J. MacGregor, Jr., in *Integration of the Armed Forces, 1940–1965*, says, "although patronizing in tone, [it] marked a bold departure from War Department policy."[4]

In an interview with Miles and Rosenblum, Lewis Weinstein, then chief of the Liaison Section of Eisenhower's staff, recalled the events leading up to this unprecedented action. "Our losses were heavy. The infantry replacements were getting lower and lower. It looked very bleak. After a tough staff meeting, I'm sleeping one night and I wake up with a start—why can't these black troops now relegated to service jobs, . . . be asked to volunteer as infantry replacements?"

Weinstein immediately took his idea to Eisenhower's chief of staff, General Walter Bedell "Beetle" Smith. He was told that though it was "a good idea, the

General Eisenhower addressing an assembly
of black troops.

old man won't buy it. But, if you want to see him, you'll see him." Among
those present at his subsequent meeting with the Supreme Commander were
General Benjamin O. Davis, Sr.—in Europe on an inspection tour—and General
John C. H. Lee. Davis, in a report to the inspector general, would state his "whole-
hearted approval" of the plan. Weinstein recalls Eisenhower listening "very
carefully" to his presentation before saying, " 'Can't do that. Nope. No, no.' I
kept on arguing more and more, and he says, 'Weinstein, you've told me enough
now. I told you that we have a policy. If you want, I'll send off a message to
Washington.' I knew that was hopeless. One of my Harvard classmates and friends
was [former Civilian Aide] Bill Hastie, and he left the War Department because
he couldn't dent the rigid policy of segregation in the army. I said, 'General, we
haven't time for that. [Before] an answer comes, men will die because we don't
have infantry replacements.' He was still stubborn, sitting there, and he said,
'Are you finished now, Weinstein?' "

Lewis Weinstein wasn't finished. In a rather remarkable display of chutzpah,
the young officer proceeded to relate to his commander a story he had been told
at General Staff Command School. It concerned a Civil War general, facing a

situation similar to Ike's, who had failed to act promptly, waiting instead for a policy decision from Washington. Seven or eight men died as a result. After the war, Weinstein continued, the general was court-martialed and found derelict in his duty. "What was his name?" Eisenhower asked. "Never knew his name," Weinstein replied. "You telling me straight stuff now, Weinstein?"

"I said, 'Would I dare do anything else to my commanding officer? But I believe I have an obligation to tell him everything I know and if I don't do it, I'm not fulfilling my responsibility. I don't belong in my job.' And he said, 'Let me hear more.' I said, 'Here is an opportunity; there are lots of blacks here, some trained [for combat]. There was a Second Cavalry Division; it was disbanded and the men are now cooks. . . . Word from you that they can volunteer will do the trick.' 'You won't get any volunteers,' he said. 'In two days, you'll know if we have or not,' I answered. 'Beetle' Smith says, 'Let's try it.' Ike says, 'All right.' "

The call for African-American volunteers went out over General John Lee's signature on December 26. They were asked "to share the privilege of joining our veteran units at the front to deliver the knockout blow. . . . It is planned

A contingent of black nurses arrives in Europe to aid the war effort, 1944.

to assign you without regard to color or to race, to the units where assistance is most needed and give you the opportunity to bring about victory. . . . Your relatives and your friends everywhere have been urging that you be granted this privilege."[5] Only privates were asked to volunteer; sergeants and corporals who applied had their ranks reduced. This was an obvious effort to avoid empowering black noncommissioned officers to give orders to white enlisted men. "We had black volunteers, two thousand six hundred of them," Weinstein told his interviewers. "They did nobly." General George Patton refused to accept any of the thirty-seven volunteer African-American rifle platoons into his Third Army. According to Bernard C. Nalty, he warned the general staff that Southern-born white soldiers would object to serving alongside blacks.[6] Interestingly, Patton was not unaware of the potential value of black replacements. He writes, in *War as I Knew It:* "In Bastogne [there were] some colored artillery; the Quartermaster men provided themselves with rifles and fought very well."[7]

In the event, Weinstein says, "They won medals. Purple Hearts, Silver Stars, Bronze Stars. They were brave. A number of them died; they were killed in action. Nobody could have been braver than those volunteers. If it were not for these brave soldiers, heaven knows what would have happened with the Bulge. Finally, after the Bulge was blunted, these soldiers—who had done their job brilliantly, side by side with whites—back they were sent to their segregated units, and these brave, heroic infantrymen became cooks and dishwashers and truckdrivers all over again."

The 761st also had to acclimatize replacements for slain and wounded comrades. New African-American riflemen were retrained at Compiègne, France, before entering combat. The rookie tankers, however, received their instruction on the job. Johnnie Stevens recalls that "there weren't enough trained replacements. So we were in a position where we were being cut to pieces, but no replacements. So we started getting people from the infantry, and we made tankers out of those guys in a few days. We couldn't teach them the technical things, but they could learn to be bow gunners or cannoneers in a short time."

In February, the battalion moved into Holland; now they were attached to the Ninth Army's 79th Infantry Division. "We fought with almost every division on the western front," Johnnie Stevens said. "They'd pull us out of one, and we'd go right to another. Out of one, right to another. We never got any rest. See, with other units, they'd pull them out, send them back. Not with us; we spearheaded all the time."

With two hundred new men in their ranks and with Colonel Paul Bates—recovered from his wounds—back in command, the Panthers took the town of

Volunteer combat soldiers on the way to the German front, 1945.

End. They rolled to Milich, where they cut the Roermond-Jülich railway line before moving on to Erkleinz. There, on March 3, they crossed over the German border in pursuit of the Wehrmacht's 2nd Armored Division, wiping out pockets of resistance and taking a considerable number of prisoners. Chief among the prizes captured by elements of the 761st and the Ninth Army during the battalion's fifty-five-mile foray into the Reich was the city of München-Gladbach, the home of Joseph Goebbels, Nazi minister of propaganda and one of the more ardent proponents of the "Final Solution." These operations appreciably reduced the Germans' ability to bring meaningful pressure on Ninth Army positions at Jülich and Geilenkirchen.

Several hundred miles southeast of München-Gladbach, in the concentration camp at Dachau, the impending collapse of Hitler's army, his Reich, and his nightmare was not impeding SS officers' progress toward the Nazis' goal of a *Judenfrei* planet.

It was at Dachau, according to Leni Yahil's *The Holocaust: 1932–1945*, that Gestapo chieftain Heinrich Himmler witnessed his first "medical experiment" on a living human being. Afterward, he asked his Führer to approve the practice.

201

| Main entrance to Dachau.

Hitler replied that "in principle, experiments on humans should be allowed when the matter at hand is the good of the state. . . . It is unreasonable that anyone in a concentration camp or prison should not be harmed by the war."[8]

Though Jews constituted the largest group among the prisoners, members of more than thirty nationalities shared their fate at Dachau. All—regardless of ethnicity—could be subject to the tortures of the laboratory, which ranged from infecting some two thousand prisoners with malaria, in a futile search for a cure, to using human guinea pigs to determine the length of time it takes a person to freeze to death.

In the winter of 1944–45, thousands of prisoners perished during a typhus epidemic that swept the camp. Their numbers, however, were soon replenished. As the Red Army continued its relentless advance in the east, the Nazis took steps to prevent the liberation of concentration camp inmates by the Soviet troops. Prisoners by the tens of thousands were relocated from camps in Poland to those within the borders of the Reich.

Buchenwald and Dachau experienced an influx from the east. During the first five months of 1945, nearly 25,000 inmates—half of them Jews—were brought into Buchenwald from Auschwitz alone.

Remains of victims of "medical experiments."

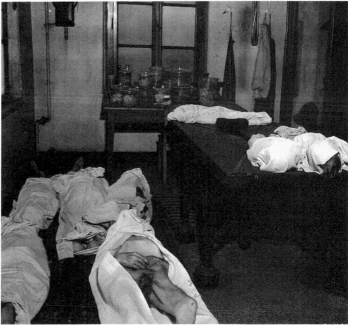

Remains of beheaded Germans:
the Nazis treated their "criminals" no better than they did the Jews.

Ben Bender remembers standing at roll calls during that frigid winter: "The air was bluish, translucent, crisp. The flakes of snow were swirling in the air. Thirty thousand people waiting to be counted. Often for hours. Many dropped dead before they were counted. The SS officials were never in a hurry. The dead were counted along with the living."

Buchenwald, like Dachau, had its share of mad and murderous "physicians." As Bender recalls, "Building 50 was for research for producing a virus against typhoid. They used human beings for this kind of purpose. All experiments were done without anesthesia, and they were cutting off a leg or a hand or even popping out eyes, because they tried, like Mengele in Auschwitz, to create blue eyes. [In one room] I saw human heads the size of an orange. They were put in a special chemical liquid, which shrinks the head. And I looked at the heads and it was terrible."

But despite the degradation surrounding him, the teenage Bender clung to a dream of liberation: "One day in Buchenwald was a lifetime in hell. But hope is invincible, because it clings to cliffs, barbed wire, iron bars, and human thoughts. Hope must be bottomless. In the abyss of Buchenwald, in the depths of an abyss called despair, I saw the blue reflection of the sky."

Frozen American soldier.

After blunting the German attack in the Ardennes, the American ground forces on the western front mounted a sustained and deadly offensive in which the 761st would play a prominent part. The basic objectives of land war are to kill or neutralize enemy forces and to capture enemy territory. From the west, this would be accomplished by pushing into Germany via France, penetrating the Siegfried Line in the process, then moving through the plains and across the Rhine River. This maneuver would set the stage for an American campaign, spearheaded by the Panthers, deep into Bavaria, then eastward through Austria to within hailing distance of the Czechoslovakian border. During these weeks, elements of the Red Army would rapidly move west, avenging the monstrous depredations inflicted on their homeland by the Führer's legions. The meeting of victorious American and Russian troops—fighting in the service of contradictory ideologies yet yoked together in a mighty crusade against fascism, a mutually despised third force—would resonate with extraordinary political symbolism.

On March 8, the 761st was pulled out of Germany and Holland. Their post-Bulge orders called for the battalion to proceed to Saverne, in France's Alsace-Lorraine region. There they were to spearhead for the Seventh Army's 103rd Infantry Division, now commanded by General Anthony C. McAuliffe, of Bastogne fame. During the latter stages of the war, elements of the 761st would be, more often than not, operating with many ground units, scattered over great distances.

The tankers would now fight their way toward the Harz mountains; their first mission was an assault on the Germans' vaunted West Wall defensive positions, known to the Allies as the Siegfried Line.

CHAPTER 9

I came into that camp an angry black soldier.
Angry at my country and justifiably so.
Angry because they were treating me as
though I was not good enough. But [that day]
I came to the realization that human suffering
is not relegated to me and mine. I now knew
that human suffering could touch us all. . . .
[What I saw] in Buchenwald was the face of
evil . . . it was racism

Leon Bass

Buchenwald, 1945. (The third soldier from
the left is Sergeant Leon Bass.)

In its most fortified sections, those most likely to be attacked, the Siegfried defenses consisted of a two-to-three-mile belt of "concrete bunkers, pillboxes, fire trenches and gun positions, protected by forests of barbed wire, deep mine fields and concrete anti-tank obstacles. Some of the amenities were of a most elaborate character: there were water closets, showerbaths, underground barracks, and every conceivable convenience including electricity and an enormous telephone installation . . . [protected by] cupolas ten inches thick and impervious to American 90mm shells."[1]

The Panthers' assault on the approaches to the West Wall began on March 14, 1945, at Gundershoffen. Over the course of the next five days, the tankers and the 103rd Infantry Division fought their way through heavily mined fields to Bobenthal, in the Harz mountains. The German land mines caused major casualties among the riflemen and knocked more than a few tanks out of combat.

During the move toward the Siegfried Line, Leonard "Smitty" Smith earned the Bronze Star for bravery. Smith, in the matter-of-fact manner of most of the tankers as they described their exploits, told Miles and Rosenblum that he received the medal for "knocking out some gun emplacements and helping a crew." His citation describes his deeds in a bit more detail:

> For heroic achievement in action . . . Private Smith, tank gunner, displayed outstanding devotion to duty in closely supporting the 411th Infantry. On one occasion, Private Smith successfully assisted in the evacuation of a disabled tank in the face of enemy artillery, mortar and small arms fire. He materially assisted in destroying the 23 pillboxes, and effectively reduced enemy automatic weapon and sniper fire. Private Smith's actions reflected the highest traditions of the military service.

At Bobenthal, Task Force Rhine was organized, under Lieutenant Colonel Bates's command. Consisting of the 761st, the 2nd Battalion of the 103rd's 409th Regiment, a detachment of combat engineers, and a reconnaissance platoon from the 614th Tank Destroyer Battalion, the task force was charged with cracking the Siegfried and advancing to the Rhine River.

On March 21, C Company rolled to Reisdorf and, for the entire day, fired round after round at the Siegfried's heavily reinforced defenses in the hills surrounding the town. At the cost of one tank, its first platoon put seven pillboxes and one antitank gun out of commission, while killing fourteen of the enemy and taking ninety prisoners. The second platoon, meanwhile, was causing similar damage to emplacements around Nieder Schlettenbach, before their replacement by a platoon from A Company. Through the course of an all-night battle, these tankers destroyed ten pillboxes and some twenty machine gun nests. During this clash, the company's commander, Lieutenant Maxwell Huffman from Newell, South Dakota, was killed by snipers.

From Nieder Schlettenbach, A Company moved on toward Erlenbach. En route they encountered dense fortifications—pillboxes (one every fifteen yards), antitank guns, and machine gun nests. The Panthers attacked these barriers to their progress by first dispatching two war machines toward the target at top speed, under cover of heavy fire from the remaining tanks. When the two lead vehicles reached their objective, two more would follow and help them secure it. This tactic was repeated until the pillboxes or machine gun nests were neutralized. Along the stretch of mountain road connecting the two towns, the Panthers destroyed twenty-four pillboxes and seventeen machine gun positions while killing 265 enemy troops and taking 1,500 prisoners.

From Bobenthal, Task Force Rhine moved on to Reisdorf, which fell to the Americans following several hours of intense fighting in the streets. The task force was then divided into two sections, one to head northeast toward Birkenhardt, the other to strike out due east in the direction of Bollenborn.

As the Birkenhardt contingent approached its objective, it encountered extremely heavy fire from German artillery and mobile antitank guns. The advance, for the moment, was halted in its tracks. Colonel Bates called for additional artillery support from the 103rd Division. Soon nine battalions of American artillery were firing barrage after barrage into Birkenhardt. The town was virtually obliterated, and those of its defenders who were left alive quickly surrendered to the U.S. troops.

The second column met such strong resistance from German artillery and antitank guns at Bollenborn that it was forced to withdraw. Task Force Rhine regrouped on the Birkenhardt-Lauterburg road and received orders to meet the 10th Armored Division near Silz, a few miles away. The two units were then to attempt to shatter the Siegfried Line. However, for reasons still unclear, the 10th was not at the rendezvous site. Bates decided that his task force would make the final assault on its own.

Night had fallen as they advanced, through dense mortar and artillery fire, on Silz. An exploding ammunition dump turned the town and its environs into an inferno. As the tankers continued on toward their next major objective, the large town of Klingenmünster, their way was lit by the roaring blaze.

They were supposed to be joined in the attack on Klingenmünster by the 36th Division. There was another communications failure, however, and, as Trezzvant Anderson reports, "the 36th was not advancing towards Klingenmünster." Again the 761st would go it alone.

They reached the town of Münchweiler at fifteen minutes past midnight on March 23. The Panthers attacked German antitank positions, and the defenders retreated. As the task force proceeded toward Klingenmünster, they encountered a fleeing column of German mechanized and horse-drawn units. Anderson describes what followed:

> The column was fired on with devastating effect and many Germans were killed. The road was . . . for five miles . . . so littered with debris, dead horses, shattered anti-tank and self propelled guns, artillery pieces, dead Germans and wrecked motor vehicles, it became necessary for Colonel Bates to order his tank-dozer forward to clear a way for his tanks to proceed. Following the successful completion of its task, this tank-dozer was hit by an anti-tank gun at Klingenmünster and knocked out. But it had done its work and Task Force Rhine proceeded in high gear.[2]

The attack on Klingenmünster began at 4:00 A.M. The first attempt by a platoon from Lieutenant Gary's B Company to blast its way in was repulsed. The tankers then, with the assistance of two assault guns barraged the town until it began to burn. At 4:35, the Panthers and the 409th Infantry Regiment entered, and Klingenmünster was quickly secured.

This victory successfully completed the task force's mission. The Siegfried Line had been broken open. Ahead lay the Rhine River plains and Germany's southern heartland.

For their bravery during this campaign, two of the 761st's tankers, Sergeant Ervin Latimore and Colonel Bates, received Silver Stars; twenty Panthers were awarded Bronze Stars. Among the Bronze Star winners was Sergeant Theodore W. Windsor from Cleveland, Ohio. He was cited for

> heroic achievement in action . . . [as he] successfully led a section of tanks, destroying fourteen pillboxes, neutralizing automatic and sniper fire, capturing one anti-tank gun intact and directing successful

evacuation of his crew members. On one such occasion when his tank was disabled in an enemy tank ditch, Sergeant Windsor remained calm under intense mortar and automatic fire and directed the remaining tanks of his section to cover his vehicle while he succeeded in evacuating his crew without casualties. He then relieved another tank commander and proceeded to exploit the successes gained. Prior to this action Sergeant Windsor had lost two tanks as a result of enemy anti-tank fire and in each instance he successfully returned with his crew to the organization despite extremely dangerous conditions.

Windsor was particularly attached to one of his tanks, which he nicknamed "Taffy." After the war, he remembered his favorite war machine in a poem.

> *To Taffy*
> Oh! Noble tank who bore my name,
> How bravely you did fight!
> In the Saar, the Ardennes, at the Rhine,
> You proved your armored might!
>
> Your guns had roared destruction,
> Your crew had named you well!
> You'd still be in there hitting,
> But the bridge that held you fell.
>
> It tore your turret from you,
> It cracked you like a shell—
> And yet you let your men escape,
> The men you've housed so well!
>
> Mighty tank that is no more—Oh
> Tank that my name bore,
> You'll not be known like "Ironsides,"
> But I shall mourn you more!

The tankers and infantry had, in the words of the 103rd Division's report, "formed a task force which overcame almost insuperable obstacles in shaking loose through the Siegfried's mountain barriers and then made a courageous dash deep into the plain." Major General McAuliffe would write to the men of Task Force Rhine after they reached the river and completed their assignment: "You have fought gallantly and intelligently and you have led all the way. I congratulate you."[3]

If the tankers were receiving the plaudits of their immediate comrades and commanders, they remained—save for Anderson's dispatches to the black press—invisible men in magazines, newsreels, and newspapers back home. "They never recognized the black soldier and what he accomplished," Johnnie Stevens recalls. "We'd complete a mission," he told Miles and Rosenblum, "and up would roll the cameras and they'd roll right past all of those big tanks . . . roll right past us to where the white infantry were gathered and start taking pictures, asking what were their names and where were they from. Then they would show it on the newsreel back here. Not once did they ever stop and take our pictures or get our names or ask where we were from. . . . I even had a sergeant ask me about it. He says, 'Hey! Why the hell don't they take pictures of the tanks?' This was a white sergeant. I just said, 'ummph.' I didn't want to talk about it. . . . See, we had just spearheaded into the town with the infantry and blew up the town and took the town. And then when they came to take the pictures, they took a picture of all the white people. They didn't even stop to say, 'Hiya guys' or nothing, you know? That's just how it was."

Twenty-five years after World War II's conclusion, Hollywood was still denying the facts of African-American participation in combat. As Johnnie Stevens puts it: "The thing that burned me up most of all, they made this picture *Patton*, and after I saw it, I told everybody, 'Don't go!' We spearheaded for Patton all the way across Germany. We took the Maginot Line, the Siegfried Line, the Saar basin, the Remagen Bridge, all of it! Did all that stuff! They didn't show not one black tanker in that picture. Patton's personal driver was a black soldier. Went all the way through Europe, Africa, every which way with him. They didn't even show him in that movie!"

After punching through the Siegfried, the Panthers were ordered to join the 71st Infantry Division at Lagenselbold, on the other side of the Rhine, for the final sweep through Germany. The battalion road-marched for some 130 miles, crossing the river at Oppenheim on March 30 and rendezvousing two days later with the 71st. The tankers went into action immediately; Lieutenant Harold B. Gary's platoon killed three hundred German infantrymen and captured five hundred more.

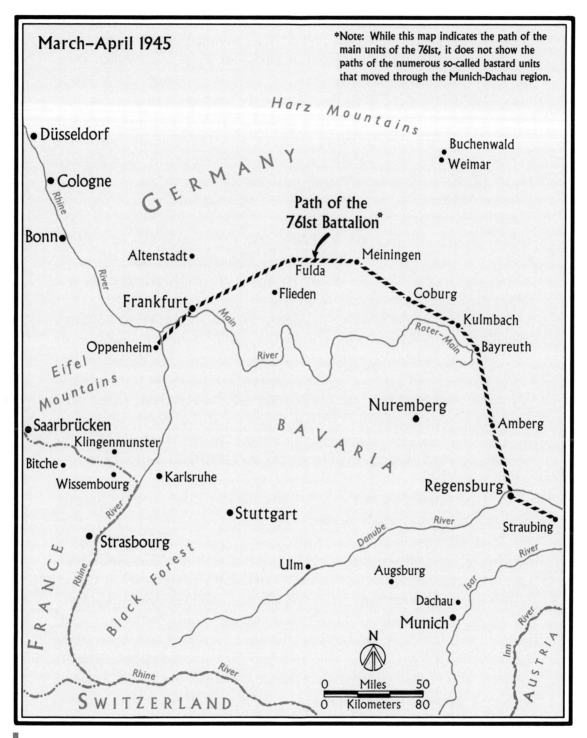

March–April 1945

*Note: While this map indicates the path of the main units of the 761st, it does not show the paths of the numerous so-called bastard units that moved through the Munich-Dachau region.

Harz Mountains

Düsseldorf

Buchenwald
Weimar

GERMANY

Cologne

Rhine

Bonn

Altenstadt

Path of the
761st Battalion*

Meiningen

Fulda

River

Frankfurt

Flieden

Coburg

Kulmbach

Main

Roter-Main

Bayreuth

Oppenheim

River

Eifel
Mountains

Nuremberg

BAVARIA

Saarbrücken

Amberg

Klingenmunster

Bitche

Karlsruhe

Wissembourg

Regensburg

River

Stuttgart

River

Straubing

Danube

Strasbourg

Rhine

Black Forest

Ulm

Augsburg

River

Isar

FRANCE

Dachau

Munich

N

Inn River

AUSTRIA

Rhine   River

0   Miles   50

0   Kilometers   80

SWITZERLAND

The 761st led the American march through Bavaria in the final phase of the ground war.

213

Although the Reich's impending defeat had been clear since the Bulge, many of the Wehrmacht's battle-hardened soldiers were not about to lay down their arms. Few units were more loyal to the Nazi cause than the 6th SS Mountain Division, Nord, the Panthers' adversaries during this stage of the conflict. These troops were desperately attempting to fight their way through the American lines while, at the same time, the 71st and the 761st were trying to encircle them and prevent their escape.

Over the Easter weekend, fighting raged through the forests and small towns in the region. German casualties were heavy; thousands were taken prisoner. By April 3, the encirclement operation was complete. Soon the 6th SS Mountain Division, Nord, was no more, its SS stalwarts dead, captured, or in disorganized retreat, with the Black Panthers in pursuit.

The chase ranged eastward to Fulda, a small city near the Czechoslovakian border. B Company continued its exemplary performance, clearing the woods outside the town of SS defenders, knocking out ten machine gun nests, and taking five hundred prisoners in the process.

After Fulda fell, the tankers continued east to Meiningen. There, Trezzvant Anderson reports, Sergeant Jonathan B. Hall and his crew witnessed a grisly scene that demonstrated, in equal measure, the fanaticism and the racism that characterized the SS troopers. As Hall prepared to take one of them prisoner, the soldier declared that he would never surrender to blacks. He pulled out a razor and, while the astonished tankers looked on, slashed his throat from ear to ear. The German fell, writhing, to the ground. Slowly, agonizingly bleeding to death, the Blackshirt sacrificed himself to his Führer's demented dream.

As most of the battalion's elements now turned south toward the Bavarian cities of Coburg, Kulmbach, Bayreuth, and Regensburg, "bastard platoons" of the 761st were spearheading for infantry units throughout Germany. On the morning of April 11, one such platoon—fighting with the Third Army—was approaching the historic city of Weimar. Weimar had been renowned as a center of high German culture. In the eighteenth and nineteenth centuries, it was home to Goethe, Schiller, Bach, and Liszt. In this century, Weimar had been the original site of Walter Gropius's Bauhaus, the most influential institution in the history of modern art, architecture, and design. It was also the birthplace of Germany's short-lived attempt at democracy, the Weimar Republic, whose turbulent existence was brought to an end by Adolf Hitler and his Nazi followers. To many people today, however, Weimar has a single association: Buchenwald.

214

On April 5, 1945, Ben Bender, suffering from a high fever, made his way to the camp hospital. "I thought I was dying," he told Miles and Rosenblum, "and to look for help in Buchenwald was almost impossible. Whoever got sick and went to ask for help was killed with an injection of carbolic acid into his heart. In a matter of two minutes, the person was dead. But I was naive. I departed from my brother [Berick] and I went to this hospital. And I was accepted. It was all sheer luck."

Bender waited in the admissions area with a hundred other seriously ill prisoners. A young female doctor entered, looked the group over, then announced that there would be no hospitalizations that day. "I began to walk out. Then I heard, in German, 'Du!' which means 'you.' A lot of people responded. He said, 'No, *you*!' I say, 'Me?' He answers, 'Yes.' He was dark, maybe thirty-five, and balding. He looked at me and said, 'Are you a Jew?' 'Yes,' I said, 'I am a Jew.'

Children of Buchenwald.

He looked at me, and he said, 'You know, there is a resemblance between you and my brother. I will try to save your life, even though I am endangering my-self, because if they find out that you are a Jew and I did it, they will kill me right away.' "

Bender was placed in a tiny room with a little mirror. "I looked into the mirror and then looked back," he said. "I didn't recognize myself. . . . This was the way a person—when he dies—looked. I looked back again and then I moved forward so I can be sure this was myself. . . . The doctor came back and I got a beautiful bed, with white sheets. . . . The feeling was unbelievable. I went to a rest room because that was the first time I could sit on toilets. In Buchenwald, there were no toilet seats."

On April 10, Ben Bender watched from his hospital room window as SS guards attempted to evacuate the camp. The Nazis had planned to murder all of Buchenwald's inmates before the American forces arrived. "This was the in-famous death march, where they took about three thousand Jews and six hundred

Russian prisoners of war. And they killed them in cold blood outside Buchenwald. It was a horrible scene," he recalled. "I saw thousands of inmates refusing to go and lying on the ground, covered with blankets. And the SS soldiers were shooting them, one by one. And dragging them, with force. And those people went to their death." Among the doomed, though Ben did not yet know it, was nineteen-year-old Berick Bender.

The next morning, Ben Bender was again at his window: "I saw Germans escaping on foot, on bikes, on horses. Shots were being fired. And then an airplane appeared in the sky for a few minutes. It lowered and then disappeared. And then I saw soldiers and then a tank. And I saw soldiers moving by the hundreds into this place."

The tankers from the 761st broke through the Buchenwald gates and, with their accompanying infantrymen, quickly ended resistance from the SS guards. Ben Bender's recollections "are still vivid—black soldiers of the Third Army, tall and strong, crying like babies, carrying the emaciated bodies of the liberated

Ben Bender.

prisoners. I was seventeen, and my life was almost extinguished. For me, it was an instant awakening of life after a long darkness. . . . I was seeing black soldiers for the first time in my life, crying like babies, carrying the dead and the starved and trying to help everybody. That's the way it was."

Johnnie Stevens recalls: "We were only there a little while, because as tankers we didn't stay anywhere long, we'd keep on moving. We shot up the place and chased the guards out of there. It was a sight I never want to see again, I'll tell you that. I jumped out of the tank, and there were people all over the place. . . . They could barely walk, and they're coming at you with their hands held halfway out, their eyes all

Abe Chapnick.

sunk in their heads. They're skin and bone. The women looking like something out of a horror movie—you know how they make those horror movies with women with long hair but their faces are all drawn and eyes sunk in their faces. It was an awesome sight. And I'd been used to death and killing; that was just something you're trained for. You weren't trained for this kind of inhumane treatment of people. They train you to kill a person or you let him go. You don't torture him, you just shoot him—which I didn't mind doing. It was just my job."

Elie Wiesel, Nobel laureate in peace, has written that "the most moving moment of my life was the day the Americans arrived. It was the morning of April 11. I will always remember with love a big black soldier. He was crying like a child—tears of all the pain in the world and all the rage. Everyone who was there that day will forever feel a sentiment of gratitude to the American soldiers who liberated us."[4]

Abe Chapnick had been born in Lodz, Poland. Transported to Buchenwald in January 1945 from a Nazi labor camp in his native land, he was one of the thousands of prisoners who—as the Red Army continued its westward advance—were transported in cattle cars from Polish labor and death camps to similar installations on German soil. Chapnick was fifteen years old on that April morning.

"They were a rarity to me because I never saw a black person before," Chapnick told Miles and Rosenblum. "It was as if someone came from the outer limits and would want to save us. They were like any other person who would take me out of bondage. We smiled at one another, made eye contact. We understood each other without speaking a word."

The tankers and riflemen rapidly subdued the SS guards and, within hours, moved on out of the camp. The terrible task of burying the dead and sanitizing the area fell, in the main, to the African-American members of the 183rd Battalion of Combat Engineers. William Scott, an Atlanta journalist in civilian life, photographed the scene. Leon Bass also entered Buchenwald with the 183rd. "When we walked through those gates," he says, "I saw in front of me the walking dead. There they stood. They were skin and bone. They had skeletal faces with deep-set eyes. Their heads had been clean shaved. They were holding each other for stability. I couldn't understand this. I just couldn't. So I walked around the camp; I wanted to see more. To understand more. I went to a building where they stored body parts from 'medical experiments' in jars of formalde-

William Scott III.

hyde. I saw fingers and eyes and the hearts and genitals. As I was leaving this building, I saw mounds of little children's clothing. Little children who didn't survive. I saw their sweaters, their caps, their booties. All of those things that belong to little children. But I never saw a child. . . . If this could happen here, it could happen anywhere. It could happen to me. It could happen to black folks in America. . . . I often wonder what I would have done if, in 1939, my family and I had been caught up in this and for all those years nobody, but nobody, would help us. I would have been a bitter man . . . and I thought about how many times my people were lynched and mistreated across this country and nobody raised a voice."

Abe Chapnick remembers seeing General George Patton at Buchenwald: "He came into camp with his two pearl-handled .45's. I didn't know what they were at the time. I thought they were like toy revolvers, but I found out afterward that they were .45's. He came in sitting on top of the jeep like a real cowboy."

The general's reaction to the horrific sights of Buchenwald can be categorized, at the least, as bizarre. His biographer Martin Blumenson writes:

Black soldiers view remains in a crematorium.

In his gloom he worried over questions looming large in his mind. Why had he not been allowed to seize Berlin ahead of the Russians? Who was going to curb the power of the Bolsheviks? What was to be the future of Europe, the fate of Germany? How could he enforce de-nazification when he was out of sympathy with the concept? The authentic non-Nazis were those liberated from the internment camps, and they seemed to be labor leaders, Jews, and communists. Unable to differentiate among them, he came to believe that they all formed an international conspiracy working for the downfall of the United States. It must be they who were setting detestable policies and ruining the prospects for stable social order. He could no longer repress the more or less natural anti-Semitism endemic to his milieu and he lapsed into the neurotic comfort of old and stereotyped attitudes.[5]

Patton's beliefs were reflected in a letter to his wife, Beatrice. "I had never heard that we fought to de-nazify Germany—live and learn. What we are doing is to utterly destroy the only semi-modern state in Europe so that Russia can swallow the whole . . . actually the Germans are the only decent people in Europe." The troublemakers, he believed, according to Blumenson, "must be the Jews who wanted revenge and whose newspapers were shaping public opinion to their ends. He made no secret of 'my personal feelings against them.' "[6]

His position on denazification brought the Third Army's leader into sharp conflict with his commander, Dwight D. Eisenhower. Ike was committed to the destruction of Nazism. He was determined to "uproot [and punish] the whole Nazi organization." Only then, he believed, could victory be assured.

In his diary, Patton recorded his innermost thoughts on the Nazis' victims: "Everyone believes that the displaced person is a human being, which he is not, and this applies particularly to the Jews who are lower than animals. Either the displaced persons never had a sense of decency or else they lost it during their period of internment by the Germans. My personal opinion is that no people could have sunk to the level of degradation these have reached in the short space of four years."[7]

German citizens forced to witness the mass burial of camp victims.

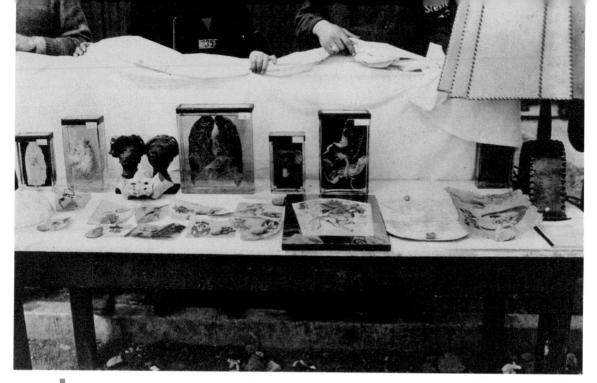

Soldiers display Nazi "trophy table."

Wedding rings
confiscated by
Germans from
camp victims.

In September 1945, while serving as military governor of eastern Bavaria, "Old Blood and Guts" went public with his views. The venue was a news conference. The reaction in the States was harsh. Eisenhower, in response, transferred Patton to a much less visible post, at Fifteenth Army Headquarters in Bad Nauheim. Patton wrote in his diary: "There is a very apparent Semitic element in the press."[8] This element, he believed, was in the service of the Communist cause.

Clearly, the great American general had little empathy with the likes of a Ben Bender. Leaving the Buchenwald hospital on liberation day, Bender went first to the camp's main gate. "When I departed from my brother, we made a promise that we would meet at the gate. I walked there looking for him. But he didn't keep his promise. I never met him again. He had been killed." Then Ben walked to Weimar, a mile or so away.

"I remember trucks were moving back and forth, honking. I didn't hear anything. For the first time, you know, I realized how lonely I was. All by myself, seventeen years old. No parents, no brother. To whom do you turn? To whom do you talk? I came to a bridge, and it was half destroyed. I looked over the rail. I wanted to commit suicide. I just had the urge to jump into this murky, oily water and to finish, you know? I just wanted it to end. I even envisioned the fall. I was thinking liberation should be a matter of joy, of laughter. Not like this . . . when you are almost destroyed. But then, in a flash of a second, I realized that

A newly liberated "enemy of the Reich."

this would be a very easy solution, after so many years of struggle and deprivation and despair. Why now? If I am alive, I have to give the message to other people. When you share joy, you share suffering too."

Ben, weak from his exertions, gaunt, head shaven, wearing prison garb, took a train back to the camp. No one tried to collect his fare. In his compartment was a German girl, blond, blue-eyed, and seventeen. She looked at him and asked a question: "Are you from . . . ?" He answered, "Yes, I am from there." She told him how sorry she was. Her expression of sorrow infuriated him. Then she said, "My father was in the Wehrmacht." Ben Bender remembers his reaction: " 'Yes, Yes!' I responded. 'Everyone was serving in the Wehrmacht. The SS was nonexistent!' I explained [it] all to her, and when the train stopped, she stretched out her hand to me. And at that very moment, I didn't know what to do . . . if I should shake her hand, if I should look at her and say, 'Thank you for . . .' But I saw tears in her eyes and I shook . . . I shook her hand."

On the morning of Buchenwald's liberation, the primary elements of the 761st Tank Battalion approached the historic city of Coburg. The Germans were not prepared to surrender the city without a struggle. Throughout April 11 and well into the following day, the Panthers blasted Coburg's Wehrmacht defenders. In the late morning of the twelfth, the tankers and infantrymen from the 71st Division took the city. The conquerors ate dinner, Trezzvant Anderson reports, "in the shadow of a monument in the city square depicting a Negro Dominican friar [Saint Maurice] who had been sainted hundreds of years before. . . . The tankers were refreshed by spirits from a factory that had been making the stuff that goes in 'the cup that cheers.' Fresh eggs, chicken and wine added to the comfort along with the opportunity to get into a good warm bed [in requisitioned houses] for the first time in many days."[9]

Good food was always a prized commodity to the men on the front lines. Walter Lewis writes of one of his "very best buddies in the war," Sergeant Samuel Allen of Richmond, Virginia:

[He] worked in the maintenance department and operated a tank retriever and was another of our unsung heroes, going up to the front many times under heavy artillery fire and bringing the disabled tank back and making it ready for combat once again. Sam could be depended on for many things. Good repair work, something to eat, something to drink and shelter. He would always have some smoked

Coburg, Germany.

meat, fresh eggs or a bottle of Schnapps ["liberated" from farms and shops] when we pulled back for a short rest or maintenance on our tanks.

During the battalion's two-day breather in Coburg, Sergeant Johnnie Stevens received some long-delayed news about an event half a world away. "It took so long for mail to catch up with us, because we were moving so fast," he told his interviewers, Miles and Rosenblum. "I was told to get back to headquarters. So I jumped in a jeep and [went there]. The guy said, 'We've got a message for you.' It came through the Red Cross. He says, 'Your brother's been killed at Tarawa.' I just went on back to my tank, [saying to myself] yeah, my brother just got killed, taking the beachhead at Tarawa in the South Pacific. See, the war did our family bad. I had a brother killed, an uncle killed, a cousin shot down. I had another cousin, he was shot down over Italy. My dad was a soldier. We came from a family of soldiers. All fighters, all of us."

225

Black soldier with captured German soldier.

Moving out of Coburg toward Bayreuth—a key objective because of its location on the Berlin-Munich Autobahn—the Panthers and their infantry cohorts attacked the city of Kulmbach on April 14. Resistance was at first stiff, but after a few hours, the Germans surrendered. The American forces, now moving along a front bounded by the Weisse River on the east and the Roter Main River on the west, reached Bayreuth on April 16. The Wehrmacht defenders rejected an American demand that they yield. They fought fiercely, for the better part of two days, before capitulating. The capture of Bayreuth, a city devoted to the memory and works of one of Hitler's icons, the composer Richard Wagner, gave Patton's forces another direct access to Munich and beyond to Austria while the Red Army continued its inexorable movement across Eastern Europe.

On April 18, one week after he learned of his brother's death on a Pacific island, Johnnie Stevens earned a Bronze Star for his actions in the vicinity of Neu, a village near Bayreuth. His citation calls attention to Stevens's ordering his tank platoon to support the infantry elements to which it was attached.

> He unhesitatingly brought them to the scene of the action. By prompt and vigorous action his section, advancing to the head of the infantry, eliminated the enemy's position without casualties among our troops. The aggressive action of Sergeant Stevens and his platoon resulted in eight enemy dead and thirty-four taken prisoner. His courage and devotion to duty reflect the highest credit upon himself and the Armed Forces of the United States.

Colonel Paul Bates related to William Miles an incident that took place during the battalion's push through Bavaria, spearheading for the 71st Infantry. Bates received a call from a regimental commander at division headquarters, who angrily complained that one of his units, caught in a mine field, had been abandoned by a 761st tank crew. Bates hurried to the scene of the alleged desertion. There he saw some fifteen or twenty dead infantrymen lying in the field. He also saw one of the battalion's tanks.

"You tell the guys [in training] that if you hit a mine, get the hell out of that tank as fast as you can. Because [an artillery shell] is going to hit you because they want to burn that tank up or explode it so it can't be repaired and used again. We beat it into their heads that when you get out of the tank, you'll see your tread marks and you can walk away by walking in those treads, because if any mines were there, they would already have detonated." Bates walked through the tread marks to the tank. He saw that it was empty and that it had been disabled by a mine.

"I went back to division headquarters and I told them that whoever complained 'is a goddamned fool. He's simply got badly trained soldiers. You're going against a fortified position, so you know damn well there's going to be a mine field. If you've got any sense, you tell your infantry to go behind the tank; it's a shield. Walk down the tread marks. Don't blame my tankers, they did what they were supposed to do, but *you* didn't tell your people what *they* were supposed to do.' So the guy says, 'Well, you know, it's all right. It's all right.' Those are the kind of thanks they gave you."

American soldiers in mess line, Camp Breckinridge, Kentucky, 1943.

For a few days the tankers' campaign through Bavaria was almost a romp as they rolled through towns where the good burghers had festooned their windows with the white flags of surrender.

Along the highways, the 761st now encountered masses of bedraggled, emaciated Russian prisoners of war, newly freed by Nazi captors who could no longer maintain their prison camps. Trezzvant Anderson remembers them as "frail, thin, tired and drawn. Hunger marked their countenances with cheek bones showing through the skin, with some of them so weak they could hardly walk, and being supported by comrades who were equally as weak as they. It was a pathetic scene."

One day toward the end of April, Walter Lewis writes:

We were slowly moving in column formation down a road somewhere in Bavaria when the very sad news came. Large contingents of German prisoners of war, prodded by U.S. infantrymen, were march-

228

ing past us, hands over their heads in total evidence of defeat. We had a fifty-gallon drum of raw cognac encased in a wicker basket strapped on the back of our tank. This was taken from a cognac factory we had overrun sometime earlier. Some infantrymen asked us for some, and we told them to jump on the back of our tank and help themselves. One of them said, "Too bad about Roosevelt, isn't it?" We learned then that he was dead.

The tankers continued on toward one of the German military's most important centers in Bavaria, the ancient city of Regensburg, situated where the Danube and Isar rivers meet, at the hub of a network of highways that reached to many of the Wehrmacht's installations in southeastern Germany.

On the way, the Panthers took eight towns, at the cost of many German lives. At Bernath, for example, B Company alone killed three hundred infantrymen, wounded another hundred, and took seventy-five prisoners.

"We were east of Regensburg and had just crossed the Danube," Paul Bates recalled. "We had a pontoon bridge in, and of course, as the tanks were approaching the thing, the ground kept getting softer and softer, and some of the guys found a gravel pit not far away. While we're putting the damn stuff in, there's a siren, and here's Patton in his jeep with his big silver helmet and his two pistols and a fifty-caliber machine gun manned by his aide. And he comes right up toward this damn pontoon bridge and the jeep sinks down to its frame in the mud. There isn't a word spoken. Every guy ran to that jeep. They picked the thing up and carried it over, put it on the bridge and [held their breaths]. The only thing Patton did, he had a riding crop, and one of the guys helping was a warrant officer of mine, and he patted him on the back with his riding crop and said, 'Nice going, man.' "

The Black Panthers had, by mid-April, fought their way through five European nations against the best the Wehrmacht and the Waffen SS had to offer. The "bastard platoons" that had liberated Buchenwald were still fighting in Prussia, hundreds of miles removed from the main elements in the south. Therefore a large majority of the tankers, though they had seen death—of friends and foes—in its many hideous guises, were still totally unprepared for the sights awaiting them at Dachau.

CHAPTER 10

I saw this large gate. SS soldiers were in front of the gate, shooting people with machine guns. My bow gunner knocked them out. . . . And there were more SS soldiers, shooting people in what looked like a big barn . . . and bodies were stacked on top of one another. And they were burning—you could see the smoke coming from the bodies—and the people were trying to climb over one another, trying to get out. And as fast as they were trying to get out, the SS were just shooting them.

William McBurney

Charred bodies are all that remain after mass burning of inmates by Nazis.

Each morning at Dachau, the inmates were lined up for roll call. From everywhere in the installation, they could see—in large white letters painted on the side of a building—the camp's cruelly ironic motto:

Es gibt einen Weg zur Freiheit. Seine Meilensteine heissen:
Geohorsem, Sauberkeit, Nüchternheit, Fleiss.
(There is a road to freedom. Its milestones are:
obedience, cleanliness, sobriety, industry.)

During Dachau's twelve-year existence, some 230,000 prisoners were interned there and at its subsidiary camps. During the war years, the facility's population fluctuated between 22,000 and 30,000 prisoners—three times its intended capacity. In the first months of 1945, as prisoners were brought in from the east, Dachau's population ballooned to more than 60,000; many of these new arrivals, from Auschwitz and other camps, would die of starvation and typhus.

Samuel Pisar was transported to one of Dachau's satellite installations late in 1944. "We arrived in winter," Pisar—who had been imprisoned first at Auschwitz and then at Buchenwald—told Rosenblum and Miles, "and there were a few barracks but no other facilities. So we had to dig the ground and pour the cement and cut the logs. And it was freezing cold and we were very hungry. The German SS men were our guards. . . . There was tremendous violence going on here, every day and night. They had vicious German shepherd dogs, and it was no fun. Many of my friends died right there. And of course, I still don't know how I made it. I was barely fifteen years old.

"This was a hard-labor camp," Pisar continued. "People died here through hard work, hunger, punishment, freezing cold. Smelly, thin soup and a tiny piece of bread, twice a day. There has never been such slave labor, not even in the Deep South. And Uncle Tom, whatever he suffered, he didn't suffer like that. . . . I'd been to school, and I had read *Uncle Tom's Cabin,* and I always remembered Simon Legree and Tom. Except for us it was probably many, many times worse, because here the Simon Legrees were the greatest monsters that ever lived. Sadistic, violent. Kill a human being at the drop of a hat. [They] didn't have a gas chamber; here the executions were by firing squad and through hanging."

Early in April, the SS started moving inmates from subsidiary camps to the main facility at Dachau. Samuel Pisar was one of them. "I don't know the exact date, because not only did I have no watch and no sense of time, but I was hallucinating with hunger. We knew we were close to the end of the war be-

April–May 1945

Torun

Wista River

GERMANY

Berlin

Magdeburg

Poznan

POLAND

LODZ

Elbe

Oder

BUCHENWALD

Leipzig

River

Giogau

Breslau

River

Weimar

Dresden

Chemnitz

AUSCHWITZ

Prague

Nuremberg

CZECHOSLOVAKIA

BAVARIA

N

Danube   River

Danube

DACHAU

River

Linz

River

Isar

Munich

River

Vienna

Salzburg

Inn

Enns River

AUSTRIA

0   Miles   100

0   Kilometers   160

Elements of the 761st joined in the liberation of Dachau and Buchenwald.

cause we could hear cannon shots in the distance. . . . And we saw American and British planes flying in for bombing missions. And while to our captors this was something that inspired fear, to us it was a message of hope. [The move] back to Dachau was something that worried us, because we felt that Dachau was a place where they would be extremely likely to do away with us. They lined us up and marched us away. The main roads were clogged by military convoys, so they had to take us the long way through side roads, forests, fields . . . I think for three or four days. But this was the way it had always been, and we were used to that."

During the trek, Sam Pisar and his two close friends, Ben and Nico, kept together in the column of three or four thousand marchers. "While many were falling like flies from exhaustion, from hunger," Pisar says, "we kept at it. And one bright morning, three American planes came down very low, thinking we were a military column, and started strafing us. The guards hit the dirt, and Nico, who was the oldest of the three of us, suddenly said to Ben and me, 'Get up and run after me.' And we started to run. As we discovered later, fourteen of us made a break for the forest as the American planes were machine-gunning the entire column. And as we ran, nine were shot. Of the five who made it into the forest, Nico, Ben, and yours truly were among them. And we ran and ran and ran until we couldn't run any longer. And deep in the forest, we stopped. It was early spring, and we simply fell asleep, and we must have slept for hours and hours, because we woke up in the middle of the night."

Waking from their exhausted sleep, Samuel Pisar and his fellow escapees could hear the distant rumbling of artillery fire. Where those guns were, they reasoned, must be the battlefront, and there lay hope of finding refuge with Allied forces. Despite their debilitated condition, the five young men began to walk in the direction of the sounds of warfare. They traveled only at night; their days were spent hiding in the forests and woods. Food was scavenged whenever possible. One rainy night, the young men stumbled upon a very heavily guarded German military airstrip. But their good fortune held, and, undetected, they stealthily fled the area.

The bedraggled group walked on through the rain. "We were tired," Pisar told his interviewers, "and there was danger all over the place. Suddenly we came upon a barn. So we broke in and discovered it was paradise, full of straw and it had a loft upstairs, so we climbed up and went to sleep. And we slept and slept and slept. We decided not to take any risks. We decided this was where we could try and sit it out. Occasionally I would go out and steal some food from the farms. I was a young kid and I had already stolen for myself some Bavarian leather pants. I looked like a peasant boy, except that my head was completely shaved. But I would come back regularly with loaves of bread, eggs, which we ate raw, tomatoes, and cucumbers. For once, we were not hungry, and there was water outside in a trough. Most of all we stayed still. Even though it was peaceful and quiet, it was also dangerous. From time to time, armed German soldiers would come downstairs—take a sleep, have a smoke—while we would sit paralyzed, trying to stay still. They could hear nothing. Then they would leave. No one knew we were there."

Pisar is not sure how many days passed this way. "We were very, very content." On the sunny afternoon of April 24, he was awakened from a deep sleep by the noises of occasional cannon fire and an ever louder humming sound. "I ran down the ladder and looked out through the slats and I saw a tank. I tried

Elements of the 761st in Germany.

to find the hated swastika, and I couldn't find it. Instead, all I could see was a white star. What is a white star? Why a white star? And suddenly it blew my mind; I realized that after four years of slavery, torture, hunger, I was actually looking at the insignia of the U.S. Army. I started to yell. 'Nico, Ben! Come here and take a look!' And like a madman, I ran out toward the tank. It was a stupid thing to do, because I was in the middle of a battlefield. Machine guns were barking, bullets were flying on all sides. But by then I thought nothing could destroy me; I had taken so many risks and been so close to death, and freedom was coming at me and I couldn't just stand there. I couldn't stop; I was just running and running, closer to the tank. Suddenly its cannon let out a belch. And all the firing ceased. And as I approached, the hatch opened and a tall, helmeted black man climbed out. I had never seen a black man before. I thought, Maybe he has soot on his face."

The tanker came up to young Pisar, who was in the line of fire, swearing in a language he did not understand. "I didn't know how to signal him . . . how to explain that I was a prisoner, that I needed help. He must have seen that I was weak, maybe sick-looking, with a shaven head. But it was a dangerous situation, so the only thing I could think of was to kneel, to put my arms around his legs and begin to yell, in the few words of English my mother had sighed when she prayed for our deliverance, 'God bless America!' And that he understood. He picked me up in his arms, he led me to the tank and took me with him through the hatch and into the womb of freedom."

235

Death march from Dachau.

It would be nearly forty years before Pisar learned the name of his African-American liberator, from whom he was soon separated. In 1982, Pisar, now a prominent international lawyer and the author of *Blood and Hope*, a memoir of his experiences, received a letter from a Los Angeles woman, Mrs. Valerie Crowley, who had been watching as he recounted history in a television interview. It resembled, she wrote, stories that her brother used to tell about how, on a German battlefield, he had saved the life of an emaciated kid with a shaven head. Mrs. Crowley and Pisar corresponded, and he ascertained that her brother, the late Bill Ellington of the 761st Tank Battalion, was indeed his rescuer. Pisar could no longer thank his "savior" in person, but, he says, "I cannot forget the moment when a black man gave me freedom and life. It's an automatic process. I feel it in my guts."

By the week of April 16, Dachau officials, knowing that the American forces, advancing rapidly through Bavaria, would inevitably reach the camp, began to destroy records and documents in a futile attempt to dispose of the paper evidence of their crimes against humanity. By April 27, the decision had been taken to destroy the human evidence as well.

The masters of Dachau adopted the death march strategy that had been employed at Buchenwald two weeks earlier. On the morning of the twenty-seventh, nearly six thousand near-starving Jewish, Russian, and German prisoners were trooped out of the camp. South of Munich, their SS guards machine-gunned the captives. Only sixty prisoners survived this massacre. "They lined us up and marched us away," one survivor testifies. "The main roads were clogged by military convoys, so they had to take us the long way through side roads, forests, fields . . . I think for three or four days. We lacked water. We lacked food. We were marching in wooden clogs and striped uniforms. The guards were having a field day taking potshots at prisoners from time to time. But this was the way it had always been, and we were used to that."

In the early hours of April 29, Adolf Hitler, in his Berlin bunker, wrote and signed his so-called Political Testament. "The war," he wrote, "was wanted and provoked only by those international statesmen who were either of Jewish origins or worked for Jewish interests." The Führer finally realized that the war was over, but, he wrote, it had not been in vain, for "the seed has been sown that will grow one day . . . to the glorious rebirth of the National Socialist movement in a truly united nation. . . . Above all, I enjoin the government and the people to uphold the racial laws to limit and to resist mercilessly the poisoner of all nations, international Jewry."[1] At 4:00 A.M., he called in Joseph Goebbels, Martin Bormann, and two generals to witness his signature.

Not many hours later, tankers from the 761st, rolling some distance ahead of a column of infantry, were unknowingly approaching Dachau.

Dachau wasn't an objective, William McBurney recalled, "it was an obstacle. I didn't know where the hell I was. I was just going through the place."

"We didn't know what it was," Leonard "Smitty" Smith told Miles and Rosenblum, "until the firing stopped, and all of a sudden, we see these prisoners come back out. Buck naked, looked like skeletons, just crawling."

Prisoners remove body with ice tongs.

237

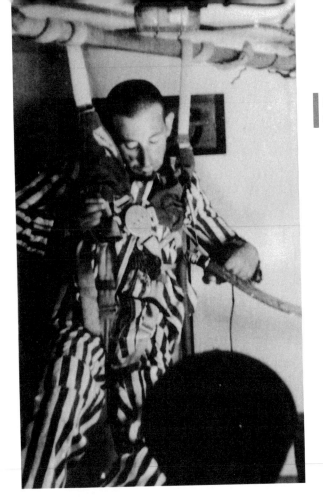

Inmate subjected to low-pressure experiment.

Disinfection room at Dachau.

The tankers, confronting this mass of starving human beings, followed their natural impulses and began to offer them food. Several of the men, however, realized that this was dangerous and shouted to their comrades: "Don't feed them! Don't feed them!"

Walter Lewis's crew did not get that message in time. "We didn't know better," he writes, agonizingly, in "Diary of a Gunner." "We gave them some of our food. They ate and fell to the ground, writhing in pain. Natural food, at this stage of starvation, [brought] death! What this did to our morale words cannot describe and I am unable to record. Here we were unwittingly killing human beings who had done us no harm. Oh! The pity of it all, and may God have mercy on our wretched souls for our stupid blunders."

"We pulled into Dachau, after the medium tanks had taken it," Lewis recalled. "I was commanding a platoon of five light tanks. One of my drivers says, 'Sarge, go in there and see what's happening.' So I got down and went into a building, and the smell of burnt bodies stifled you. I said, 'Oh, my God, I can't stand this.' I put my handkerchief to my nose and walked to a furnace. I opened it and I saw a burnt body. . . . I said, 'Oh, no, it can't be.' I went to the next one and opened it and . . . 'it can't be.' Against the wall were people, I guess the ones who would have gone into the furnaces if we hadn't got there, and they were moaning and groaning. I just looked at them; they were dying from malnutrition. Then I went in the back to what they called the shower room. I didn't go in, I just peeked through the window because I feared that maybe the gas was still on. I came out and went to my tank, and I sat and I cried. My gunner says, 'What's happening, Sarge?' I said, 'Oh, nothing.' The tears came out of my eyes. I cried and I said to God, 'How could a man give such an order, so cruel to human beings?' Regardless of the war."

The tankers received orders to head out of Dachau in pursuit of German troops elsewhere in the vicinity. Other American forces entered to finish the task of liberation. The first of these, in another of the war's incredible ironies, were members of the 442nd Regimental Combat Team, most of whose members had enlisted out of concentration camps established by the United States government. They had joined the army, according to Rudy Tokiwa, because "if we wanted to live in this country—and it is the only country we know—we had better show that we are as loyal as anyone else. If there are no volunteers, it will give the President a real good reason to say, 'It's a good thing we put them there. See: they're not loyal.' So we joined."[2] Indeed, these Japanese-Americans more than proved their point; the 442nd was the most decorated, and had the highest casualty rate, of any unit its size in World War II.

An article in the November 11, 1991, issue of *The New Yorker* magazine describes the reaction of one inmate, Janina Cywinska:

> I was standing with a blindfold waiting to be shot, but the shot didn't come. So I asked the woman next to me, "Do you think they're trying to make us crazy, so we'll run and they won't have to feel guilty about shooting us?" She said, "Well, we're not going to run. We'll just stand here." So we stood and stood and suddenly someone was tugging at my blindfold. He tugged this way and that way, and then he jumped up because he was short and he pulled it off. I saw him and I thought, "Oh, now the *Japanese* are going to kill us." And I didn't care anymore. I said, "Just kill us, get it over with." He tried to convince me that he was an American and wouldn't kill me. I said, "Oh, no, you're a Japanese and you're going to kill us." We went back and forth, and finally he landed on his knees, crying, with his hands over his face, and he said, "You are free now. We are *American* Japanese. You are free."[3]

The army ordered the Nisei soldiers never—under pain of court-martial—to reveal their role in the liberation of Dachau, so that soldiers of Japanese descent would not receive their rightful share of credit for this heroic effort.

Nisei soldiers.

Dachau prisoners cheering their liberators. (Prisoners wearing striped suits were destined for the crematorium.)

As at Buchenwald, the job of cleaning up the camp fell, in large part, to elements of the 183rd Battalion of Combat Engineers.

Paul Parks, a combat engineer from Indianapolis, remembered that on arriving at Dachau, "we assumed that it was an army camp, because we didn't know anything about concentration camps. No one had briefed us or told us about them. I had read William L. Shirer's *Berlin Diary* before I went into the army, so I knew a bit about the problems the Jews had in Germany, but I didn't know about the camps. We entered Dachau, and [the inmates] wanted to hug us or hold us. We felt uncomfortable because they were dirty and had sores and were in all kinds of states of emaciation. Later we felt embarrassed about our being uncomfortable, but at that moment, we didn't know what we were dealing with, and our officers were aghast."

A man came out of one of the barracks and, speaking English, approached Parks. "He said, 'Just sit down for a minute.' So we sat on the ground and I asked, 'Why were these people killed?' He answered, 'Only because we're Jews.' I said, 'That doesn't make any sense to me.' So he kept talking and explained to me how they had come there and what had happened. And finally I told him—he was a rabbi—'I think I begin to understand,' because there's one other

Inside a bunker at Dachau.

great incident of inhumanity that I'm very familiar with, the three hundred years of slavery in my own country, where people for generations were not allowed to be free, subject to the dictates of another race. Held in bondage, forced to work, and forced to do what another person wanted you to do. And if you didn't obey, there were no laws against killing you and destroying your family. So I said, 'As you talk, I see that there's a close parallel between the history of my people in America and what's happened to the Jews in Europe.' "

His experience in the camps had a profound effect upon Parks, who in later years would be closely associated with Dr. Martin Luther King, Jr., and the civil rights movement, both as an activist and as a public official who served as secretary of education in Massachusetts during the height of the school busing battles in Boston during the 1960s. "Emotionally and psychologically, seeing the camps and being involved in Dachau said to me that unless we do something about seeing that more people have their rights and freedoms, this can occur again. That whenever we acquiesce to the point where we say it is reasonable to do *this* to someone, that is wrong. So when I came back to the States I had one thing in mind—that I had a legitimate right to fight for my freedom and rights, because I had served this country and served it well."

Colonel Lewis Weinstein, from General Eisenhower's staff, arrived at Dachau several days after liberation. He had previously inspected the killing grounds at Buchenwald. Weinstein recollects: "My driver didn't want to go into the camp. He said, 'Colonel, I can't take it here anymore.' I said, 'Well, you stay here with your jeep.' I found a young captain who took me over the camp . . . the enormity of the number of bodies around, thousands and thousands of bodies. Then we came to piles that had been heaped up, orderly in some cases, like a stack of logs; other places, helter-skelter. Many people died before my eyes. I stood beside one medic who was working on a victim, and the man finally died. The medic said to me, 'Why is it that there's no respect for life?' We both said a prayer together. Mine was partly in Hebrew and partly in English. I said the prayers for the dying and the dead, the Sh'ma Israel and the Kaddish. And when we finished, we threw our arms around each other, and he said, 'Why do humans have to do this to other humans? Why can't they just be human?' "

Weinstein—a longtime partisan of liberal and civil rights causes—could not bring himself to relate his experiences in the death camps when he returned to civilian life. "If I was asked a question, I'd say, 'Yes, I was at these camps,' but

The last victims before the liberation.

Eisenhower with Colonel Weinstein (second from left) at liberated camp.

I wouldn't talk about them. Then one night, twenty years later, my wife shook me, woke me up. She said, 'You've had a nightmare, you've been screaming, you've been saying Sh'ma Israel. What happened?' I said I was dreaming about my standing there in front of the crematorium in Dachau, and I was waiting there. I was next in line. That afternoon I spoke about this with two of my closest friends, a Harvard philosophy professor and his cousin, my physician. And each of them said, 'You've got to talk about it; you've got to bear witness. One said, for the sake of history and truth and helping others; and the other one said, for the sake of your own health.''

At three-thirty in the afternoon of April 30, as the Red Army blasted its way through the bomb-ravaged streets of Berlin toward his bunker, Adolf Hitler put a pistol to his head and pulled the trigger. His wife, Eva Braun, took

244

poison. William L. Shirer, in *The Rise and Fall of the Third Reich*, describes the "Viking funeral" that followed:

> Their corpses were carried up to the garden and during a lull in the bombardment placed in a shell hole and ignited with gasoline. The mourners, headed by Goebbels and Bormann, withdrew to the shelter of the emergency exit and as the flames mounted stood at attention and raised their right hands in a farewell Nazi salute. It was a brief ceremony, for Red Army shells began to splatter the garden, and the survivors retired to the safety of the bunker, leaving the gasoline-fed flames to complete the work of eradicating the last earthly remains of Adolf Hitler and his wife.[4]

Chancellor Adolf Hitler had ruled his "Thousand Year Reich" for exactly twelve years and three months. The Führer, in his "Political Testament," expelled his longtime henchmen, interior minister and SS chief Heinrich Himmler and Reich Marshal Hermann Göring, from the Nazi Party and named Admiral Karl Dönitz to succeed him. "He believed," Shirer writes, "that the Army, the Air Force and the SS had betrayed him, had cheated him out of victory. So his only possible choice of successor had to be the leader of the Navy, which was too small to play a major role in Hitler's war of conquest."[5]

Putting Dachau behind them—though its terrible sights and smells would remain forever engraved upon their memories—the Panthers, spearheading for the Third Army's 71st Infantry Division, moved east toward Austria. Town after town was captured or surrendered as the American troops pressed on to the Inn River, the boundary between the two nations. Despite their leader's ignominious end, Hitler's more fanatical followers in the Wehrmacht still obeyed his oft-repeated call for devotion to duty unto death.

At Ering, a dam with a roadway at its summit crossed the river. Its approaches were guarded by German troops, whom the tanks of A Company quickly dispatched. Upon examination, the roadway was found too weak to bear the weight of the battalion's Shermans. Lighter vehicles and infantrymen traveled over, while the tankers lobbed covering fire at enemy troops presumed to be on the Austrian side. "Gazing across the water," Trezzvant Anderson reports, "they could see the red and white Austrian national colors hung out by townspeople, peasants and farmers so that these relentless Americans would know that here lived not the hated Germans."[6] This attempt at instant historical revisionism sought to deny the reality of most of the Austrian people's fervent support of Nazi doctrines and Nazi goals.

Following the infantry's successful crossing, the Panthers moved upriver to Egelfing, where there was a strong span. On May 4 at 7:30 A.M., they rolled into Austria, the sixth nation in their European odyssey. The tankers had covered so much ground so quickly that the battalion's supply lines were now two days behind them. Out of food, they went hunting and fishing for their sustenance. Walter Lewis writes: "By pulling the pin out of a hand grenade and detonating it under the surface, whole schools of fish would come up. All we had to do was gather in the harvest. We took out carbine rifles, killed a number of deer and made barbecued venison. The Germans couldn't kill us and Providence would not let us starve."

As the Panthers moved through towns and villages, they were often greeted with both white flags of surrender and the Stars and Stripes. "The Austrians," Lewis noted, "were very clever people. . . . Upon close inspection, we found they also had a supply of Nazi flags, as well as French, British and American. Whoever was invading at the time got a white flag of surrender and the flag of their respective country hung from the windows."

The tankers, as usual, went immediately on the offensive. B Company struck Braunau am Inn, the town where, on April 20, 1889, Adolf Shicklgruber, aka Hitler, was born. In *Mein Kampf* he wrote: "Today it seems to be providential that fate should have chosen Braunau am Inn as my birthplace. For this little town lies on the boundary between two German states which we of the younger generation at least have made it our lifework to reunite by every means at our disposal. . . . This little city on the border seems to me the symbol of a great mission."[7]

That "great mission," like the man who conceived it, now lay in ashes. In that symbolic town, B Company took the lives of two hundred German troops, wounded one hundred fifty more, and took three hundred of the "Führer's finest" captive.

Moving swiftly along the Vienna-Salzburg highway, the battalion headed for the city of Wels. On its outskirts, C Company devastated a Luftwaffe air base. Hangars were blasted to bits, pilots killed in their cockpits as they attempted to take off and escape the onslaught. One plane, a Junkers transport filled with enemy troops, managed to get airborne. Second Lieutenant Frank C. Cochrane caught it in the sights of his 50-caliber machine gun and blew it out of the sky.

Major General Wyman of the 71st Infantry
decorates members of the 761st.

From Wels, the 761st moved south toward Steyr. At Lambach, A Company blasted the Wehrmacht forces into submission. Three thousand German soldiers laid down their weapons and surrendered. Southeast of that town, in woods along the twisting road to Steyr, the enemy had set a trap for the advancing tankers. However, in a brief but furious battle, the Panthers destroyed two Mark IV tanks and twenty machine-gun emplacements, while killing four hundred of the enemy and taking three hundred prisoners.

Since the entry into Austria, rumors had run through the battalion that their objective was to rendezvous with Red Army units that had swept through Czechoslovakia. Now the 761st received the official word: "You will advance to the Enns River, and you will wait there for the Russians."

CHAPTER 11

We took bridges, we took towns . . . and the Germans respected us. They knew us all over the front. They called us *"schwarze Soldaten"* [black soldiers]. The word had passed back through Germany that these black soldiers were coming, and they were afraid. And they were told not to take any black tankers prisoner: "Kill them."

E. G. McConnell

Black French soldiers greeting their black American counterparts.

The move to Steyr, a few miles from Austria's border with Czechoslovakia, marked another historic milestone for the 761st: they fought farther east than any other U.S. Army unit on the western front. For the Panthers, the trip from Wels to the Enns River was not without its share of problems. Lieutenant Horace Jones from Detroit remembered an attempt by white troops to prevent the battalion from keeping its date with the Russian tankers of Marshal Ivan Koniev's First Ukrainian Army:

Lieutenant Horace Jones (right).

"This was an instance where the army let its prejudices show. The war was just about over. I went to pick up the gasoline, and at the depot, they said, 'No gas for the 761.' 'What the hell do you mean?!' 'I don't know, sir. That's just the way it is.' So I found some black guys who were working there, and they gave me some gas, two or three thousand gallons. So we got to Steyr anyway. But what was happening was that the brass didn't want the blacks to meet the Russians. They didn't want us to gain the honor of having fought further east than any other American outfit. They were going to take pictures, and they didn't want us dirty blacks, being months in combat, looking like hell—raggedy clothes, raggedy equipment—they didn't want that in their pictures. They couldn't kill us, so the only way they could stop us was take the gas away."

For many of the tankers, the stop in Steyr was their first respite in six months.

"The only time I stopped in 183 days, except when I was wounded," E. G. McConnell recalls, "was at the Enns River when we met the Russians. That's the only time I stopped. Change clothes? I had socks rot off my feet. For a while we were wearing German clothes that we could scrounge out of houses, because we were moving so fast the supply trucks couldn't keep up with us. They had to drop us ammunition and gasoline from the air. I never saw the Red Cross."

250

Hanging out the wash in Coburg, Germany, May 1945.

Leonard "Smitty" Smith confirmed: "They talk about how the Red Cross gave the troops on the front lines clothes—we never saw them."

On May 5, 1945, as the tankers were reaching Steyr, Admiral Hans von Friedburg, Dönitz's successor as chief of the German navy, entered General Eisenhower's headquarters—a small schoolhouse in Reims, France—to negotiate his nation's formal capitulation. The previous day, the Armed Forces High Command had surrendered its troops in northwest Germany, Denmark, and Holland to British Field Marshal Bernard Law Montgomery. On May 6, Friedburg was joined in Reims by the Wehrmacht's chief of operations, General Alfred Jodl. William L. Shirer reports in *The Rise and Fall of the Third Reich* that the "German aim . . . was to stall for a few days in order to have time to move as many German troops and refugees as possible from the path of the Russians so that they could surrender to the Western Allies"[1]—who presumably would treat them better than the Soviets. Their effort was in vain. Eisenhower responded to the delaying tactic with an ultimatum: Sign the surrender declaration or he

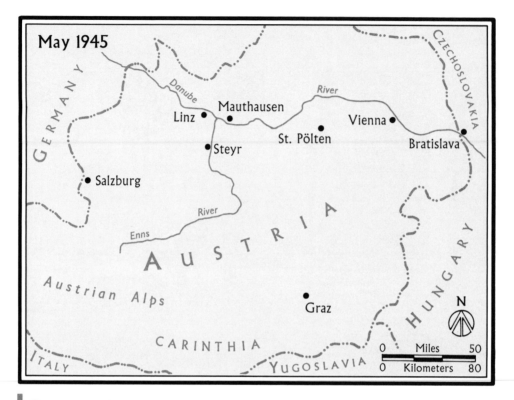

May 1945

CZECHOSLOVAKIA

GERMANY

Danube

River

Linz Mauthausen

Steyr St. Pölten Vienna

Bratislava

Salzburg

AUSTRIA

River

Enns

Austrian Alps

Graz

HUNGARY

N

CARINTHIA

ITALY YUGOSLAVIA

0 Miles 50
0 Kilometers 80

The war ended for the 761st on the banks of the Enns River near Steyr, Austria.

would close the entire western front to prevent any Germans from crossing the American lines.

"When we reached Steyr, we started cleaning our tanks because we heard that the war was just about over," "Smitty" Smith recalled. "And these Germans or Austrians were coming across the bridge in droves. It was like the closer the Russians were getting, the more people were coming across. And then, all of a sudden, we had orders to stop them. No more Germans could come across. And that's when the Russians finally came. And I'll never forget: a big Russian broad shouting, 'America! America! America!' damn near broke my ribs hugging on me. And I have never seen it written anywhere [except in Anderson's book] that blacks were there when our soldiers met the Russians."

The image of these final moments remains crystal clear in the memory of Johnnie Stevens, as well: "When the last little pack of Germans gave up, the Russians came up one side of the river, we came up the other. And they had lady tankers! This is what knocked me for a loop! And that's where I learned my first Russian words. The meeting was real friendly, full of joy and understanding. Lot of hugging and kissing and all that stuff. And they brought out the vodka. Yeah, it was nice."

No film, no photographs preserve that historic moment. "The [white] divisions," Smith continued, "they had Signal Corps people [to record their exploits]. We didn't have anybody. There's a lot of things that we did and places we went, people have to take our word, because we were there. But we had no documentary proof. Like when we went into Dachau, we didn't have any Signal Corps or any officers. A lot of times when we went into combat, the highest-ranking person we had was a sergeant—the tank commander. So, therefore, when you did something like that, there was no one there—a lieutenant or other officer—who could say, 'Oh, yeah, they were there.' But we know what we did. We know what happened. Because we were there."

"The way we were split up," Smith added, "they must have thought there were thousands of us . . . so many platoons here, so many over there. And

Paratroopers and tankers with captured Nazi flag.

Allied forces link up at Torgau, Germany, 1945.

much of the time we weren't even fighting in a platoon, just two or three tanks. We were stretched all across the front. We never fought as a battalion, except in the Bulge. We hardly ever fought as a whole company."

May 6 was a day for celebration, not for waging war. During the Soviet-American festivities at Steyr, word came that the cease-fire order had been issued. The party took its toll on E. G. McConnell. "We gave them hundred-octane gasoline and sugar, and inside of a few hours they had made this witches' brew. They wanted to celebrate, and everybody was trying to explain in English—which is hard—that I didn't drink. Finally, one of the Russians gave me a slab of bacon and told me to drink and chew the bacon. We were drinking that rough vodka—it'd knock the top of your head off. When I went back to camp, I got a rifle and tried to shoot everybody I could see. They had to tie me to the bed. I didn't get court-martialed, due to the fact that our captain knew I didn't drink. [The other guys] gave him the story that I was forced to drink and it just made me go crazy."

Allies celebrate their victory.

There were other pleasures available that day in addition to the Russians' rotgut. Colonel Paul Bates remembered that "when the thing broke up, we were forming up a convoy to go, and one of our sergeants didn't form up with us. We sent somebody back to get him. He came out, and there was this big Russian sergeant—a woman—all over him. And I was yelling, 'For Christ's sake, speed it up! What's the matter with you!' And he came over to me and he says, 'Colonel, you have no idea what I did for my country tonight.'"

At 2:41 A.M. on May 7, with Germany's cities reduced to rubble and millions of her citizens—military and civilian—dead, the Nazi dream of world conquest came to a final inglorious end in Reims. Jodl and Friedburg affixed their names to the document of unconditional surrender. The Allied signatories were General Walter Bedell Smith for the United States, General Ivan Susloparov for the Soviet Union, Lieutenant General Sir Frederick Morgan for England, and General François Sevez on behalf of France.

The momentous business completed, Jodl addressed his conquerors: "With this signature the German people and the German armed forces are, for better or worse, delivered into the hands of the victors. . . . In this hour, I can only hope that the victors treat them with generosity."

During the middle of the night, in a French schoolhouse, the Allied occupation of Germany—and the subsequent division of the European spoils—was launched. Nearly six years after it had begun, the most terrible war in mankind's history had ended. Though the participants that evening may not have realized it, a "cold war" that would last for four and a half decades was now under way.

In mid-June, the Panthers took to the road, en route to their first peacetime assignment—the occupation of five towns near Bissingen, Germany. As they pulled out of Steyr, the men were not alone. Anderson writes of "fräuleins who walked and rode bicycles for many miles to follow the 761st to their next camp."

They remained in Bissingen until July 30, when they were reassigned to guard strategic factories in the area around the Bavarian town of Teisendorf, located some fifteen miles across the border from Salzburg, Austria. Anderson reports that when they departed for Teisendorf, 175 miles distant, "there were

Tankers Harry Tyree and Robert Burrell in Teisendorf, Germany.

fräuleins (and fraus also) who left their fathers and mothers and their husbands and followed the trail of these brown tankers, whose gentle ways, mannerly dispositions and tender natures, so bitterly opposed to their battlefield conduct, had caused German women of the Third Reich to fall in love, madly, with many of them."[2]

From their first combat in Germany after the Siegfried Line breakthrough, the Panthers had established a very good relationship with the civilian population. Preston McNeil remembered: "The German people didn't see many blacks, and the white American soldiers in World War I had told the German people that we were monkeys and had tails. . . . So we'd roll into a town, and they'd send their kids out. They were hungry, so we'd give them food. It's hard to see kids down in the garbage cans, getting food. So I used to take my mess kit, put food in there, and give it to them. And the next day, [the kid] will come out looking for you, and then he'll invite you to his house. And you'd bring the food and everything. So they came to love us. We didn't treat them cruel, like a lot of soldiers did. We got along with the German people. They worshiped us! They didn't even want to see us leave town after they got to know us. But the war went on, we had to move on to the other fights and other sights."

Soldier and new friend, Germany, 1945.

The good feelings between black tankers and enemy civilians continued during the postwar months of occupation. The ironies implicit in having to travel six thousand miles from home to be treated like human beings by white people were hardly lost on the men of the 761st. "Smitty" Smith asked himself, "How come we didn't run into [prejudice] overseas? Now we're over there fighting for

257

A black soldier bidding German children farewell.

our country, and the same people that were our enemy hosted us better after the war than they would down South." A headquarters report summarizing the 761st's occupation activities notes that "relations between battalion personnel and German civilians have been very agreeable. This might be attributed to the exemplary conduct of the men." As Johnnie Stevens saw it:

"We were treated better by the civilian population than we were treated in America. See, in our own country, we couldn't buy a hot dog when we were in uniform, had to ride in the back of the bus when we were in uniform—you were nothing in uniform. But over there, you were treated like a king. We ate together, slept together. After the war was over and [the Germans] had dances again, you were invited. That's why a lot of black GI's took their discharges in Europe. They said, 'Look, ain't nothing in America for me. I can't get a decent job when I go back, I know that. I'm not gonna have any privileges, I can't even vote. So what the hell do I want to go back there for?' "

In July, the battalion submitted to General Eisenhower's headquarters, over the signature of Captain Ivan Harrison, a recommendation that it be awarded the Distinguished Unit Citation, also known as the Presidential Citation, the highest honor the nation can bestow upon a military outfit. Paul Bates recalled the events leading up to the application:

"The last division we fought with was the 71st, and [its commander] General Wyman, who was a hell of a nice guy—and we'd been in combat a lot longer than that division—asked me how did I feel about decorations? I said, 'My God, we're the most underdecorated people I've ever known.' He said, 'Put in any deserving decoration that can be verified; two other people have to see what happened, and I'll approve it.' . . . There's no question but what we deserved [the DUC]."

But though Wyman could and did approve the awarding of many individual honors, it was not in his power to authorize a Presidential Citation. That was the province of the commander of the U.S. forces in the European Theater.

Standing, third and fourth from left: Paul Robeson and Johnnie Stevens in the backyard of Hitler's home, June 1945.

Included as exhibits with the document requesting the DUC were the tributes to the battalion—already noted in this volume—from Generals Eddy, Paul, and McAuliffe. Also submitted was the commendation directed to Colonel Bates on May 15 by General Wyman:

1. Now that the end of this great war in Europe has been reached, it is appropriate that recognition be given to the superior manner in which you and the members of your battalion have performed during the period of 29 March 1945 to 15 May 1945, the time you were closely affiliated with the 71st Infantry Division.

2. The combat missions which were assigned your battalion were performed magnificently, which unquestionably made possible the rapid advance of the entire division, and you share generously in the honors which are ours through the phenomenal progress which was made through Germany and Austria. The splendid way in which you and the members of your command responded to the tasks assigned you is worthy of high praise.

3. The excellent combat record of your unit as veterans has been further extended while operating closely with this command. Please extend to all the members of your battalion my congratulations and my sincere thanks for a job well done.

The award was merited, the petition stated, because "this unit has distinguished itself by extraordinary heroism in battle and has exhibited great gallantry, determination and esprit de corps in operations against the enemy, overcoming such hazardous conditions as adverse weather, mountainous terrain and heavily-fortified positions." The document went on to enumerate the battalion's yeoman effort in the Ardennes campaign, the cracking of the Siegfried Line, and the battle through Bavaria to Steyr, the easternmost objective of any American outfit on the western front.

Third Army headquarters, asked by Eisenhower's office to evaluate the 761st's petition, replied on August 18: "After a careful study of the action of the 761st Tank Battalion . . . it is considered that the action, while commendable, was not sufficiently outstanding to meet the requirements for a unit citation." The letter was signed: "For the Commanding General [George S. Patton] by Lt. Col. R. W. Hartman, Assistant Adjutant General."

A black GI dancing with his girl.

On August 6 and 9, 1945, the United States detonated atomic bombs over the Japanese cities of Hiroshima and Nagasaki. One hundred fifty thousand people were killed; tens of thousands more were horribly maimed. Following the Nagasaki strike, the imperial government of Japan declared its intention to capitulate. On September 2, representatives of the Japanese armed forces formally surrendered to General Douglas MacArthur, Supreme Allied Commander of the Pacific Theater, aboard the U.S.S. *Missouri.* World War II was over.

That fall, the army instituted a system of "Adjusted Service Ratings," a formula that assigned each GI points for length and type of service. Those achieving high scores were sent home for honorable discharge.

It was time for many tankers to say farewell to their German lovers. Anderson writes:

> When the first large shipment of men for discharge left Teisendorf there were fräuleins who openly wept in the streets; crying, not quietly to themselves, but aloud, little caring that former red-hot Nazis, who had taught them that the "schwarz soldat" was nothing less than a fiend, should see that their hearts were broken, because the end of the trail had also come for love and romance.
>
> And [as] I listened to "Maria" (we won't tell her last name) say with tears rolling down her cheeks: "Ich lieben das Mann; Ich wohlen das Mann; Ich wohlen das Baby," there was a tug at my heart, for here was a lovely girl of twenty-three, married, who had left her home, her parents and her husband a German like she, to be with this Negro soldier, and had become pregnant! The tragedy of it: the soldier is married and has a wife in a great Midwestern metropolis in the U.S. But his case is no different from many others.[3]

By the time European Theater Headquarters rendered their verdict on the citation issue, most of the original tankers were stateside. Paul Bates had gone home to New Jersey in November, to be succeeded as battalion commander by Captain Ivan H. Harrison from Detroit. Harrison had been one of the first three black officers assigned to the 761st at Camp Claiborne in July 1942. Now he would become the first African-American to command a combat battalion in the European Theater of Operations.

On Sunday morning, December 9, General Patton, in Bad Nauheim, had completed preparations to return to the United States on a thirty-day leave. He had a date to go pheasant hunting with a close friend, General Hobart Gay. Patton had recently been assigned a new driver, nineteen-year-old Private Horace Woodring, as the replacement for now discharged John L. Mims, the African-American sergeant who had chauffeured the general, without mishap, throughout the war.

At 11:45 A.M., en route to the hunting grounds, the general's Cadillac limousine pulled away from a railroad crossing. It was struck by an army truck, making a sudden and sharp left turn at a speed of no more than twenty miles an hour. Neither Woodring nor Gay was injured. Patton, however, bled profusely from a head wound and had difficulty moving his limbs.

The general was taken to the U.S. Army hospital in Heidelberg. For twelve days, he lay paralyzed from the neck down. He was, however, conscious and able to converse with medical staff and visitors. The latter included his wife, Beatrice, who had been flown in from the States. Patton had suffered serious neurological damage, and though he rallied periodically, his doctors were not optimistic about his prospects. Plans were made to evacuate him to a hospital in Massachusetts. On the night of December 20, he suffered a pulmonary embolism. At five o'clock the next afternoon, Patton told his wife, "It's so dark," then he added, "It's so late." Forty-five minutes later, George Smith Patton was dead. His legend, a curious mix of fact and fiction, like all such, survived him, as "Old Blood and Guts" knew it would. In May, speaking to the Third Army's 6th Armored Division, he had delivered what amounted to his own epitaph:

> There is one great thing you men will be able to say after this war is over and you are at home once again. And you may thank God for it. You may be thankful that twenty years from now when you are sitting by the fireplace with your grandson on your knee and he asks you what you did in the great World War II, you won't have to cough, shift him to the other knee and say, "Well, your Granddaddy shovelled shit in Louisiana." No sir! You can look him straight in the eye and say, "Son, your Granddaddy rode with the great Third Army and a son of a bitch named Georgie Patton."[4]

General Patton's funeral, December 1945.

The final decision regarding the 761st's Distinguished Unit Citation, signed by General L. S. Ostrander, the ETO's adjutant general, was forwarded to Captain Harrison on February 12, 1946. It was twenty-five words long and echoed the Third Army's position: "Disapproved. While the operations of the 761st Tank Battalion were commendable, it is not felt that they meet the requirements for a Distinguished Unit Citation."

Trezzvant Anderson, in a War Department press release dated August 6, 1945, compiled the recorded combat accomplishments of the 761st. It must be emphasized that these statistics, impressive as they are, cannot present a full and accurate accounting of the damage inflicted upon the enemy by the Black Panthers, as they do not take into account the activities of many of the battalion's bastard platoons that fought all across the western front:

> Fifty-eight pill boxes knocked out. Three hundred thirty-one machine gun nests eliminated, ninety-nine anti-tank guns were knocked out, six anti-aircraft guns were destroyed, twenty-four bazooka teams and fifty-one [armored personnel carriers] put out of action, thirty-one tanks destroyed, as were . . . eight self-propelled guns. Three enemy ammunition dumps were blown up, two fully stocked armored supply dumps were blown up, two fully stocked armored supply dumps were captured, as were four air fields and one enemy radio station. Enemy casualties inflicted by the guns of the 761st alone were 6,246 killed, 650 wounded and 15,818 captured.[5]

Anderson went on to enumerate the honors garnered by individual members of the battalion: eleven Silver Stars, sixty-nine Bronze Stars, two hundred eighty Purple Hearts. Eight tankers received battlefield commissions as second lieutenants. Thirty-six Panthers—three officers and thirty-three enlisted men—paid the ultimate price in defense of their nation. Anderson noted that the 761st Tank Battalion—along with the 24th Infantry Regiment in the Pacific—had been cited by Under Secretary of War Robert L. Patterson as the "two outstanding examples of the success of Negro troops in combat."[6]

Walter Lewis's reaction typified the Panthers' anger upon learning that their battalion had been refused the Presidential Citation. "This was an unfortunate occurrence," he wrote, "and something must be done to rectify it. It does not reflect the democratic principles on which this country is founded. I will not be at rest until the day of adjustment for this fiasco comes." As E. G. McConnell saw it, "Three generals had recommended this unit for the Presidential Unit

Citation. There again, discrimination took over. The system wouldn't permit it. It's pitiful to think of what my comrades in arms died for and how they tried to ignore us."

Well before the army chose to disregard their accomplishments, the Panthers had been deeply concerned that their deeds on the battlefields of Europe should not be forgotten. They were acutely aware, as previously noted, that while they were in the field, their very existence had been ignored by both the civilian and the military media. The tankers came to realize that the only way their story would be truthfully told would be for them to tell it. Trezzvant Anderson, in consultation with a committee, produced *Come Out Fighting*. The title was taken from the battalion's quite appropriate motto. It was intended as "our report to the world of what these brave men did . . . and how they did it." In the late fall of 1945, two thousand copies were published in Salzburg. They were distributed to all present and former members of the 761st. The tankers chipped in to cover the printing cost of $1,040.

As the liberators prepared to return to America, those to whom, in Ben Bender's words, "they had given the gift of life" were reentering a world of normal reality, a world whose existence they could barely recall. As Ben stood on the bombed-out bridge in Weimar, contemplating suicide, he meditated on past and future:

"I had lost a lot. I lost my childhood. I lost my parents. I thought: You are the only one who bears the name Bender. You could be the beginning or you could be the end. The beginning means new life, means family, means children, grandchildren, new generations. I decided I had to do something with my life. I had to create a family and I had to create something for generations to come . . . that they should learn from my experiences."

Ben Bender places flowers on site of last meeting with his brother in 1945.

265

Forty-seven years later, Bender considers his goal achieved. Now he says: "I have a grandson, he's ten years old. His name is Michael."

Abe Chapnick was resettled, with the help of relief agencies, in an orphanage in France. This, he says, "was the beginning of my life." While in the orphanage he met an American correspondent, who included Abe's story in articles that were published in the United States and Poland. Remarkably, his mother—who had survived in a Polish work camp—saw the article in Poland. His uncle saw the one in America. Abe was reunited with the two other survivors of the extended Chapnick family, which had once numbered some sixty people. His uncle brought him to America.

"To an extent," Chapnick said, "we [liberated prisoners] tried to cut our experience out of our minds. We tried to obliterate it. Eventually, it came to a point where we started to realize that this was part of life, that it transpired, that it really did happen."

Over the decades, Chapnick kept in touch with many of his fellow former inmates, now widely dispersed in the United States, Canada, Australia, South America, and Israel. "Most of them wound up in Israel," Chapnick recalled. "There's a few—very, very few—that returned to their country of origin. Just about every single one of them has made some kind of mark in life for themselves. There are a few that never really made it. They never got their bearing afterward. But most of the boys that came out of Buchenwald made their mark.

Ben Bender returns to Buchenwald forty-six years after liberation.

They have all not really succeeded moneywise . . . but they made their mark in that they became real human beings."

The tankers, too, had memories they wished to erase. "We returned to civilian life," E. G. McConnell said, "trying to forget the past, the horror of the atrocities we'd seen in Europe."

"War," Walter Lewis wrote,

> is the devil giving birth to ten thousand imps, influencing men's minds to rain death, destruction, devastation, and famine upon mankind. War is Christ being crucified over and over again.
>
> War is mangled bodies piled high in village streets, chickens eating at their entrails, the stench unbearable to human nostrils. War is women screaming. War is raped and ruined cities, wide-eyed hungry children, bewildered old men, sudden death, bloody gutters, fear beyond definition.
>
> War is the helplessness of the good and the monstrosities of the wicked. War is a chain reaction of evil. . . .
>
> If you have not been in war, you should thank God for your good fortune. You should get down on your hands and knees and pray for peace and dedicate yourself to doing all in your power to prevent it.

Though the remembrance of such horror could, perhaps, be banished during the daylight hours, it would surface—hauntingly—at night. Walter Lewis wrote his "Diary of a Gunner" as a "therapeutic exercise because of hallucinative nightmares after World War II. When the incidents were recorded on paper, the hallucinations subsided."

"I dream I'm back in combat a lot of times," Johnnie Stevens says. "But not as much as I used to. I dream that I've got a gun, but it just won't fire. I'm trying to fire it, but it won't go off. I feel like I'm helpless. Dreams like that. They keep coming back. They never go away."

EPILOGUE

I, for one, know of no sweeter sight for a man's eyes than his own country.

Homer,
The Odyssey

Memorial Day: mothers tend newly dug graves in black section of cemetery.

The more than one million African-American servicemen returning to civilian life in late 1945 and 1946 came home to a land that had changed in many ways during their absence.

Though a majority of blacks remained mired in poverty, the economic circumstances of many African-Americans had improved markedly during the war years. A million more blacks had found employment in the private sector, and the number of black women in industrial jobs had risen by 400 percent. In government service, the picture was similar; black employment in the public sector jumped fivefold, from 60,000 workers in 1941 to 300,000 by VJ Day. The return of millions of demobilized white servicemen, however, would seriously erode some of these gains.

The African-American exodus from the South had continued during the war: some 330,000 blacks left their traditional homes below the Cotton Curtain. However, unlike the prewar migrants—the overwhelming majority of whom had settled in the industrial cities of the Northeast and the Midwest—fully two thirds of the wartime departees made their new homes in cities and towns on the West Coast, mainly because of the huge expansion of jobs in defense industries. But if the economic prospects of a portion of the black community had brightened somewhat, relations between African-Americans and their white countrymen—particularly in the South—remained at a dismal status quo. In 1946, six blacks were lynched, and racial rioting erupted in the streets of Columbia, Tennessee; Athens, Alabama; and Philadelphia, Pennsylvania.

"We knew," Johnnie Stevens said, "that we were coming back to the same prejudice we left. I was waiting at Fort Benning [Georgia] to come home, and I had all those medals and decorations on my chest, all of my stripes and stars. There were eight [white] soldiers at the bus stop from the 26th Division, whom I had spearheaded for. The bus came, and the driver says, 'Hey, boy, you got to wait a minute!' I said to myself, 'Here we go again.' There was a big tough-looking sergeant, and he says, 'Hey, don't you see the goddamned medals on that man's chest? He was with us in combat. Now he's gonna get on this damn bus, and he's gonna ride up front with us!' Then he says to me, 'Sarge, get on the bus.' I got on and I sat down beside him. I talked and drank with these guys all the way to Atlanta. And all those people that didn't want me to get on the bus, they didn't open their mouths."

But, Stevens reflected, "though we came back to the same identical thing that we had left, in a way World War II was good for the black soldier and the black people, for the simple reason that we really learned a lot. We learned what

Recipients of the Soldier's Medal for Heroism,
Belgium, January 1945.

it was to live without prejudice. And believe it or not, we learned it from other countries. We didn't encounter any prejudice in France, Austria, Holland, Belgium, Luxembourg; none of those places did we encounter prejudice. But we had to come right back to the United States and bump into it again."

One whose clash with Southern racism captured the attention of the nation was Sergeant Isaac Woodard, Jr., a veteran of fifteen months service in the Pacific Theater.

In February 1946, Woodard, after receiving his discharge at Fort Gordon, Georgia, boarded a bus bound for his North Carolina home. He was still wearing his uniform. There was a rest stop in South Carolina. On returning from the "colored" rest room, the young man was cursed by the driver for taking too much time. At the next town, Batesburg, the driver demanded that the local sheriff arrest his passenger. Bernard C. Nalty writes in *Strength for the Fight*:

The charge was drunkenness, even though Woodard did not drink. In making the arrest, the lawman beat the prisoner with a blackjack, and someone, either the sheriff or a policeman, thrust the end of a nightstick into his eyes. Denied medical care, locked overnight in a cell, the former sergeant was found guilty and fined fifty dollars. When Woodard at last reached an Army hospital at Spartanburg, South Carolina, doctors found his corneas so badly damaged that he was permanently blind. . . . President Harry S. Truman was shocked by the outrage in South Carolina. "My God!" Truman told [NAACP head] Walter White, "I had no idea things were as terrible as that. We've got to do something."[1]

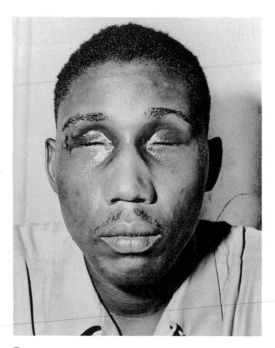

Isaac Woodard, Jr., blinded by South Carolina police, 1946.

The attack on Woodard—heavily reported by the media—generated widespread outrage and brought protests from Americans both black and white. When the case against Sheriff Linwood L. Shull came to trial in U.S. District Court (it was a federal matter because the bus was traveling interstate), Southern justice took its course. The defendant claimed self-defense. The United States attorney offered only the merest semblance of a case in behalf of the black GI. The FBI found no evidence corroborating Woodard's contention that he had been blinded in the course of a vicious unprovoked assault by Batesburg's peace officers. An all-white jury of his peers acquitted Sheriff Shull; courthouse spectators raucously cheered the verdict.

Though injustice triumphed in the Woodard case, it would have unforeseen long-range implications for black America's centuries-long struggle for equal protection under the law. The judge in the case was a "reconstructed" South Carolinian named J. Waites Waring, who, as Nalty reports, was so disgusted by the defense counsel's racist appeals to the jury that he cut the lawyer's summation short. Waring became a stalwart activist from the bench on the side of

African-Americans deprived of their constitutional rights. Sitting in an environment extremely hostile to liberal racial perceptions, Waring would be a beacon in the "judicial revolution" that led to the U.S. Supreme Court's *Brown v. Board of Education of Topeka* decision in 1954 and the subsequent judicial and legislative actions that dismantled the legal, if not the psychological and socioeconomic, foundations of apartheid American-style. In the forefront of the courthouse attack on segregation were William Hastie, former civilian aide to Secretary of War Stimson, and future Supreme Court Justice Thurgood Marshall.

Black leaders and white progressives brought pressure on President Truman to pay tribute to the sacrifices of black servicemen by ending segregation in the nation's fighting forces. The result was Executive Order 9981, issued in July 1948:

> It is hereby declared to be the policy of the President that there shall be equality of treatment and opportunity for all persons in the armed forces without regard to race, color, religion or national origin.

Lewis Weinstein, General Eisenhower's former aide who was in large part responsible for converting African-American service troops into combat forces, returned to Boston after the war to practice law and become an influential member of the Democratic party's liberal wing. "I was a factor in [Truman's edict]," he recalled to Miles and Rosenblum. "Three or four of us together saw Truman and told him to get the army desegregated. And he issued an order. And do you know what happened to that order? It was treated by the army, the navy, the air force and marines as just being a suggestion. And they stalled and stalled, and before long Truman's term ended. Then Eisenhower came in. Eisenhower was never interested in integrating the army. . . . And, unfortunately, Eisenhower, who had a lot of good qualities, also had some unhappy qualities. He didn't give a damn about racism."

During the Korean War, however, there was some integration of combat forces, particularly in the Eighth Army. The effort, according to Morris J. MacGregor, Jr., in *Integration of the Armed Forces, 1940–1965*, "moved Secretary [of the Army Frank] Pace to call the integration of the Eighth Army 'a notable advance in the field of human relations.' "[2] Yet there were charges that Negro troops were mistreated and discriminated against during the conflict. *The Negro Almanac* notes that "Thurgood Marshall of the NAACP conducted an investigation of one such accusation and ultimately issued a highly critical report of the court-martial procedures involved in the sentencing of some thirty-nine Negro soldiers, most of whom were later released or given less severe sentences."[3] Though MacGregor considers integration to have been "an established fact in Korea . . . the question remained: could an attitude forged in the heat of battle be sustained on the more tranquil maneuver grounds of Europe and the South?"[4] Public facilities in the South remained segregated, and justice continued to be rendered there in a discriminatory manner. As the war in Korea ended, in 1953, the opportunity to vote still eluded the South's African-American population.

"Came John F. Kennedy," Lewis Weinstein stated. "I had helped him during his campaign, I was a friend of his, and I told him that one of the first things you've got to do is desegregate the military of the United States. . . . He wasn't in office but [a few months] when the desegregation order came down. He was able to desegregate the whole army."

That directive came from Defense Secretary Robert McNamara on July 26, 1963—fifteen years, to the day, after Harry Truman had promulgated Executive Order 9981. It clearly assigned "responsibility and authority for promoting equal opportunity for members of the Armed Forces" to the assistant secretary of defense (manpower). McNamara's directive continued:

> In the performance of this function he shall (a) be the representative of the Secretary of Defense in Civil Rights matters, (b) give direction to programs that promote equal opportunity for military personnel, (c) provide policy guidance and review policies, regulations and manuals of military policies and (d) monitor their performance through periodic reports and visits to field installations. 2. In carrying out [these] functions . . . the Assistant Secretary of Defense (Manpower) is authorized to establish the Office of Deputy Assistant Secretary of Defense (Civil Rights).

The directive further called on all military departments to institute in each branch of the service a "system for regularly reporting, monitoring and measuring progress in achieving equal opportunity on and off base." Finally, it charged "every military commander" with the "responsibility to oppose discriminatory practices affecting his men and their dependents and to foster equal opportunity for them, not only in areas under his immediate control, but also in nearby communities where they may live or gather in off-duty hours."

One hundred ninety-three years after Crispus Attucks was slain in the Boston Massacre, African-Americans had been granted the right to die an equal-opportunity death in the service of their nation.

Kennedy's decision was undoubtedly prompted by the continuing success of the civil rights movement—begun in the wake of the Brown decision and the refusal of a Montgomery, Alabama, seamstress, Rosa Parks, to move to the back of a bus—in galvanizing, through violently resisted nonviolent protests, interracial support for its goal of attaining full human and civil rights for African-Americans throughout the nation. One month after the Defense Department decree, half a million citizens marched on Washington to hear of Martin Luther King, Jr.'s, soul-stirring dream. Three months after that historic occasion, the President was gunned down on a Dallas parkway.

The Panthers returning to civilian life—E. G. McConnell taking a job with the City of New York, Walter Lewis going to work at the Philadelphia Naval Shipyard, Johnnie Stevens becoming a cook in Atlanta—were acutely aware of their second-class status, and in the immediate postwar period they were not looking to nonviolence as a method of redressing their righteous grievances.

Stevens remembered: "After the war, I made it a habit of carrying a gun. It was a war souvenir—a German P-38. I was working at Western Electric as a cook, and I got into a little altercation with one of the white fellas there. My mother, God bless the dead, says, 'Johnnie, if I were you, I just would not go back to work. You know how those white people are.' See, my mother was never taught to fight back. I said, 'Mom, I don't care how they are. I've just come from overseas; I've been shooting and killing people for this country and

Johnnie Stevens, 1947.

275

the right to do that job. Nobody wants to die, but I'll tell you one thing, I'm not gonna die alone.' "

The next day, Stevens put his pistol in his belt and went to his job. The white workers were gathered in the parking lot. "I got out of my car and said, 'Look, I don't want trouble and I'm not looking for it. But I'm going to work.' And they knew this guy must mean it. Nobody bothered or touched me, because nobody wants to be the first to die. And I had made up my mind—knowing the way they would shoot black guys in the South then—I had made up my mind that if they're gonna shoot me, there's gonna be some widows out there moaning along with my mother.

"No progress in any nation or race has ever been won without bloodshed," Stevens believes. "Somebody has to die to accomplish something for future generations. That's the way the world is, and it'll never change. Look how many of us had to die in our civil rights struggle. Look how many unaccounted-for blacks were lynched or hung up or shot at night in the South, and nobody ever knew about it. *We'd* known it! We just couldn't prove it."

Stevens's anger at Southern racism caused him to abandon his native Georgia and migrate north to New Jersey. "I believe that if I had stayed there, I'd probably be dead now," he said. "A lot of guys lost their lives down there because they just couldn't take it and they fought back, and they'd get killed and you'd never even hear about it. It didn't make any newspaper headlines." Settling in the town of Carteret, across the Hudson from New York City, he immersed himself in civic affairs and working with local youth. In 1947, he integrated the New Jersey Transit Bus Company's work force, becoming the first African-American to be hired as a long-distance driver.

"Sometimes people would get on and say, 'By golly, we got a nigger bus driver,' because they'd never seen a black bus driver before. I was the only one out there. . . . A bus is a large vehicle; so is a tank. And sometimes late at night, driving through the mountains when all the passengers were sleeping, I would have a flashback. . . . It would seem like I was in a tank again. It would all come back. A lot of times. . . . See how far we've come? We've come a long way and most of it because of the war. The war did black people more good than anything in the world, because it taught America there was a need for us. Not only on the front lines, not only in tanks, but as workers. Blacks were elevated to jobs that they had never had a chance to get. For example, how many black welders could you find before World War II? If I had to fight that war again, I'd do it, for the simple reason that I think it was worthwhile. In

America, people got it made. That's why they should try to get together and pull together and stay together and keep what we got."

The men of the 761st stayed together. As Horace Jones put it: "We became, more or less, like brothers. We trained for three years together, and then, when we went through combat, we really tightened up with each other . . . a feeling that you don't even have with your own brother, because he wasn't there. We were close. . . . A comrade would lose a friend or just have a deep feeling, and he would go to you . . . sobbing, tears running down his face, and throw his arms around you, and you'd console him. When's the last time you had a man run up to you and cry on your shoulder? It's a bond that you don't share with anybody. It's a wonderful feeling of comradeship that you don't find anywhere else. That's why this unit has stayed together for more than forty years."

The men of the 761st began early on to convene in various cities for yearly reunions. As many as 25 percent of the veterans would take part. "This," said Jones, "was the highest number percentagewise to take part [in such affairs] of any World War II outfit." One topic constantly discussed was the perceived injustice involved in the army's denial of the Distinguished Unit Citation to the Black Panther battalion. They decided to try to rectify the situation. "In 1978," E. G. McConnell said, "several of our comrades went into the archives, dug out the record of our unit, and presented it to President Jimmy Carter."

Members of the 761st after receiving the
Distinguished Unit Citation, 1978.

Historian Walter Lewis, Congressman Raymond Lederer, and Judge
James Lightfoot after receiving Distinguished Unit Citation from President Carter.

Times, as Paul Bates puts it, had changed. "There can be a time and place
when you try to get a particular thing done and it won't work at all. And there's
another time or place when it'll work perfectly, because you can get all the
doors open. We had four or five guys working in different directions . . . con-
tacting prominent people—senators and congressmen. So the second time around,
they were able to get all the doors open . . . plus the fact that we had a secretary of the army, Clifford Alexander, who was black."

August 20, 1978, was a day E. G. McConnell recalls with pride: "Those of
us surviving were invited to Fort Myer, Virginia, where the 761st were finally
awarded the nation's highest unit award. God, we were choked up with joy!
And I thought of those who'd passed on, who weren't here to share the glory of
this glorious moment, when the Black Panthers were finally acknowledged for
their deeds in Europe."

It was a beautiful sunny afternoon as the army's ceremonial "Old Guard"
unit trooped the colors across the fort's parade grounds. Secretary Alexander
addressed the veterans and their families:

> . . . the 761st had to endure a climate of racial discrimination which,
> for millions of Americans, blemished the accomplishments of our na-
> tion in the war against Nazi oppression. In a war where enemy pris-

oners were frequently granted more respect than black American soldiers, these men and hundreds of thousands of other blacks answered their country's call. . . . A pernicious aspect of the discrimination that existed was the reluctance or even refusal to recognize the achievements of black units. Such institutional racism is deep-rooted and only through perseverance can it be reduced or eliminated. It is a sad commentary that earlier efforts to recognize the valor of these men may have been thwarted by such attitudes. In many respects the Army today is much different from the Army of the 1940's. At the same time certain core values endure. Courage will always be a necessary attribute of soldiers, and the wartime exploits of the soldiers of the 761st provide an example of courage which serves us well in the Army of today. I salute the men of the 761st Tank Battalion. For over thirty years you have lived with the knowledge that you did something out of the ordinary. The Army and the Nation share that knowledge today.

Let the final words come from James Earl Carter, Jr., the thirty-ninth President of the United States:

The 761st Tank Battalion distinguished itself by extraordinary gallantry, courage and high esprit de corps displayed in the accomplishment of unusually difficult and hazardous operations in the European Theater of Operations from 31 October 1944 to 6 May 1945. Throughout this period of combat, the courageous and professional actions of the "Black Panther" Battalion, coupled with their indomitable fighting spirit and devotion to duty, reflect great credit on the 761st Tank Battalion, the United States Army and this Nation.

NOTES

Chapter 1

1. Harry A. Ploski and James Williams, *The Afro-American* (New York: John Wiley, 1983), p. 794.

2. Laurens to Washington, May 19, 1782. In Morris J. MacGregor, Jr., and Bernard C. Nalty, eds., *Blacks in the United States Armed Forces—Basic Documents*, vol. 1 (Wilmington, Del.: Scholarly Resources, Inc., 1977), p. 146.

3. Thomas to John Quincy Adams, November 24, 1775. In MacGregor and Nalty, vol. 1, p. 34.

4. *Diary of a Hessian Officer*, October 23, 1777. In Harry A. Ploski and James Williams, comps. and eds., *Reference Library of Black America*, vol. 3 (Detroit: Gale Research, Inc., 1990), p. 816.

5. Heath to Adams, August 27, 1777. In MacGregor and Nalty, vol. 1, p. 104.

6. *Reference Library of Black America*, vol. 3, p. 815.

7. *Black Americans in Defense of Our Nation* (Washington, D.C.: U.S. Government Printing Office, 1990), p. 30.

8. Jackson to Claiborne. In *Reference Library of Black America*, vol. 3, p. 831.

9. Jackson Proclamation, December 18, 1814. In Harry A. Ploski and Roscoe C. Brown, Jr., comps. and eds., *The Negro Almanac* (New York: Bellwether, 1967), p. 542.

10. General Order, Adjutant General's Office, February 18, 1820. In MacGregor and Nalty, vol. 2, p. 218.

11. Frederick Douglass, Broadside, Rochester, N.Y., March 21, 1863. In Philip S. Foner, ed., *The Life and Writings of Frederick Douglass*, vol. 3 (New York: International Publishers, 1952), p. 318.

12. Thomas Wentworth Higginson, *Army Life in a Black Regiment* (New York: Collier Books, 1962), p. 115.

13. Foner, p. 14.

14. March 6, 1863. In MacGregor and Nalty, vol. 3, p. 29.

15. Colonel J. M. Williams to General T. J. Anderson, January 1, 1866. In MacGregor and Nalty, vol. 3, p. 51.

16. December 1, 1888. In MacGregor and Nalty, vol. 3, p. 53.

17. July 13, 1898. In MacGregor and Nalty, vol. 3, p. 192.

18. August 20, 1898. In MacGregor and Nalty, vol. 3, p. 197.

19. Washington to Taft (telegram), November 20, 1906. In MacGregor and Nalty, vol. 3, p. 226.

20. MacGregor and Nalty, vol. 4, p. 2.

21. Bernard C. Nalty, *Strength for the Fight* (New York: The Free Press, 1986), p. 106.

22. MacGregor and Nalty, vol. 4, p. 39.

23. *New York Tribune*, July 1917. In MacGregor and Nalty, vol. 4, p. 114.

24. October 20, 1917. In MacGregor and Nalty, vol. 4, p. 117.

25. March 28, 1918. In MacGregor and Nalty, vol. 4, p. 277.

26. In MacGregor and Nalty, vol. 4, p. 278.

27. May 1919. In MacGregor and Nalty, vol. 4, p. 282.

28. May 6, 1919. In MacGregor and Nalty, vol. 4, p. 288.

29. Harry A. Ploski and Ernest Kaiser, comps. and eds., *Afro-USA* (New York: Bellwether, 1971), p. 575.

30. MacGregor and Nalty, vol. 4, p. 295.

31. April 13, 1920. In MacGregor and Nalty, vol. 4, p. 329.

32. *New York Post*, November 11, 1991.

Chapter 2

1. *Negroes of New York*. Writers Program, Works Progress Administration (microfilm, reel 4). (New York: Schomburg Center for Research in Black Culture, n.d.), n.p.

2. Mark Naison, *Communists in Harlem During the Depression* (Urbana: University of Illinois Press, 1983), p. xvii.

3. Ibid., p. 152.

4. *Negroes of New York*.

5. Robert Weisbrot, *Father Divine and the Struggle for Civil Rights* (Urbana: University of Illinois Press, 1983), p. 177.

6. Ibid., p. 37.

7. Letter, Houston to Roosevelt, July 15, 1937. In MacGregor and Nalty, vol. 4, p. 469.

8. *Crisis*, October 9, 1940.

9. Ibid.

10. Daniel S. Davis, *Mr. Black Labor* (New York: E. P. Dutton, 1972), p. 115.

11. Ibid., p. 107.

12. *New York Age*, December 26, 1941.

13. Weisbrot, p. 203.

14. Ibid., p. 205.

15. James Farmer, *Lay Bare the Heart* (New York: Arbor House, 1985), p. 81.

16. Bayard Rustin, *Down the Line* (Chicago: Quadrangle Books, 1971), p. 50.

17. C. Eric Lincoln, *The Black Muslims in America* (Westport, Conn.: Greenwood Press, 1982), p. 12.

18. Ibid., p. 14.

19. Malu Halasa, *Elijah Muhammad* (New York: Chelsea House, 1990), p. 60.

20. Lincoln, p. 206.

Chapter 3

1. Stimson Diary, October 25, 1940. Henry L. Stimson Papers, Yale University Library. In Morris J. MacGregor, Jr., *Integration of the Armed Forces, 1940–1965* (Washington, D.C.: Center of Military History, United States Army, 1981), p. 20.

2. Memo, Marshall to Stimson, December 1, 1941. In MacGregor, p. 21.

3. Nalty, p. 179.

4. Letter, Eleanor Roosevelt to Henry L. Stimson, September 22, 1942. In MacGregor and Nalty, vol. 5, p. 170.

5. Graham Smith, *When Jim Crow Met John Bull* (London: I. B. Tauris, 1987), p. 46.

6. Memo, Davis to Inspector General, U.S. Army, December 24, 1942. In MacGregor and Nalty, vol. 5, p. 174.

7. Ulysses P. Lee, *The Employment of Negro Troops* (Washington, D.C.: Center of Military History, United States Army, 1986), p. 367.

8. Nalty, p. 167.

Chapter 4

1. Memo, Hastie to Stimson, January 5, 1943. In MacGregor and Nalty, vol. 5, p. 178.

2. MacGregor, p. 27.

3. War Department Bureau of Public Relations release, July 10, 1941. In MacGregor and Nalty, vol. 5, p. 51.

4. Memo, Hastie to Stimson, January 5, 1943.

5. *Time*, July 10, 1944.

6. *New York Age*, August 21, 1943.

7. B. J. Widdick, *Detroit: City of Race and Class Violence* (Chicago: Quadrangle Books, 1972), p. 95.

8. *Life*, August 2, 1942.

9. Widdick, p. 101.

10. *Detroit Tribune*, June 26, 1943.

11. Widdick, p. 103.

12. Ibid., p. 107.

13. Ibid., p. 111.

14. *The New Republic*, August 16, 1943.

15. *Chicago Defender*, August, 1943.

16. Lee, p. 371.

17. Ibid.

18. Memo, Chief of Staff to the Commanding Generals Air Force, et al., July 3, 1943. In MacGregor and Nalty, vol. 5, p. 270.

19. Lee, p. 374.

20. Memo, Gibson to Davis, July 16, 1943.

21. Letter to Hastie, August 8, 1942.

22. *Dachau* (United States Seventh Army, 1945; reprint, Atlanta: Center for Research in Social Change, 1979), p. 31.

Chapter 5

1. MacGregor and Nalty, vol. 5, p. 269.

2. Ibid., p. 332.

3. Letter, Eleanor Roosevelt to Stimson, November 23, 1943. In MacGregor and Nalty, vol. 5, p. 299.

4. MacGregor and Nalty, vol. 5, p. 288.

5. Ibid., p. 291.

6. George S. Patton, *War As I Knew It* (Boston: Houghton Mifflin, 1947), p. 160.

7. MacGregor and Nalty, vol. 5, p. 307.

8. Ibid., p. 326.

9. John D. Silvera, *The Negro in World War II* (New York: Arno Press, n.d.), n.p.

10. MacGregor and Nalty, vol. 5, p. 262.

11. Ibid., p. 340.

12. Jules Tygiel, *Baseball's Great Experiment: Jackie Robinson and His Legacy* (New York: Vintage, 1984), p. 60.

13. Ibid., p. 61.

14. Ibid.

15. Ibid., p. 60.

16. Ibid., p. 39.

17. Ibid., p. 62.

18. Sugar Ray Robinson with Dave Anderson, *Sugar Ray* (New York: Viking, 1970), p. 123.

19. Deposition, Virginia Jones, July 19, 1944.

20. Captain Gerald M. Bear, Court-martial proceedings, August 2, 1944.

21. Jules Tygiel, "The Court Martial of Jackie Robinson," *American Heritage*, January 1985.

22. Ibid.

23. Ibid.

24. MacGregor and Nalty, vol. 5, p. 257.

25. Robert L. Allen, *The Port Chicago Mutiny* (New York: Warner Books, 1989), p. 42.

26. Ibid., p. 43.

27. Ibid., p. 69.

28. Ibid., p. 85.

29. Ibid., p. 130.

30. *Los Angeles Times*, September 17, 1991.

Chapter 6

1. Silvera, n.p.

2. Nalty, p. 171.

3. Lee, p. 611.

4. Nalty, p. 187.

5. Ibid., p. 195.

6. Trezzvant W. Anderson, *Come Out Fighting* (Salzburg: Salzburger Druckerei und Verlag, 1945), p. 17.

7. Smith, p. 121.

8. MacGregor and Nalty, vol. 5, p. 299.

9. Smith, p. 165.

10. Ibid., p. 133.

11. Ibid., p. 143.

12. Ibid., p. 197.

13. Ibid.

14. Ibid., p. 168.

15. Ibid., p. 187.

16. Lucy S. Dawidowicz, *The War Against the Jews, 1933–1945* (New York: Holt, Rinehart and Winston, 1975), p. 129.

17. Leni Yahil, *The Holocaust: The Fate of European Jewry, 1932–1945* (New York: Oxford University Press, 1990), p. 606.

18. Nora Levin, *The Holocaust Years* (Malabar, Fla.: Robert E. Krieger, 1990), p. 267.

19. David S. Wyman, *The Abandonment of the Jews* (New York: Pantheon, 1984), p. 304.

Chapter 7

1. Martin Blumenson, *Patton: The Man Behind the Legend, 1885–1945* (New York: William Morrow, 1985), p. 210.

2. Ibid., p. 211.

3. Ibid., p. 213.

4. Patton, p. 160.

5. Ladislas Farago, *The Last Days of Patton* (New York: McGraw-Hill, 1981), p. 239.

6. Blumenson, p. 13.

7. Charles B. MacDonald, *A Time for Trumpets* (New York: William Morrow, 1985), p. 18.

8. Anderson, p. 28.

9. Ibid., p. 29.

Chapter 8

1. William L. Shirer, *The Rise and Fall of the Third Reich* (New York: Simon & Schuster, 1960), p. 1090.

2. MacDonald, p. 79.

3. Anderson, p. 54.

4. MacGregor, p. 51.

5. Ibid.

6. Nalty, p. 177.

7. Patton, p. 195.

8. Yahil, p. 538.

Chapter 9

1. H. Essame, *Patton: A Study in Command* (New York: Charles Scribner, 1974), p. 237.

2. Anderson, p. 75.

3. Ibid., p. 76.

4. Elie Wiesel, "Facing Hate," Public Affairs Television, November 27, 1991.

5. Blumenson, p. 280.

6. Ibid., p. 281.

7. Ibid.

8. Ibid., p. 287.

9. Anderson, p. 83.

Chapter 10

1. Shirer, p. 1126.

2. *The New Yorker*, November 11, 1991, p. 32.

3. Ibid., p. 33.

4. Shirer, p. 1134.

5. Ibid., p. 1126.

6. Anderson, p. 89.

7. Shirer, p. 6.

Chapter 11

1. Shirer, p. 1138.

2. Anderson, p. 129.

3. Ibid.

4. Farago, p. viii.

5. Anderson, p. 134.

6. Ibid.

Epilogue

1. Nalty, p. 204 and p. 205.

2. MacGregor, p. 447.

3. Ploski and Brown, p. 551.

4. MacGregor, p. 447.

BIBLIOGRAPHY

Allen, Robert L. *The Port Chicago Mutiny*. New York: Warner Books, 1989.

Anderson, Trezzvant W. *Come Out Fighting*. Salzburg: Salzburger Druckerei und Verlag, 1945.

Blumenson, Martin. *Patton: The Man behind the Legend, 1885–1945*. New York: William Morrow, 1985.

Dachau. United States Seventh Army, 1945; reprint, Atlanta: Center for Research in Social Change, 1979.

Davis, Daniel S. *Mr. Black Labor*. New York: E. P. Dutton, 1972.

Dawidowicz, Lucy S. *The War against the Jews, 1933–1945*. New York: Holt, Rinehart and Winston, 1975.

Essame, H. *Patton: A Study in Command*. New York: Charles Scribner, 1974.

Farago, Ladislas. *The Last Days of Patton*. New York: McGraw-Hill, 1981.

Farmer, James. *Lay Bare the Heart*. New York: Arbor House, 1985.

Foner, Philip S., ed. *The Life and Writings of Frederick Douglass*, vol. 3. New York: International Publishers, 1952.

Halasa, Malu. *Elijah Muhammad*. New York: Chelsea House, 1990.

Higginson, Thomas Wentworth. *Army Life in a Black Regiment*. New York: Collier Books, 1962.

Lee, Ulysses P. *The Employment of Negro Troops*. Washington, D.C.: Center of Military History, United States Army, 1986.

Levin, Nora. *The Holocaust Years*. Malabar, Fla.: Robert E. Krieger, 1990.

Lincoln, C. Eric. *The Black Muslims in America*. Westport, Conn.: Greenwood Press, 1982.

MacDonald, Charles B. *A Time for Trumpets*. New York: William Morrow, 1985.

MacGregor, Morris J., Jr. *Integration of the Armed Forces, 1940–1965*. Washington, D.C.: Center of Military History, United States Army, 1981.

MacGregor, Morris J., Jr., and.Bernard C. Nalty, eds. *Blacks in the United States Armed Forces — Basic Documents*, vols. 1, 4, 5. Wilmington, Del.: Scholarly Resources, Inc., 1976.

Naison, Mark. *Communists in Harlem during the Depression*. Urbana: University of Illinois Press, 1983.

Nalty, Bernard C. *Strength for the Fight*. New York: The Free Press, 1986.

Negroes of New York. Writers Program, Works Progress Administration (microfilm, reel 4). New York: Schomburg Center for Research in Black Culture.

Patton, George S. *War As I Knew It*. Boston: Houghton Mifflin, 1947.

Pisar, Samuel. *Blood and Hope*. New York: Macmillan, 1982.

Ploski, Harry A., and Roscoe C. Brown, Jr., comps. and eds. *The Negro Almanac*. New York: Bellwether, 1967.

Ploski, Harry A., and Ernest Kaiser, comps. and eds. *Afro-USA*. New York: Bellwether, 1971.

Ploski, Harry A., and James Williams. *The Afro-American*. New York: John Wiley, 1983.
———, comps. and eds. *Reference Library of Black America*, vol. 3. Detroit: Gale Research, 1990.

Robinson, Sugar Ray, with Dave Anderson. *Sugar Ray*. New York: Viking, 1970.

Rustin, Bayard. *Down the Line*. Chicago: Quadrangle Books, 1971.

Shirer, William L. *The Rise and Fall of the Third Reich*. New York: Simon & Schuster, 1960.

Silvera, John D. *The Negro in World War Two*. New York: Arno Press, 1947. Reprint 1969.

Smith, Graham. *When Jim Crow Met John Bull*. London: I. B. Tauris, 1987.

Tygiel, Jules. *Baseball's Great Experiment: Jackie Robinson and His Legacy*. New York: Vintage, 1984.

Weisbrot, Robert. *Father Divine and the Struggle for Civil Rights*. Urbana: University of Illinois Press, 1983.

Widdick, B. J. *Detroit: City of Race and Class Violence*. Chicago: Quadrangle Books, 1972.

Wyman, David S. *The Abandonment of the Jews*. New York: Pantheon, 1984.

Yahil, Leni. *The Holocaust: The Fate of European Jewry, 1932–1945*. New York: Oxford University Press, 1990.

PHOTO CREDITS

KEY:
CPI = Culver Pictures, Inc.
LC = Library of Congress
NA = National Archives
SCRBC = Schomburg Center for Research in Black Culture
USHMM = U.S. Holocaust Memorial Museum
USSC = U.S. Signal Corps

Half-title page: USSC; **title page:** NA; **introduction:** USSC; **chapter 1:** page 2–NA, 8–NA, 11–NA, 12–NA, 15 (top)–LC, 15 (bottom)–NA, 16–LC, 18–LC, 21–NA, 23–NA, 24–NA, 27–NA; **chapter 2:** 30–CPI, 32–Jim Jacobs Collection, 36–NA, 37–CPI, 39 (top)–LC, 39 (bottom)–LC, 40–NAACP Collection, 41–SCRBC, 45–LC, 46–LC, 47–LC, 49–NA, 50–SCRBC, 51–NA, 54–SCRBC; **chapter 3:** 56–USSC, 59–LC, 60–LC, 62–LC, 63–LC, 64–NA, 65–NA, 67–NA, 68–NA, 70–LC, 71–LC, 72–NA, 73–LC, 74–LC, 77–courtesy Franklin D. Roosevelt Library, 78–USSC,

79–NA, 80–LC; **chapter 4:** 82–NA, 84 (top)–E. G. McConnell, 84 (bottom)–Leonard Smith, 85–NA, 86–LC, 87 (top)–LC, 87 (bottom)–NA, 89–Alexander Jefferson, 90–USSC, 91–LC, 92–NA, 93–LC, 95–CPI, 96–SCRBC, 101–LC, 102–NA, 105 (top)–NA, 105 (bottom)–NA, 106–LC, 108–Museum of Contemporary History; **chapter 5:** 110–LC, 114–SCRBC, 116–NA, 117–SCRBC, 118–NA, 121–SCRBC, 122–CPI, 125–USSC, 127–Lieutenant Colonel Paul L. Bates, 130–UPI/Bettmann, 131–UPI/Bettmann, 132–SCRBC, 133–NA, 134–Yad Vashem, Jerusalem; **chapter 6:** 136–USSC, 139–USSC, 140–NA, 141–USSC, 142–USSC, 145 (top)–LC, 145 (bottom)–NA, 146–USSC, 148–LC, 149–NA, 151–NA, 152–NA, 155 (top)–NA, 155 (bottom)–Walter Rosenblum, 156–Museum of Contemporary History, 157–Iaenderpress, 158–Museum for the Labor Movement (Budapest), 159–Archiv Dachau; **chapter 7:** 160–NA, 162–USSC, 163–Joseph T. Wright, 165–NA, 166–NA, 169 (top)–USSC, 169 (bottom)–NA, 172–NA, 173–Patton Museum of Cavalry and Armor, 175–NA, 176–Johnnie Stevens, 178–USSC, 181–NA; **chapter 8:** 184–CPI, 187–USSC, 189–USSC, 190–Leon Bass, 193–CPI, 198–USSC, 199–USSC, 201–USSC, 202–NA, 203 (top)–NA, 203 (bottom)–NA, 204–NA; **chapter 9:** 206– William A. Scott III, 215–Louis Held, 216–NA, 217–Ben Bender, 218–Abe Chapnick, 219–William A. Scott III, 220–Ghetto Fighters' House, Kibbutz Lohamei Haghetaot, Israel, courtesy USHMM, 221–USHMM, 222 (top)–NA, 222 (bottom)–NA, 223–NA, 225–NA, 226–NA, 228–USSC; **chapter 10:** 230–The Bettmann Archive, 235–E. G. McConnell, 236–Archiv Dachau, courtesy USHMM, 237–NA, 238 (top)–NA/courtesy USHMM, 238 (bottom)–Archiv Gedenkstatte KZ Dachau/courtesy USHMM, 240–NA, 241–UPI/Bettmann, 242–William A. Scott III, 243–NA, 244–courtesy Dwight D. Eisenhower Library, 247–NA; **chapter 11:** 248–NA, 250–E. G. McConnell, 251–NA, 253–Courtesy Harry S. Truman Library, 254–Lee Miller Archives, 255–Lee Miller Archives, 256–Harry Tyree, 257–William McBurney, 258–Henry Ries Studios, 259–Johnnie Stevens, 261–photo by Ed Clark, *Life* magazine, Time Warner, Inc., 263–NA, 265–Simon Chaput, 266–Simon Chaput; **epilogue:** 268–NA, 271–NA, 272–CPI, 275–Johnnie Stevens, 277–761st Tank Battalion Collection, 278–761st Tank Battalion Collection.

Some of the U.S. Signal Corps photos are from the collection of Jesse J. Johnson, Colonel (retired).

PERMISSIONS

The epigraph in Chapter 1 is from the poem "Crispus Attucks" from THE COLLECTED POEMS OF ROBERT HAYDEN, edited by Frederick Glaysher. Reprinted with the permission of Liveright Publishing Corporation. Copyright © 1985 by Erma Hayden.

The lyrics in Chapter 1 from "Buffalo Soldier" are copyright © 1983 by Kenemo Music and Bob Marley Music. Used by permission of Noel George Williams and the estate of Bob Marley.

The epigraph in Chapter 2 is from the poem "Little Lyric" from SELECTED POEMS by Langston Hughes. Copyright 1942 by Alfred A. Knopf, Inc. and renewed 1970 by Arna Bontemps and George Houston Bass. Reprinted by permission of the publisher.

INDEX